SIMPLE FUNERAL

A.R. Eguiguren

SIMPLE FUNERAL

Sun on Earth Books

Publisher's Cataloging-in-Publication Data

Eguiguren, A.R., 1962-
Simple funeral/A.R. Eguiguren.—Ist ed.
I. Title.
PS3555.G85S56 1993   813'.54—dc20
Library of Congress Catalog Card Number: 93-85168

ISBN 1-883378-38-9 (pbk.): $13.85

Cover design by Cristián I. Eguiguren

For A & B

*When a crime is committed, the guilty man threatens
any indiscreet persons with death, and that is enough.*

—Paul Gauguin

Part One

Chapter I

1

Martin knew they had caught up with him again. It never failed. With every new identity, an old familiar face emerged to haunt him.

He forced his pace but his feet ignored him. The sand did it. A beach was no place to flee from a murderer. He plodded on, occasionally turning back for a look at the short man who followed.

It must be Alfie, he thought. The limp was unmistakable. Martin had never verified it, but the rumor was that Alfie had an artificial leg, that one of his brothers had blown off the real one with a shotgun years ago. Supposedly an accident. At any rate, the limp was a giveaway. If the Souzas' idea had been to surprise him, sending Alfie to do the job had failed.

Moore Beach was always deserted outside tourist season. The surf came in with a monotonous splash, as if to underscore the loneliness. No one to approach for help.

Martin had no choice but to head for the cabin and blow Pete's cover. Pete Lane, his half brother, had fled the false safety of the Witness Protection Program to create his own identity. And for two years, his efforts had paid off.

They had kept in touch since the Souza trials by occasional correspondence—more out of curiosity than affection. They had little in common other than the parochial boarding schools they had been forced to attend as children.

Their parents had always insisted on a religious education. The teachers were better, they claimed. They taught about God. But the experience had only left Martin with a mixture of doubt and cynicism about religion.

Pete had agreed to meet Martin secretly, after so long, only to share advice on how to go solo. Somehow, Martin had brought the Souzas to the meeting.

If we had only planned this better, he thought. But it was too late to change plans. With every step, he felt he was giving Pete a fresh stab in the back. Pete had worked hard to lose the Souzas. This didn't help.

He stepped down closer to the water. Firmer ground allowed him to move faster, at a trot. Alfie barely bothered to hurry. Artificial leg or not, he seemed to know he had Martin cornered. The lighthouse at the end of the cape blocked the way, and there was only the boardwalk leading to the cabins.

Martin looked at the ocean. The black buoy Pete had mentioned was there. This was the right place, then. The boardwalk would lead him to the other side of the dune.

Whatever happens, he thought, Pete's got to get out of this safely, before me.

He sprinted to the cabins and looked for number 16. The numbers were old and faded, only visible from up-close. All cabins had green roofs, weather-beaten shutters blocking the windows, and similar doors. Martin knocked on one, then raced to another. No answer. Where was number 16? Pete had always been meticulous. Sloppy directions were not his nature. Had he bargained with the Souzas? *Kill Martin. I'll lead you to him in exchange for my freedom.* No. Martin knew that Pete shared at least a few of his principles. Lying was acceptable. But not betrayal.

He stopped at the sight of a cabin with a sign of life. A faint plume of smoke flowed out of the chimney. It had to be number 16, Pete's meeting place.

The door was unlocked. Martin had no time to lose. He slammed it shut behind him and turned the bolt.

He first found the kitchen and rummaged through the silverware drawer for a large knife. Pete didn't seem to be around. If he was out or asleep, all the better. Martin would take care of Alfie on his own.

The counters were covered with dust. No one had cooked here in a while. The cupboards were all open, with only discrete mounds of rat poison in them.

The sound of someone trying the front door came from the entrance hall. Martin glanced at his fist, tight around the knife's handle, as if to make sure the weapon was ready. Hardened criminals had no need to double-check like that. Only liars and petty gamblers like himself handled a weapon with fear, with the insecurity of a young man's first stab at lovemaking.

He looked out at the hall. The front door remained there. It didn't come away from its frame with a violent kick—as in the movies—but with a gentle push after the turn of a key.

Martin made a dash for cover. If Pete makes it in, he thought, we're safe, and closed the bathroom door to a crack. He took a deep breath. The foul air stung his nostrils. The rat poison had probably done its deed.

The man at the door wasn't Pete.

"What took you so long, Lane? Made me go look for you." Alfie acted as though he had entered his own house. He had taken off his sweater and dropped it on the floor. A large, heavy crucifix rested on the white undershirt. It looked old and priceless, like a family trove.

"Can't you smell the stench of death already, Martin? It's *your* death—coming to you in just a moment." Alfie shot a wild shot at the ceiling. "Come on. Let me finish my job before my big brother arrives. I wanna make him proud." He stepped forward and began to check the rooms—first the kitchen, then the hall closet. It wouldn't take long before he tried the bathroom door.

Martin tried to imagine what a bullet might feel like—ripping through the innards, splintering cranial bones while voiding a brain out. With panic, he blocked the thought, whipped open the door, and sank the knife deep into Alfie's right shoulder. A shot went off but he felt nothing.

Suddenly, Alfie seemed weak and inexperienced, too young to know what to do with the pain. Martin pushed the knife to open the wound. Survival meant being violent sometimes, even against one's will. Alfie yelled with a frenzied stammer in Portuguese. The gun dropped to the floor and Martin kicked it away.

He felt sorry for Alfie, and tried to recall the first aid classes he had taken once in school: *If it's a vein, dark blood flows like a river. If an artery, cherry red blood spatters out the wound.* Or was it the other way around?

It didn't really matter. Alfie's gash had a life of its own. Martin couldn't tell what color the blood was, nor what it was doing. He dragged Alfie into the bathroom, ignoring the obscenities that poured as fluently from the mouth as the blood did from the wound. With a sense of purpose, he took off his belt and used it to tie Alfie's legs to the shower head.

"What the hell are you doing?" Alfie's face blanched. "Let me down!"

Martin ignored him. He ripped the blood-stained under-shirt and used it to tie the young man's arms against the spout in the bathtub.

The wound bled profusely. A look of panic settled on Alfie's face. "Let me go. I need a doctor."

"Shut up, Captain Ahab." Martin knocked on Alfie's artificial leg. He didn't mean to be cruel, but it amused him that getting rid of danger had been so easy. Pete would be glad when he arrived. He checked the wound one more time. No, it was not serious. The man would live.

"I'm going to bleed to death, you bastard!"

"You won't. I've taken first aid and know about these things. Just relax."

"Fuck! Let me go!" Alfie made matters worse trying to pull his arms free from the spout. The blood smeared across the sides of the tub and up to the tiles.

"If you'd only stop moving, damn it!" Martin slapped him. The crucifix's chain broke and the small figure of Christ fell with a clank in the tub.

"Kill me, then! I don't want to bleed to death. Take the gun and shoot me!" Alfie thrashed about, his face distorted with every utterance. "You can't let blood spill like this. Stop it. Stop it!"

Martin reached under Alfie's head and fit the stopper in the drainpipe. "This will save it for you."

Alfie thrust his body violently. His hips banged on the wall. "Shoot me! Shoot me!"

He'll do fine, Martin thought, and closed the bathroom door to muffle the screams.

He checked the bedroom and found Pete face down on the floor. For a moment he didn't really believe it. His nerve failed him. Only the screams from the bathroom kept him moving.

Pete's head rested on the stained carpet, moist with blood. In the low light of the room, his skin looked filthy and beaten, like a bar of soap recently used by auto mechanics.

Martin felt sick. It could have been *his* body there. He touched Pete's head, afraid that it might move. Sorry, he thought. So sorry. We should have been more careful.

It had been so long since he had seen Pete that he only felt anger, not grief. A distant half brother meant little more to Martin than a postman or a bank clerk.

He studied the room. A black address book on the night table stood out—the only thing that might be of any use to him. He pulled a pair of shorts and a shirt from Pete's duffel bag and changed. It wouldn't do to walk out of here wearing blood-stained clothes.

He tucked the black notebook in the undershorts and ran to the front door. He had to rush if it was true that Alfie's older brother was on his way.

A metallic noise came from the bathroom. Alfie was banging something against the bathtub.

Martin stopped to study the handgun on the floor. He felt an urge to shoot the bleeding man, if only to show Pete he was truly sorry about the way things had turned out.

Another clang came from inside the bathroom and Martin leaned toward the handgun. He stared at it, but he knew he didn't have it in him to kill a man.

He locked the front door from outside and stepped back. The smoke had ceased to flow from the chimney and the cabin showed no signs of life. He could barely hear the sounds coming from the bathroom.

Martin reached the sand quickly and jogged away edging the waves. When he was far enough, he flung the key into the ocean.

2

Alfie's older brother slammed shut the cab's door with visible annoyance. The car was not in good condition and had stalled several times on its way to Moore Beach. But he shouldn't blame the driver. All his life he had refused to drive a car, and had to live with the consequences.

He paid the fare and rushed to the sand. The lighthouse stood in the distance—dark and quiet, living an extinguished life.

As the oldest son of the Souza clan, he had taken the family name. Even friends called him Souza, especially now that his father was in jail. No one was sure how long the old man would be in prison, so it was up to Souza to guide the four younger sons, Alfie in particular.

He glanced at his watch. He was late. He had promised Alfie he would be there to help him, if there were a need for help. Two bodies were difficult to dispose of with only one good leg.

He started off hurriedly, with clumsy steps. Far off to his left, near the surf, a jogger passed in the opposite direction. The beach and surroundings were deserted otherwise, and he liked that. He was happy. It had taken his family long to reach this day, what he liked to call *Make-Ends-Meet* day. In his line of work, the term had more than economic connotations. On such days certain people met their ends, people like Pete and Martin Lane and their gambling parents. Killing them was as simple as making an entry in a ledger, as closing an account. The police called it murder. But the Souza family never bothered with what the police had to say.

The old man Lane and his wife had been unemployed. Souza had given them generous terms and grace periods on the loans. He understood the cyclical nature of their winnings. Gamblers had their low months, too. He could wait.

But Martin's father had decided to free himself from the debts by going to the FBI, turning in most of the Souza clan on fabricated accusations. He had lied to get himself and his family into the Witness Protection Program.

Souza kicked a moll of sand with disgust. Nobody has the right to lie about us, he thought. Especially to incriminate and jail us.

He reached the footpath and walked past the cabins, slowly. Better make sure there would be no witnesses to have to deal with later on. The trees surrounding the cabins could easily hide eyes. He looked carefully. Most of the doors had at one time been carelessly splashed with red paint. The dapples reminded him of a slaughterhouse.

He pulled a cigarette out and tucked it between his lips. The cabin was quiet. Things had come out well, apparently. He went around the building with his hand near the holster and handgun under his arm.

There were no visible signs of violence. Alfie had come through for him with a clean job. The family would be happy, and Souza couldn't be more proud of the young man.

He tried the door and found it locked. His lips quivered and the cigarette almost fell. Instinctively, he drew the automatic. Something was wrong. They had agreed the door would be left unlocked. He studied the faded number on it. The right one—number 16.

He splintered the jamb with a single kick and rushed in. The rancid air inside brought memories of the poorly refrigerated butcher shops of his native Portugal. It burned his nostrils, and he made an effort to cover them with his cuff. He noted the bloody footsteps that had upset the fine layer of dust on the floor. An oppressive silence lay on them. Only the sound of sea gulls reached from outside.

Souza stepped forward, pressing the cigarette between his lips upon seeing the feet in the bedroom. It occurred to him that Alfie might have indulged some sadistic trait of his. That would account for all the bloodstains on the walls and floor. Souza disapproved. Blood was too messy. And the Souzas were religious. They didn't go about slaughtering people like animals. To kill sufficed.

He pulled up the weight of Pete's body with his foot and recognized the face: Pete, the son of the informer. Finally, the father, mother, and one son were accounted for. Only one more left to close the account—Pete's half brother, Martin Lane.

Now where did you leave the other one, Alfie? He moved on and crossed over to the kitchen. The cabin was small. He had instructed Alfie to leave the two bodies inside. The walls and carpet would provide effective fuel for a pyre.

He opened the bathroom door and confusion held him back for a moment, before he could feel any pain.

"Alfie!" He approached the bathtub and put his hand to Alfie's neck. The body didn't seem to have enough blood left in it to be alive.

Alfie's feet were still tied to the shower head. Somehow he had managed to knock off the towel bar in his last moments of desperation.

Souza collapsed next to the lifeless man. "Alfie—you screwed up. You screwed up!" He wept freely while a dark memory came to mind.

At sixteen he had taken Alfie out for an afternoon of hunting. A bad day. They had killed nothing. The last flock of birds had flown away too quickly, and Souza's shotgun remained cocked and ready as they hiked back home. They planned the next outing. They would leave home earlier, when they might find larger flocks.

Souza studied the steps of his eight-year-old brother, who walked in front of him. He amused himself with Alfie's awkward gait. "Your feet are crooked, Alfie." But it was *his* feet that failed him. He tripped, and the shotgun blasted off an incessant shrill from the younger one.

"Jesus! Keep quiet!" Souza yelled at his brother as he slapped him to make him shut up. "Stop screaming. Stop!" He was no longer sure whether the uncontrollable shrieks came from Alfie's mouth or his own. "Stop, please. Stop. God, make him stop. Make him stop. Let me see the wound. Let me see..."

Souza could see nothing. Alfie's blood had soaked his clothes instantly. The boy's left leg was gone.

An accident, he later told his father. They were just walking, going back home—to dinner.

Alfie survived, but Souza never stopped repeating the words to himself: an accident. From that day he gave his younger brother special treatment—permanent, overbearing protection.

That had happened over fifteen years ago. Still, it had been with reluctance that Souza had given Alfie this first professional job.

The Lanes' handiwork with the FBI had landed Souza's father in jail. For that alone, Souza had decided to eliminate the foursome. No big deal, just one more chore in his daily dealings, a mom-and-pop job and their two bastard children—the type of people no one would miss.

But now this, he thought. A death in our family. A murder. That bastard killed Alfie.

He leaned closer to the corpse to examine the crust of blood in the bathtub. It had already turned dark and hard at the edges. He pulled out a handkerchief and pressed it into the red pool, farther to the center, where the mass was still gelatinous. He made the sign of the cross with it and put it back in his pocket. How ironic that Alfie had survived the hunting accident only to end up like this.

If God willed it this way, he thought, then fine. But this is a personal matter now, between me and Martin Lane. That son of a bitch is going to pay for this with much more than his life.

Souza would not rest until he himself killed Martin. No one else in the family would get this assignment. His own hands would deliver justice this time. No matter where the Witness Protection Program took Martin, he would track him down and kill him.

He composed himself and took a last look at the rooms. Too many things cluttered them, things that didn't belong in the place. He took Pete's bag and stuffed it with every piece of clothing he found in the cabin, pens, pencils, pieces of paper, and Alfie's gun. He had learned the lesson years earlier: never leave food for the police on which to feed a case. This evidence was his alone, and only he would find clues in it that would lead to Martin.

He took one last look at Alfie—a half-naked body twisted grotesquely with the panic of death.

No man deserves to die like this, he thought. Death must be sudden and clean if what's left of a man is to deserve a happy funeral.

He shut all the doors to contain the smells and pulled the cigarette from his lips. "This one's yours, Alf. I won't smoke it till Martin's dead."

Chapter II

1

Martin enjoyed a ride in a cab. He could sit back in it and observe a city from a different perspective, especially a city in which he had never lived before.

He was glad to be in Washington, D.C. He felt clean here. Perhaps that was why some people looked forward to a new job: a new start in life.

He thought with relief of his departure from the Program. After so much hesitation, he had finally made the move Pete had two years ago. Though now there would be no *Panic* phone number to call if a Souza found him again. He would have to use his own resources to escape and relocate. But that was not impossible.

I just did it, he thought, and can do it again—though it probably won't be necessary, ever. They'll never find me.

"This is it." The cab driver pointed at a large driveway to their right.

"Yes. But drive in slowly. I'm early for the interview."

The man let the car advance on the force of idle speed alone. "What a place," he said. "Some people know how to get an education."

Martin agreed silently. The school appeared to be much better than he had imagined, much better than the ones to which his parents had struggled to send him.

"Amazing, isn't it?"

Beyond the buildings, a bright hedge surrounded the property. Here one felt like the master and dweller of a sumptuous estate. In education, trees and plants made all the difference. Because of them, private schools seemed to achieve a higher state of tranquility, enlightenment and discipline—and a sort of privacy, too. Here were gardeners to keep the grounds, and students to support a landscaping budget. The beauty of the Japanese hollies and rhododendrons could never be matched by the prosaic barberry and ivy found on public-school grounds.

The driver showed no overt interest in the flowers—his eyes turned instead to the Alfa Romeos and Saabs parked on the side of the road. "Getting a job here?"

Strangers often asked what he considered rude questions. His young face gave them the incentive. None of your business, Martin thought, but said instead, "I'll try."

The crisp spring air swayed the top of the trees placidly. A gardener appeared from behind a fountain and trundled a wheelbarrow on a path of flagstones. He carried an enviable air of peace in his eyes. His shoes were old, torn and worn, but they moved with feet that loved their work.

Martin rolled down the window hoping to distract himself, to get a closer look or maybe a whiff from a flower. His hands moved restlessly and he forced them into a relaxed pose. It was more than the coming interview that made him nervous. He was about to start a new life, a whole new lie.

The granite administration building stood in front of him and his hands disobeyed him, moving first to his knees, then to his chest. He thought of the book no one had written for his benefit—*How to Lie For The Job, On The Job, and About The Job*. Lying required guidance. One had to manage countless false details well. The school's principal had probably studied Pete's résumé carefully and would be ready to question him on every point. It should be an easy interview, he thought, as long as they kept details undisturbed. If he succeeded in getting hired, it would be more than luck, a reward, even: in his years in the Program, the Justice Department had moved him around the country from one menial job to the next, despite his continuous complaints. Manual labor didn't stimulate his intellectual nature. But U.S. marshals could offer him nothing else. They claimed that any job above blue-collar level would be too visible and a constant threat to his cover. Yet the Souzas had always managed to find him even as he worked minimum-wage affairs, in what to him were obscure sweatshops. No doubt there was a corrupt marshal in the Program, one who had given away his identity and location every time. If that wasn't the case, why had Pete been safe from the Portuguese family for nearly two years *after* fleeing the Program?

How ironic that Pete's death had worked out to benefit his own effort of going solo. Martin could now assume his half-brother's pre-Program identity. The Souzas would never think of looking for a teacher, nor would Martin's ex-duty officer in the Program.

Pete had been a teacher before the family's debts to the Souzas had become unmanageable. He had not taught again after the trials, and that left a gap of more than three years between his last teaching position and now. Martin would have to justify it somehow.

The office stifled him. Thermostats often gave bosses the means to torture subordinates at will. But the principal, the middle-aged woman who sat across from him, did not seem to be the ruthless type, the intimidating superior. Perhaps she only suffered from shifts in body temperature, from a hormonal imbalance that allowed her to feel comfortable in this heat.

A colorful arras hung on the wall behind her, and a grandfather clock graced a corner. Her desk was clear of common clerical items. Only a set of crayons in a tin cup and a calendar with color-coded notations rested on it.

She studied the résumé hurriedly. "Sorry. Just trying to refresh my memory."

"Take your time." Martin was inordinately calm, sedated by the phenobarbital he had taken. He struggled to stay alert against the lulling tick of the clock.

A number of colorful notations covered the résumé, all too small to be read from his seat.

"This is very good," the woman said, as if referring to some dish he had prepared. She picked a bright orange crayon to underline some point she liked about Pete's past. Her hands were chubby and tanned and didn't go with her prim behavior. Probably a one-time convent student, Martin thought. Surely she wouldn't approve of lying.

She placed the document face down on the desk. "I've read it a few times, actually. But I didn't explain to you. This is not to be the actual interview. That will come later. I usually prefer to have a personal chat, a warm-up contact with the applicants first. The last few months have been a period of upheaval for us. I only took the helm recently, after my father, who founded the school, fell seriously ill."

"Oh—"

"Don't feel sorry for me, please. I'm taking it all with a drop of humor. God knows I wouldn't make it otherwise."

"Good for you. One must sometimes be trivial and frivolous to cope with difficulties."

"That's what I say. Now, are you aware of the situation we have here? The scandal?"

"Scandal?"

"A big one. Was even in the papers."

"I wouldn't know, being new in town." He smiled.

"Oh, good. All the better for us. Don't let anyone tell you what took place, then."

"I won't."

She retrieved a green crayon to write *Out-of-town applicant* on the back of the sheet. "The teacher who held this position was accused by several students of improprieties. He was terminated as a result of those accusations. We considered not replacing him at all, letting the psychology teacher take over instead, since we have so little left of this school year." She took a deep breath and looked lost for a moment, the crayon stuck between her fingers in the manner of a cigarette. "I'll let you in on a secret." She leaned forward. "The parents demanded a replacement, the Pee part of our PTA. Sometimes I call it Pedants and Teachers Association. But that isn't fair, really, as I have a daughter studying here myself. I understand their concerns. But the fact is—we've had a drop in enrollment in the last few years. Tuition has risen so sharply—not by our initiative, of course, but because costs in this country have gone to the clouds. Many parents have withdrawn their children and taken them back to public schools as a result. At first I thought it was my fault, as I didn't have the years of experience my father did. But before he died, he reassured me. 'It's the economy,' he said. 'Things are not right.'"

Martin assented. It's a good thing I got a talker, he thought. She'll prattle along until I decide to stop her.

She retrieved a pack of cigarettes from the drawer and lit one with seemingly measured spasms. "Don't do this in front of our students. We discourage bad habits. Anyway, we're struggling for newcomers, new revenue—*that's* my point. The scandal certainly harmed us. We've had to cut back on all sorts of expenses, even for things I consider essential for the welfare of these children. For example, the senior cook in our—"

"At least you've got a pretty garden." He'd had enough.

She smiled. "Well, Mr. Lane, I'm glad you noticed it."

"Pete, please."

"Pete. Call me Barbara, then. Yes, the garden. The school must look right to first-time visitors. The parents of prospective students wouldn't enter the grounds if all they saw from out there were fallow molehills—don't you agree?"

"Certainly. I was very impressed with the hollies."

"See! I'm glad you understand. My father loved nature, too. Now, about your salary." She gave out a laugh. Martin had the impression she had staged the meeting—prim and modest at first, gradually easing her real character, then ready to strike business toward the end.

"I must tell you I was really impressed with your résumé," she went on. "And although it's not official and the board of directors must still meet and interview you, I'd dare say it's almost certain you'll get the position. Don't tell them I said this—but remember, since it is now so near the end of the year, you'll be hired in what we call a probation capacity. That's why the salary will be low. Then, for the next school year, if you remain with us, you'll become a permanent member of our faculty, and receive full salary and benefits."

"I'm not really worried about the salary." His worry centered on the fact that he had never taught before, except for a one-day teacher assistant experience in college.

"Oh, great! Another one of those good people who don't place importance on money. We like those." She took a bright yellow crayon and made a note. "If you're wondering, yellow stands for gold. I note salary requirements with it, see?" She lifted the sheet and showed him the entry: *D.G.A.D.* He nodded out of politeness.

"It stands for Doesn't Give A Damn," she said, and gave out a gratuitous laugh that drowned the tic-tac of the clock. Martin laughed to accompany her. He couldn't imagine how anyone like her could end up in her position without a father from whom to inherit it.

"Okay, Pete. Want to see the campus? Or do you have any questions?"

He had to make an effort, think of anything that might seem relevant. "Do you have a good library? I enjoy good books."

"Of course. That's one other area in which I wouldn't scrimp. I bet you like to read them, too." She laughed.

"If they're good."

"Well, we have the latest in best sellers. You'll love it."

The gardeners were on their lunch break, but only a few students were out on the grounds. Their yelling came from somewhere beyond the buildings.

Barbara pointed north. "Sometimes the boys play soccer during their lunch hour. Our girls cling to the fence, almost like caged animals, just to cheer them. It gets so loud, you have to wonder what it is they're really cheering. Not the boys' playing abilities, I'm sure."

"You seem to have more girls than boys, judging by what I saw back in the halls."

"We should. Ours is an all-girls school. We've tried to turn it into a coed but our PTA—the Pees, you know. They say it'd be a problem, that girls would spend their time fighting over boys, and so forth. Those few boys you saw belong to the school next door. They're a menace."

Martin had lost interest in her comments. He found them as stifling as her office. To fake interest took more skill than to tell a lie, so he kept a straight face.

The students who walked past and stared at him held his attention with less effort. Their tartan uniforms were tight and short. Perhaps the girls had tampered with them, raising the hem and stitching a few pleats together so that the skirts hugged their thighs more closely. All beautiful girls to him. They talked with their arms, excitedly, as though conversation were more a contest in calling attention than a mere form of communication. He stared at the moving arms, at the young breasts heaving, and at the smiles. How fascinating, he thought. That one is very pretty. She even seemed to have read his mind as she acknowledged his interest with a wink.

"That's how that other teacher was terminated," Barbara said, as if she had also been able to read his mind. "One of the girls looked too enticing to him. He just couldn't pass her up."

Martin smiled. "I can't imagine."

She introduced him to the librarians before showing him around the shelves. The stacks were filled to capacity with books whose spines showed no evidence of use. Audio-visual equipment sat in one corner next to large planters of carefully arranged cacti. Two sofas ran along a *Periodicals* rack that was bolted to the wall.

"So where *are* you from, Pete?"

He hesitated. "All over."

Barbara puckered her brow.

"My parents moved a lot," he said. "My father—first decided to move when I was eight, then again, and again."

"You were an Army brat?"

"No. He was a businessman. It made things difficult for me. Just when life was perfect and everything was normal, when I'd grown accustomed to my new school and friends, my parents would decide to move and yank me from my safe surroundings."

"How terrible. That type of thing would really make me resent my parents. I bet you live well away from them now."

"I do. They've both passed away."

"Oh, I'm so sorry. I had no idea—"

"That's alright. It doesn't bother me." A surge of adrenaline rushed in him. Stupid mistake, he thought. Only *his* parents were both dead. Pete's father was still alive. He wondered whether the man had learned of his son's death, or whether he cared at all. Maybe no one had found the body yet. Who knew what Alfie and his older brother had done with it, with the blood, and with the cabin after Martin had fled?

Barbara led him out of the building and through an open garden. A greenhouse sat at the far end. She picked up a crumpled paper cup from the gravel. "I did notice in your résumé that you've moved a lot. Marked it in blue. Blue's for past job stability—not that you seem unstable at all. Don't get me wrong. I just like to take into consideration all factors and personal characteristics of the applicant." She placed the cup in a trash can. "And I did notice that three-year gap as well. You haven't taught in over three years."

"I had to recharge my batteries."

"One does get tired of young people, doesn't one?"

They were out on the flagstone walk. Barbara checked her wristwatch. "I'm afraid I'll have to let you go on with the tour on your own. I've got a meeting to attend in five minutes."

"I'll manage."

He watched her take a few steps and then turn back.

"Would you mind if—" she said before she checked herself: a few students walking nearby seemed to make her cautious. She drew near him and almost whispered, "Would you mind if I ask you how old you are?"

"No. Thirty-three."

"Oh," she said with a sigh of relief. "You look so young. It's that baby face you have. The girls will go crazy over you. You'll have to guard yourself." She laughed as if to discredit her suggestion, as if she really wanted him not to guard himself. Martin got the impression she had enjoyed whatever scandal had taken place. Perhaps she wanted a repeat. It kept the school's name in the papers, and possibly brought new students in—as long as the news reported that the offending teacher had been dismissed.

With Barbara gone, Martin felt a sudden urge to make a phone call, to tell someone and celebrate. He had lied so successfully that a teaching job in a prestigious private school was practically his. It showed him how little importance experience and education had to do with employment. All it took was a well-written résumé and a good, straight face to go with it.

He reached for a cigarette but checked himself. His future pupils could see him. He searched farther inside his breast pocket for coins.

The girls will go crazy over you. He flipped a coin to the words. *The girls will go crazy over you.* How about you, Barbara? Aren't you a bit crazy yourself?

Alone on the path he drew attention. Naturally he had to be going somewhere. Normal people didn't just stand in a garden for too long, especially not in a high school.

Adolescent girls were curious sorts. He didn't like the way they stared at him. He was obviously out of place here—too young to be a parent or a teacher, too strange to be anyone's brother. He had tried to look conservative for the interview, but had overdone it. His clothes were too formal and out of vogue. Fashion zealots would have a field day deriding his wide tie, his old, clumsy clodhoppers, and the ridiculous cuff links he had bought at the Salvation Army's thrift store.

He entered the cafeteria thinking how little he knew about American Literature from the standpoint of a teacher. All he had going for him was that he liked to read. And he had read most of the classics at least once. How fortunate that, if he got the job, he would be inheriting it from a disgraced man fired near the end of the school year. No one would expect great results from him under those circumstances. It would be difficult even for a good teacher to make such a class work.

He picked up the receiver and had to think of the number, though it had once been drilled into his memory for several months. Opposite the line of pay phones were rows of cafeteria tables. Only a few students sat there, but they managed to talk loudly enough to make it difficult for him to hear the dial tone.

An operator answered. "Your file number, please."

"I need to speak to Marshal Tito."

"I need your file number, sir." She was rude and impatient. "This is the emergency relocation number you have dialed. Your file number, please."

"I lost the regular business number. Please put me through to Tito."

"The regular number is 4-3-8-6-1-7-2, area code—"

"I don't have a pen. Would you just put me through!"

She didn't answer. The line went dead, and he waited. It must happen often, he thought—relocated witnesses calling their duty officers out of sheer boredom and desperation. The emergency number was the only one they remembered, like a 911, or a bank card's PIN code. Fresh in their minds, it put them through to the only person who knew their true identities. They couldn't be bothered with regulations.

"Who are you holding for?" the voice came once more.

"Marshal Tito."

And she was gone again.

Tito's name was a joke among the staff at the Program's office. U.S. marshals often came with names like John, Richard, Henry, or Joe. But Tito? His Yugoslav-American secretary had not been able to resist the political christening. Martin did not even know the man's real name. Witness relocation worked that way—a shroud of secrecy was standard procedure.

The last group of students lingered in the dining hall. They talked about boys and late-model cars with careless conviction. Their sense of insecurity was clearer in the nail polish and eye liner they wore than in their fatuous giggles. They followed convention, making fun of boys to feel better about themselves. Martin wondered if his female contemporaries had made fun of him in that same cruel way. He had lacked all the desired physical attributes of the popular boy prototype—personality and muscles. With girls out of his reach, he had filled his teen-age years lying about poor grades, forging report cards, and hiding his smoking habit and his weakness for Benzedrine. *Lie to absolutely everyone and you'll never be found out in your lie.* It had worked for him. His parents had never really had a chance to know him before their deaths.

The girls were making fun of contraceptives. How easily they talk about sex, he thought. They made a phallic gesture as readily as they waved. Sex was fun and games to them. Magazines and movies made that sort of pleasure appealing and seemingly uncomplicated. They giggled again, and he stared. One of them pulled her hair back continuously. Her thighs stood firm and tight. She was a sexual attraction, and she knew it. He could see how a mature male teacher could be enticed. That kind of thing never died in a man—that teen-age boy's lust. He felt it himself. If it hadn't made him so miserable once, he'd be tempted to try again. Kathy, and her abortion, and all the big mess. That was all the cheap thrill got you, nothing else. He had never seen her again. And she was probably still living her lie.

The girl pulled her hair back again and waved across the hall, to a friend, a tall girl with a strange haircut who waved back. Shaved grooves ran horizontally along the left side of her head and past the ear.

"This is Tito."

The voice surprised Martin. He could imagine Tito sitting in his office, that small room cloudy with cigarette smoke. Tito was overweight, with overflowing flesh too excessive to be the result of overeating alone. He was surely scraping his scalp with a fountain pen at this very moment, letting a flurry of dandruff fall onto the desk.

"It's me," Martin said with a touch of hesitation.

"Oh. Hold on." Tito's chair creaked through the line as he moved his frame somewhere, probably to close the door without getting up. "Where are you? I'll send you a relocation team."

"How do you know I need to relocate?"

"We found Pete near your current address, last address, whatever you call it now. We looked for you at work. The man said you'd split. Do you know about your brother?"

"No—I saw the Souzas in town and fled."

"Well, he's dead. My condolences. We thought you were dead, too. The cabin was completely empty, except for Pete's body and things that normally belong there. Not a piece of evidence to work on. The bathroom was a butcher shop, covered with blood—though none of it Pete's. It looked as if a body had been dragged away. We thought it was yours. There was enough blood there to fill a horse. Someone put in a stopper to collect it in the tub."

"Sounds grisly." Martin pressed his hand against his chest and wondered about Tito's description of the scene—words so casual he could have been talking about a boring painting, as though blood were only a pigment the artist had used too much of.

"We're sure, whoever's blood it was, that person's dead." Tito cleared his throat as if to put an end to one topic and go on to something else. "Now..."

Martin was no longer listening. How fragile a human life was, he thought. Alfie should have survived the cut. His older brother surely would have arrived in time to take him to a hospital.

But it couldn't be. Martin knew something was definitely wrong. Why would someone die so easily? And where *was* the body, then? Wouldn't the Justice Department know about a Souza funeral? Alfie was probably alive, and Tito was only bluffing.

He noticed a girl staring at him confusedly. He must have turned pale, he thought—a ghost leaning on the telephone.

"Where are you?" Tito said.

"I'm not telling. I'm quitting the Program."

"You can't. We still need you to testify."

"A man deserves a break, Tito. I've never had peace from the Souzas. They've found me every time. There *must* be a leak in your office. You can't trust your people. I'm going solo, like Pete." He pulled out a cigarette and lit it. He couldn't be bothered with being a good role model to students now.

"Pete ended up with a bullet in his head. There's no leak and you know it."

"Not once was Pete discovered after going solo. I was almost killed twice under your so-called expert protection."

"You're wrong. Pete *was* found out, *and* killed."

"Probably because of me. We were to meet two days after I saw the Souzas in town. Had he not tried to meet me, he—"

But what was the point in discussing? He had called to celebrate, to boast about his newly-found freedom, to tell fat Tito he didn't need him anymore.

"Tell me, Martin, where was Pete hiding all this time?"

"Good bye, Tito. I'm going out on my own."

He replaced the receiver with a shudder. His hands were cold and smelled of sweet perfume. These were the same phones the girls used to call their boyfriends.

2

Martin liked the small house. He had been lucky to find a decent one for little rent in less than two weeks. The school had not yet made a decision on his hiring after the formal interview, but he already considered himself settled. If he didn't get that job, he would look for another. He was here to stay.

The old duffel bag wouldn't take many more moves. It had accompanied him everywhere, carrying the only items he could take with him—his books, notes, some basic clothes and family memorabilia. He never had time to pack. The moves were always sudden, unexpected, and unappreciated by him. He could only hope there would be no more of them.

Perhaps this one will be my last one, he thought. If I get this job and keep a low profile, I may finally have a stable life, if only for a few years.

He unpacked every item and filled the bookshelf above the mantelpiece with his books. The volumes were a heavy load to carry for someone so much on the move as he was. But they were to hold him over while he checked the local libraries, decided on which one to use, and applied there for membership. It didn't matter that he had read these more than once already. They were classics. He compared himself to the characters and read them whenever he needed to reclaim himself.

The Bible was a large edition, old and musty. A useful book. Large and firm—a good place in which to file things. As a young boy, he had read it once. He remembered the pictures, especially the one of Lazarus coming out of a stone grave with those cadaverous eyes that had always scared him. Perhaps I should give it another try. He thumbed through the pages, all of them yellow with age. Memorabilia flickered past—a birth certificate, a photograph, a school report card—relics from the past. A blue envelope called his attention, a letter from his friend Mudoga that remained unopened. He'd had no time to read it before this sudden last move. He dropped it on the coffee table and placed the Bible on the shelf.

Martin enjoyed the warmth of this new home. He felt he could relax here, open the windows and have a drink. A bottle of beer cooled in the freezer and he sat on the carpet to make time for it. He only missed the ocean. Every other memory of his last identity made him shudder with distaste. The job had been the most boring he'd had in his time with the Program. The last house had been a squalid corner apartment in an old building—the only thing he could afford on his own. But it had been two blocks from the beach. Having an ocean nearby made up for all the injustices of life.

He opened the beer bottle and let himself down heavily on the couch. The room looked empty. His only contributions were the couch, the coffee table, and the books on the shelf. Little else dressed the rest of the house. A table and chair in the kitchen, and a mattress on the bedroom's floor—all he needed and could afford. The cash inside Pete's address book had helped pay for all this. Whenever he needed money, he thought, it somehow came his way. He wet his lips with a sip of beer before giving out a laugh: another loan he wouldn't have to pay back. It wasn't funny, but he had to laugh.

He took the black address book from the table. Pete had always kept detailed records. This had been *his* Bible.

Martin studied a few pages. They were neat and crisp, with every entry carefully hand printed.

Some people hold their whole lives in a notebook, he thought, as if afraid their days will be cut short at any moment. They think the notebook will keep them alive in the minds of others.

Everything was in it—birth dates and profiles of every member of his family, everyone's Social Security and driver's license numbers. Photographs. Instructions on how and where to get fake documentation in a rush. Bank account numbers. Civil registry locations and registration numbers of birth certificates and of his parents' wedding license. Detailed profiles of every identity Pete had assumed. Someone who didn't know better would have taken the entries for short biographies of friends of his. Martin was surprised to find even his own name and identities listed. The book contained more details about each of his past lives than he himself remembered.

I never really got to know you, Pete, did I? Here you were, noting every bit of information I gave you about my lives and identities, and I didn't know it. I'm lucky to have taken this book with me.

The windows in the house were large. A person could easily enter through them and he debated whether to close them before he went upstairs. He was always afraid that after a short visit to the bathroom or into a walk-in closet, an assailant, a burglar, or a Souza might surprise him. Part of the paranoia that fed his life in hiding. He could never really know if he was completely safe and free. The same feeling came to him when he entered the house during the night—after a long day at work—with a chance that someone might be waiting for him inside, in the dark.

He locked both windows in the living room, one in the kitchen, and turned the bolt on the front door. He could never defend himself face-to-face with a killer. He had no weapons. With the windows and doors locked, if someone tried to break in, he should at least have enough time to call the police, or somebody.

Perhaps I should buy a butcher knife, too, he thought. One like Pete's at the cabin.

He rushed to the bathroom and took Mudoga's letter with him.

Godfrey Mudoga was a happy man. His letter started with the good news of his promotion to provincial head of his ministry, a post his uncle had held for many years. Martin held the envelope against the light to study the postmark. The letter was old. Sometimes correspondence took months to reach him as a result of the intricate forwarding system he had set up. The only way to avoid letting others know of his whereabouts. This letter had also come from Africa, which added a few extra weeks to the journey.

Martin had shared college classes with Mudoga long ago. His friend had changed markedly through the years, and this letter stood as evidence. It was typed. *I have acquired a fax machine and a Dictaphone. One of my secretaries types all my correspondence now. As you can see, I'm an important man.*

With every letter the talk of power and economic means increased. The Mudoga of today was a distant man from the feeble, soft-spoken African Martin had known in college. He had come to America on a government scholarship his influential uncle had awarded him. They had met because of a statistics class. Mudoga had sought a tutor and Martin had helped. The man was forever thankful. *You're most invited to visit me and my beautiful country,* went the last

          A.R. Eguiguren

few sentences in every one of his letters. Martin never considered the invitations. They reeked of formality.

The colorful stamps were exotic, filled with butterflies. There had been other stamps before—some with rallies and masses of people gathered for a presidential speech, others with elaborate monuments, and more with the silver silhouette of the Queen of England.

He dropped the letter the moment he heard a noise from downstairs. Someone was banging on the front door, but so loudly and with so much insistence, he imagined fire fighters trying to force their way in. For the first time he noticed the pungent scent of ammonia in the bathroom. The landlord had insisted on having a crew over to clean the house before Martin moved in. The cleaning crew had left the empty disinfectant bottles blocking the kitchen door. Martin heard one of them fall and break. Someone had already entered the house.

Martin panicked. He had forgotten to lock the kitchen door. He raced downstairs for the outdoor light. At least, he thought, no one would try to murder him out there, in plain view. He unlocked the front door forcefully and pulled it away from the frame. Barbara's open hand almost hit him in the face. A cigarette burned between her fat fingers.

He turned back for a look at the kitchen door.

"That was me," she said. "I was going to yell your name in but think I broke something instead. Sorry. You weren't answering the doorbell and—"

"It doesn't work." He was indignant. It took little time to replace fear with anger.

"I was going to call you and realized we didn't have your phone number."

"I don't have it, either. The phone company keeps on making excuses."

"Well, you got the job! I just had to tell you. Didn't want you to go on out there looking for some other employment opportunities. The review board really enjoyed their interview with you, they said, and—may I come in?"

Martin hesitated. He had to mentally review every room before anyone saw it. A false identity could be revealed by the smallest detail—a photograph left carelessly in sight, an address book, even the scar on his chest. They must all be stored away at all times.

"Come in," he said, and hoped the news of his hiring had been all she had come to give him. The last thing he needed was a short, fat woman forcing herself on him sexually.

"You don't mind if I smoke, do you?"

"Feel at home." He showed her into the living room and pointed at a tin filled with cigarette butts and ashes.

Perhaps it's part of the interview, he thought, even though the job's mine already. She needs to see how her new employee lives, what vices and sins are part of his private life.

"Very nice place you have here, Pete."

"I'll show you the rest of it." He felt obligated. But there would be no harm in it—as long as she didn't make it a habit to come visit and snoop. He picked up Pete's address book and forced it between the other books on the shelf.

After the empty dining room, they moved on to the kitchen. She apologized for the broken bottle as he swept the pieces into a dustpan. He did it slowly, intent on making her feel uncomfortable. He knew how unpleasant it was to stand idly around someone performing repetitive household chores. In his childhood, his mother had done the same to him.

He rushed her through the rest of the house: a quick tour, the type real estate agents give when they are eager to sell a

     A.R. Eguiguren

property and hide its defects. And why not? Didn't he have the right to be left alone in his own house? He had to show her that he didn't appreciate unexpected visitors, banging on his doors, trying to yell in, even to tell him that a new job waited.

He concluded the tour before she finished her third cigarette. "Sorry for rushing you this way," he said. "I was actually on my way out."

"Need a ride?"

"I'll walk."

He watched her struggle with the heavy door of her old-model Cadillac, the type of car only a woman like her would drive. Her power tank, he thought. She can feel aggressive in it, throwing her weight about the road.

She waved. "You're off now?"

"Yes."

"Better lock your doors. It's a big city."

"It's a safe neighborhood," he said.

"Have it your way, then. But only fools trust their brethren." She drove off slowly.

Martin knew that she had noticed the lie, that he wasn't going anywhere. All the best, he thought. I don't want her around here.

Mudoga's letter smelled of ammonia. Anything that lingered for too long in the bathroom acquired the scent. He sat on the floor next to the coffee table and read. *But you're especially invited now—for a visit, even a sojourn. I could accommodate you in any school. You'd make a great teacher. I am living proof that you can tutor anyone well on whatever subject. So you can visit and be employed....*

Why on earth should I go to a third-world country when I have a future here with this new job? He stared at the ashtray and winced at the cigarette butts Barbara had left behind. Her garrulous lips remained on them, imprinted in bright lipstick. The mark reminded him that he would soon be seeing much of those lips, daily, as a member of the school. Students he had never met were to start learning from him, too. He knew the subject well, but could he teach it? The students would help him, surely. He would try a friendly approach—improvisation, loose lesson plans, games. Make learning fun, he thought. Make life a joke.

He checked the windows and doors again and left the house.

3

The tall man stood next to the car with an air of exasperation. His daughter had already pushed his patience to the limit. One could justify parental love only so much. He contracted his stomach muscles with anger. There, he felt the incipient nudge of an ulcer he had to keep to himself. In life, he had lost his temper too many times. The girl's mother had made an early exit as a result of his uncontrolled outbursts. He didn't want Elizabeth to follow her mother now—not at this transitional age.

His tailored suit fit him perfectly—one of dozens he owned. He brushed off the shoulders and pressed his frame against the idling car. "Just shut it off," he said to the chauffeur. "I don't know what's wrong with that stupid girl."

Rufus complied without a word.

The tall man liked that. He couldn't stand household staff participating in what was not their business. He had hired Rufus to drive him and his daughter wherever they needed to go. That was all.

"Elizabeth!" he yelled as he stepped firmly on the driveway toward the palatial house. Everything in his life was large-scale. He lived only with his daughter, but that required a fourteen-room mansion with a colonnade in front, ten acres of landscaped gardens, and the wide driveway he now walked on. The driveway surrounded the building and led to the six-car garage, the pool and tennis courts behind the house, and the service quarters that housed four maids, a gardener, and Rufus. All for his daughter, he thought. He was never home.

Elizabeth appeared at the entrance door before he reached it. A tall girl who had outgrown the innocence of her tartan school uniform. Her frame had matured beyond her seventeen years. The skirt wrapped around her hipbones tightly.

He stared at her and saw a woman, though he knew she was still a child—one who couldn't be trusted.

She's only seventeen, he thought. Nature yields adult bodies too soon, while the mind is still struggling with childhood. When did all this burgeoning sensuality come about? At twelve? Thirteen?

He had never noticed. His work left little time—and the sensuality of the women at the office was of far more interest to him.

"We're late to school again. You're making this a habit." He made an effort to sound harsh, but she seemed to pay no attention and walked past him taking a book out of her bag. He studied the left side of her head, the grooves she had shaved off with his electric razor. He couldn't think of any woman contemporary of his who would have done such a thing at Elizabeth's age. Things were so different now. Girls had developed gadding personalities. They strived to shock.

Rufus started the car quickly and got out to open a door for her. She anticipated him and rushed to get into the passenger seat.

Her father sighed. It was going to be another one of those mornings. "Sit in the back, honey."

"I'm fine here."

"I don't want you to disturb Rufus while he drives. Come back here."

"I'm not disturbing him. Am I, Rufus?" She turned to the driver and played with his cap.

"Enough of this!" The tall man put his hand on his abdomen. It wasn't worth it to fight with her. Only he would come out the loser.

"What's the big deal, dad? I get more light up front. I need to do my homework."

He didn't answer her and motioned to Rufus to go.

The car moved slowly down the driveway past a fish pond and a row of stone benches. Elizabeth wrote rapidly on a notepad. The pen produced a continuous scratch.

"Always doing your homework at the last possible minute," the father said. "That's why your grades have suffered so much lately. You take advantage of the fact I've been so busy with the move. Once the office is set up here, you're going to keep a tight schedule. And I'm going to supervise it."

She threw the pen against the pad. "Would you stop it? I'm trying to concentrate."

"It's too late to concentrate, too late for doing homework. What kind of work can you do in the front seat of the car?" He reached for the pad and ripped off the page on which she had been writing. "This is crap," he said, and crumpled the sheet into a ball. "What you have to do is ask the teacher if you can turn it in tomorrow and then do the work at home. You have a desk there, reference books, a computer—everything you need. It's better not to turn any work in than to show up with this. At least you can come up with some excuse for not having anything, while with a piece of crap like this you can't—"

"Okay, okay, okay. You've made your point." She stuffed the book and pad forcefully into the bag. "What are you so upset about, anyway?"

"You continually delay us so you can arrive late to school."

"You don't have to wait for me. I can get there on my own."

"That's not the point."

"It's not a big deal, anyway. Our first-period teacher was fired."

"The more so you should care then." He ran a weary hand through his graying hair. These were the same roles they played every time they rode together—expected behavior from both of them, a set approach to their relationship. At work, he assumed another role, and yet another at intimate moments with any of his ambitious secretaries. But he was tired of the role he had to play with his daughter. She was only being herself. Though, from where he sat, she looked like a stranger—a half-shorn head with a ponytail that bobbed with every turn the car made. It demoralized him not to have a set of eyes to face. He could deal effectively with a direct stare, but had no power when offered an indifferent back. His own parents had dealt this way with him as a child, too, with a cold back whenever his behavior slacked.

Elizabeth opened the glove compartment and took out a small flashlight. She turned it on and rotated it slowly in her fingers. The beam became visible only when it fell directly on the eyes. "Are you taking the jet?"

"Yes. I'll fly back tomorrow or on the week-end."

"Where's the key to the boat?"

"I've given you one already."

"That's for the cabins. I want the engine's."

"You're not taking it out."

"Why not?"

"Because you don't have the knowledge nor the experience either to sail or maneuver it out of the harbor." He was determined not to let her make him lose his temper. The subject of the boat had come up between them before. She often used it to prod him.

He wondered how different things might have been had he had a son, or if Elizabeth's custody had been awarded to her mother. He would have given up his fortune to take the child away from his wife. Not because he loved the girl so much, but because he believed in justice. He had to give the woman a lesson he felt she deserved.

"I'm taking it out," Elizabeth said, "whether you like it or not."

"You will have serious problems if I hear from anyone at the club that you've as much as uncovered the binnacle."

Elizabeth clenched her teeth.

They were near the school's entrance. Classes had started long ago. The car rode past a group of gardeners and flower beds. Elizabeth opened her door.

Her father started. "Would you please wait till the car comes to a full stop? Didn't you learn that in driver's ed?"

"It would have sunk in had you given me a car to drive to school."

"Grow up first. Children aren't allowed to drive."

"Who talks about children. You, with your two-million-dollar boat permanently moored at a yacht club, all wrapped up in plastic inside as if it was some museum piece. What's so adult about *that*!" She slammed the door shut and ran to the building.

The tall man looked at Rufus for a facial reaction, but got none.

4

Martin held the doorknob for several seconds as he summoned the courage to go in. He could hear the noise from inside—the sounds of adolescent girls talking and yelling and occasionally laughing. The bell had rung long ago. He was late to his first class.

A girl stood at the front of the room, mocking a lecture. She stopped cold the moment he came in. The others laughed.

"You *do* have a teacher now," he said, not sure whether it had been loud enough for all to hear. The girl took her seat.

An awkward silence followed as he studied the names on the roll sheet.

It's no big deal, he thought. They're just children. The fact that teenagers are more perceptive than adults doesn't mean one can't lie to them. They won't be able to tell I have no teaching experience.

Girls intimidated him. He had never made friends with them in his school days. They grouped easily and made merciless fun of you. He saw them as creatures who would not hesitate to stab someone in the back or heartlessly end a friendship. Even as an adult, he still lowered his gaze every time he walked past a group of them. He was terrified of being chosen as the butt of their jokes.

"My name is—" He looked for a piece of chalk on the board but didn't see any. "—Pete Lane." He checked in the desk's drawer. A few loose pieces lay there.

A voice said, "Could you repeat, please?"

He spoke louder and wrote the name on the blackboard. "You can call me Pete. I dislike too much formality." A thunderous applause greeted the statement.

He motioned for silence. "However, I *do* care for discipline, and *will* demand it here." He surprised himself. How easy it was to assume a position of power. The students were quiet and responded to his words. It would be a cinch to lie to them after all, a simple act of politics.

He thumbed through his textbook. "It's unfortunate your school year, in this class, was interrupted by—whatever it was that happened here."

"A sex scandal," a voice said. "Everyone knows about it."

"Well, I don't. I'm new here." Already they were putting him on the defensive. It wouldn't do, he thought. He had to show them who was in charge.

"We had a male teacher just like you," the girl went on. "Tried his hand at more than education with one of the students." Some of them giggled mildly at the joke. "He became *too* informal."

Martin managed a pensive look, so serious that it effectively made them stop. No one said another word. Perhaps they felt sorry for him already. He was paralyzed in his own form of stage fright, unable to make a move.

A sex scandal? Surely the label exaggerated the truth. He had already heard the story from Barbara. From the girls, though, it somehow sounded like an invitation. The scandal had chipped at their innocence.

"Does anyone here know what's been covered in class?" No one spoke. "Any takers?" He didn't want it to be up to him to carry the class. One's not a teacher to teach but to guide. What had *his* teachers done? His memory produced only a few hateful characters—yelling, unstable spinsters—not their teaching methods. No more than the frequent floggings came to mind.

"No takers?" he said. "Then I'll pick one." He experienced a vague form of pleasure in choosing a name from the list. This one. What does she look like? What can she offer me? "Joanna?" No one acknowledged it. "Is she absent?"

Someone said, "There's more than one Joanna."

"Fine. I want the one in the tartan skirt."

They laughed, and he wondered whether it was at the joke or at the fact that he had said he wanted her, without being specific. He stared at them at length. Many of the girls had hair no longer than shoulder length. "The Joanna with the long hair," he said, and waited. A girl with wavy brown hair stood. She wore a large pair of glasses and had eyebrows so thin she must have shaved them.

"That's me," she said.

"Give us an overview of the course, Joanna." He opened his book to the Table of Contents. "Whatever you've covered so far this year of the syllabus."

"We've seen the various periods." Some of her classmates laughed.

"Come on. Give her encouragement."

"The Classical Period," she went on. "The Romantic, Realistic—"

He flipped the pages. "Name some Romantics." Someone made a joke that made part of the class laugh. Martin looked up and caught her. "It was you, wasn't it?"

"Me?" she said.

"Yes, the joker. Tell us, who are the Romantics?"

She stood. Her teeth were even, with the perfection only an orthodontist can give. Perhaps the perfect smile gave her greater confidence than Joanna. She listed the authors as Martin followed the names in his book. But she was going too fast. He lagged behind as his mind trailed off onto a lists of quotations the book had in every chapter. He liked quotations. Something that amused him made him interrupt the girl suddenly: "Who said this?: 'Lying is universal—we all do it; we all must do it. Therefore the wise thing is for us diligently to train ourselves to lie thoughtfully.'"

They didn't follow him. "What's wrong?" he said. "Don't you have the book? What good is it if you don't read it? Page fifty-two. Look it up." A flutter of sheets filled the room as though hungry scavengers had been told that food was on one of them.

The girl with the even teeth said, "Mark Twain."

"Good." Martin smiled. How easily they could cooperate. "So where were we?"

"I was about to mention Emily Dickinson," Joanna said. "We were to declaim her poems when the sex scandal took place."

"Yes," he said, "when the scandal took place. It must have been a spectacle. Everyone's still talking about it. But such an event is part of life and thus part of poetry." He surprised himself at his own words. For the first time in years he felt talkative, in a position to talk. If he wanted, he could speak through the period and no one would complain. He had been kept quiet in school by louder and more assertive children. Now he had a chance to compensate for it. He browsed through the poems. One more touched his character. "Who was to declaim The Truth is Stirless?" The students turned their heads as if to find a thief among them.

"She isn't here," a voice said.

"Too bad. We'll keep it for when she is. Who had, then, The Soul Selects Her Own Society?"

"I did." A tall girl with short hair stood up in military fashion.

"Let's hear it."

The girl seemed flustered. "Do you expect us to recite by rote after all the emotional stress we've been through?" Everyone laughed.

He couldn't control the jesting atmosphere, he thought. Nervous laughter was the way in which they were dealing with the scandal. He would have to either become a stern disciplinarian or follow the flow of jokes and laugh with them. The tall girl stared at him disrespectfully, with eyes that demanded an answer.

He waved her down. "Take your seat, please. Sometimes it's easier to memorize things while under stress. I want you all to know that." He spoke from experience. For every one of his identities, he had been forced to learn pages of details, of fabricated family histories, numbers, codes, names—all under the pressure of knowing his life depended on it.

He took the book closer to his face and read, "The soul selects her own society—"

Someone had entered the classroom at that very moment, and Martin turned to look as he finished the verse, "—then shuts the door."

Elizabeth shut the door and her classmates responded with a thunderous wave of laughter.

"I was fighting with my father," she said, and walked on to a seat after making a bow and throwing him a kiss. Another roar of laughter came.

Martin put the book down. What is this? he thought. Have things changed so much? Or do I look too young to be a teacher? What happened to respect for adults, to reverence?

He stood with hands locked on his hips. "And who are you?"

"Can't you tell? I'm the class joker. People have the habit of laughing every time I perform."

Martin was taken by her beauty. Why had she chosen to ruin it by shaving one side of her head? She was taller than the military girl. Despite her hairstyle, she had the presence of an experienced woman. The only one in class.

He decided which road to follow—the one with the jokes, the one of the friendly professor. He might as well enjoy the job while he had it. He said, "You can't take that title—that of the joker of the class. I already gave it to—" He looked at the roll for a moment, then ignored it. "To the girl with the perfect teeth." They laughed again.

"Then I'll have to fight to get it back," Elizabeth said.

Someone said, "She's The Truth is Stirless."

"Oh," he said. "I suppose you forgot your poem, too."

"I know it."

"Let's see you perform, then. Come up here and recite it."

The girl with the even teeth said, "How about The Soul Selects Her Own Society?"

"We'll finish that later."

Elizabeth stood next to him. He caught himself turning his eyes away from her legs. It wouldn't be difficult for the other girls to misinterpret looks, not after their experience with their previous teacher.

She declaimed the poem fluently, with the visual skill of a thespian, allowing her legs to go feeble as she said, "How excellent a body/That stands without a bone."

Martin applauded alone. "Thank you. Please show up on time tomorrow."

The bell rang immediately after and no one cared to remain in the room. First period was the hardest to endure, and they scrambled out. He heard Elizabeth ask someone who he was, but he didn't catch the other's answer. They moved along past him in single file, occasionally staring at him as if he were a deformed mass of human flesh in a freak show.

At the last moment Elizabeth drew near him. "Let's see how long *you* last, Pete." She blew him a kiss, then rejoined the rank and was out of sight.

He stared at the door and wondered whether it had been a threat.

Chapter III

1

Souza was about to light the cigarette when he remembered his resolution—not to smoke it until Alfie's killer was dead. His hands itched. This would be a long night. He felt tired and looked for something to distract him. The wads of money in his pocket formed a visible bump, like a large tumor that had grown there and he had never bothered to have removed. He put his hand in and felt the tight rubber bands that held the bills together. He was playing with them when he heard the steps on the creaky stairwell.

A man's shadow came through the diffusing glass and pushed on the door. He wore an old, stained cap that he took off upon entering.

"There you are." He seemed surprised to find Souza sitting near the corner, away from the light.

Souza stood. "You got it?"

"Yes, but—" The man seemed disturbed. "Talk only to the men wearing caps like mine. And be discreet, please. If you're seen handing them over, everyone will want some."

"Don't you think I know that?" Souza made for the door. "Come on, let's go."

"You'll have to leave your gun here."

Souza hesitated. He had expected to be asked for his weapon, so he had slung two automatics around his chest. The indecision came from which one to give up. He drew the one on his left side and handed it over. "Don't let any filthy hands touch it."

The man didn't pay much attention. He seemed worried about something else as he placed the automatic in the corner desk's drawer. He extended his hand out to Souza—a dirty hand with grime packed under long nails. Souza retrieved one of the wads and placed it on the desk. "Let's go," he said.

The man took the wad and smiled: he had probably just earned four months' worth of salary. "Follow me."

They walked through a narrow corridor whose walls had once been light blue. The porous concrete had absorbed nearly all the color. It gave Souza the idea of a soggy sponge. He let his hand slide over it but couldn't feel a thing. His eyes were not much use either. The bare bulbs high on the ceiling were few and far apart—just enough to cast shadows and contrasts to allow a man to walk through.

Souza studied the man with the cap in front of him as he advanced with a measured stride. What miserable slime work in these places, he thought. Prison guards stand at even lower rungs than the prisoners they keep.

For a moment he imagined that it was Martin there giving his back to him. Souza went through the motions quietly: he held the air as if it were the automatic and drew his hand closer to the man's back, then up to the nape. He thought, Die, bastard—and quietly let the sounds escape his mouth. "Wooph—wooph."

The man with the cap stopped and turned briskly. "What is it?" He seemed edgy.

"You are hearing things. Walk. I don't have all night."

They moved on. Souza scratched his hands against the wall. His fingertips were reacting again. The itching and swelling came back periodically, like a woman's menses.

The quack who had done this to him was dead, but it had been no sweet revenge to kill him. Souza's hands were still ruined forever.

He recalled the events distinctly: he was a young Souza in trouble with the law. His criminal record contained nothing more serious than larceny, but the young scare more easily at the idea of spending their prime in a cell. He and his friends had ruined a job. While Souza burrowed through the drawers for drugs, the others had accidentally shot and killed the pharmacist. No one else had touched a thing in the store except him. He didn't know better. His fingerprints were everywhere. It would be an easy match.

After going into hiding, he grew desperate in the loneliness of his underground life. It finally drove him to see the quack.

The thought brought back the uncontrollable anger he had felt periodically since the operation. He scoured his hands with increasing force against the wall as he visualized the small clinic—a clandestine practice with a gilded caduceus on a glass door and no nurse to glare at. The front office had been made to look half legitimate with a row of fake degrees hung askew on sooty walls. The doctor, in his battered white robe, explained the procedure: *It's a simple surgical graft.* Souza's fingertips were to be sliced off, easily and expertly, then someone else's sewn on. Once the seams sealed, the doctor said, it would be impossible to tell a scalpel had ever touched them. *And don't worry. I've done this before. Some of the most famous families in town are my clients.*

Souza had believed it.

The allergic reactions to the grafts forced Souza to visit the doctor a few more times. The man reassured him that the puffing up was only temporary. He even gave Souza soothing pills to relieve the itching. But the discomfort never stopped. Souza tired of promises and itchy hands that swelled and turned red often. The doctor had time to move his practice to one more address before the police found him, his fingers chopped off and a bullet lodged in his brain.

The porous wall gave Souza no relief. He made a fist and rammed it against it with anger. Damned quack, he thought. Messing with us—a Portuguese family. Bastard. Let him use Italians for experiments next time.

The man in the cap pushed open a wicket on a large barred gate. They walked through. A group of men huddled over a small black and white TV set on a corner. The screen flickered between the scrambled image of white noise and a few naked bodies acting out pleasure. The men had turned the volume down but Souza could still hear the faint, artificially prolonged moans of a woman.

The man in the cap said, "Come this way." They turned a corner and the stench of urine immediately reached them. It occurred to Souza his father had been living in this filth long enough—and Martin was to blame.

They reached a smaller gate where another man in a cap waited. The first one said, "This is as far as I go. Come by my office on your way out to retrieve your property." Souza nodded. He and the new man watched the other go back into the maze of cell bars. The new man said, "You got something for me, sir?" Souza drew another wad of bills from his pocket and placed it in the man's hand. This hand was much cleaner than the other's. The gate then clanged shut and they lost themselves in the darkness.

His father's eyes were red with mourning. The old man remained quiet for minutes at a time. Souza waited. The cell looked somber under the light of a candle, and the smell of mold now overpowered that of urine. He could feel years of water absorption in the cold concrete supporting his feet. He watched his father light a cigarette and craved one for himself.

The old man burned the tip slowly, as if enjoying a pyromaniac fantasy. He let the flame burn through the length of the match even after the glowing embers of the cigarette had a life of their own. He was not burning the cigarette but a worry doll, one in the image of Martin. The old man swallowed the venomous spittle he had accumulated in his mouth and said, "The marshal, he doesn't have any clues?"

"Only that Martin called his duty officer once, to dismiss him." Souza twirled his fingers, playing with a cigarette.

"He went the way of his dead brother, then. If he's hiding on his own, we may never find him. We never could find Pete until Martin led us to him." The old man wiped his bushy brows with a slow rheumatic hand. It was as if mold constantly built up on them and he had to rub it off every other minute. He said, "Maybe the marshal is lying?"

"No. Martin has left the witness program for good. I'm sure of that. He's on his own now—and so are we."

Some frantic yelling reached them from far off inside the building. Souza drew a silver flask from his inside breast pocket and offered the old man a drink. "I don't have many ideas. I took everything I could from the cabin and went over every piece at home. Didn't find a thing in—"

"What was there to take?"

"Clothing. Toilet items. Books."

"Anything in the books?"

"I thumbed the pages. Nothing."

The old man shifted his weight. He wasn't comfortable and let his back down on the mattress as if the bed were a searing grill. The bedstead creaked. "Do we know where Martin worked?"

"That boat store near the beach."

"They may know something. Go visit, and look in the bag again too. Check what you took from the cabin—in the pockets, pill bottles, the inside covers of books—check it all again with different eyes. You'll find something."

They remained still, like stone sculptures of a deathbed scene. Only the cigarette smoke gave life to the shapes. The old man exhaled it in faint gasps as if each were his last. He said, "Get out of here. I don't want you to see me like this."

Souza was not ashamed. It meant nothing to him. Some of the best men spent time in jail. His father was just one more of them. He put out the candle and left the old man wheezing quietly in the darkness.

2

The sedan rolled slowly down the street bordering the seaside. The driver craned his head out the window looking for an address. Not an easy thing in small resort towns. Rows of building ran along blocks in confused, uneven shapes. He pointed and drove the car to a stop.

Souza got out and instinctively turned both ways to check for traffic. He rushed to cross the street while the wind flapped his raincoat against his legs. A few drops fell and he turned to the clouds to curse them. It had been in weather like this that he had found Alfie's body in the cabin.

He tapped on a window that read *The Dream Marine*. The building looked quaint, too old to be still standing. Only the zeal of a historical society could have kept it alive.

An old man unlocked the door from the inside. A set of bells jingled as he opened it. His worn mustache had turned yellow, like an old piece of scrimshaw. "Sorry," he said, "I try to lock for a few minutes while I have my midday sandwich."

Souza put his gloves on quickly to hide his hands.

"It's chilly out there today, isn't it?" The old man limped back behind a counter and took a bite off a large sandwich.

"Yes. It hurts my hands, this weather." Souza stepped in and studied the galvanized shelves. Plastic crates filled them in an organized pattern. He walked behind them to make sure he couldn't be seen from the street and picked up a small pulley from one of the crates.

The old man limped toward him. "Something I can help you with?"

"I have a photograph." Souza took it out—a grainy and creased picture that had been enlarged from a smaller print. Martin's features were easily distinguishable.

"Oh yes, yes. Is he in trouble?"

"He's in danger."

"Used to work for me. Someone else came looking for him, too. He had a much better picture than yours. An old friend of his, he said." The old man trailed off back to the counter for another piece of his meal.

"Did he leave his name?"

"He wore a pair of round glasses," the old man said as though the information were of any relevance. "No one wears those anymore. I used to sell them to sailing buffs when they were in fashion."

Souza dropped the pulley back in the crate noisily, with the intention of drawing the man back behind the shelves. Merchants, he thought, like their customers to mistreat the goods. It means they might end up buying something.

The old man limped back with a curious face. "You don't want that pulley?"

"It's overpriced." Souza moved on. "Tell me about my friend in the photograph. What did he do here?" As he spoke, he played with the merchandise. He picked up what caught his eye, studied it, and put it down with a violent thrust.

The old man's hands jumped with every bang. He didn't have the nerve to insult a client. Customers can be jerks whenever they please.

"Did he ever tell you much about himself?" Souza said.

"He was quiet, well spoken, overqualified for his job as a stock clerk, I thought." The old man spoke quickly, as though he knew that the more information he gave the sooner Souza would leave. "He brought books with him all the time and tried to read them every moment he had a chance to. The best clerk I ever had. Reorganized the store like this. Even taught me—" He seemed to be struggling to remember more details. "He disappeared just like that." The old man snapped his fingers for emphasis.

Souza stepped into the stock room. The methodical way in which the spare parts had been arranged stood out. He recalled the loan payments Martin had sent to him, when the Lanes had still been paying. Every payment had included an explanatory statement—with interest amounts listed in separate columns—as though Martin were the creditor, telling him what it all meant.

The old man said, "Sir. You can't go in there. Employees only."

Souza didn't pay attention. His eyes were enthralled with the tidiness of the room. He got the impression that the store never sold anything, that the spare parts in the stock room were museum pieces the owner only dusted occasionally. He noticed a rack of spools and nylon rope. "I like these," he said, and approached the rack to unwind a few feet of rope. He stepped back with it toward the wall, like someone taking the length of a room with a measuring tape. "Do you happen to know where my friend might be?"

"No, sir—listen, I'll go back now to—"

Souza whisked the old man by the shirt's collar and slammed him against the wall.

The man winced. "I don't know, sir. I don't know, I swear. Please, don't hurt me."

"Shut up." Souza released the shirt but kept his gloved hands near the man's stomach. "That's okay. Don't get so worked up, old man. I just want to make sure you're telling the truth."

"I don't know who he was or where he is. Please—"

The bells on the door played their pleasant jingle and stopped. Someone had walked into the store.

Souza lowered his voice and said, "You want to be left alone? Then keep quiet now, *and* later." He rushed along the galvanized shelves to the other end of the store, from where he could still see the immobile old man inside the stock room. He drew his automatic and crossed his lips with it, to show the man he meant business.

"Anybody in?" the customer called out.

Souza studied him. He looked familiar—an overweight man who, facing the counter, brushed a few dandruff flakes from his shoulders and took off a pair of round glasses before calling again. "Hello?"

Souza waved the gun at the store owner as a sign that he attend the customer. The old man walked past the shelves and toward the counter as Souza headed for the back door.

"May I help you, sir?" the man said to the customer with exaggerated volume. His hands shook uncontrollably.

Souza stepped outside before the other could reply, but he did have enough time to hear the store owner say, "Oh, it's you again."

Chapter IV

1

The Deep Black Café teemed with the afternoon tea wave. Martin was glad to recognize no faces. Most of the patrons were either older women in fancy outfits or bored young mothers with bratty children. He approached the counter and ordered a cup of coffee. Was this a safe place? He worried about an overdose of good luck. At times one needed to fall through the cracks of misfortune, to drag oneself through the mud.

The coffee burned his tongue and he set the cup down with force, suddenly annoyed with himself. Sometimes, nothing he did satisfied him. He had ordered coffee when he really wanted tea. His hands moved heavily and clumsily, as if resisting him—harbingers of bad luck. And he believed it. Luck had always run out whenever he thought it had. His mind took care of that.

He approached the counter again to order tea. The bagels behind the glass reminded him of the last time he had eaten one near the beach, the morning he was to meet Pete.

It looked as if a body had been dragged away. He recalled Tito's words. *We thought it was yours.*

The murder didn't leave Martin alone. But he wasn't sure which murder—Pete's or the one he had committed.

When his order arrived, he sat and stared at the steam from the bagels. It blended in with the tea's as he waited for it to cool. He closed his eyes and walked through the cabin, as he had done hundreds of times in the last week. What was there? In the kitchen, the knife. In the bathroom, the blood. In the bedroom—he had failed to check the cabin thoroughly. What if there had been other clues in Pete's room that he had overlooked, clues that could give away his new hiding place? After all, Pete had lived in this very city during his two successful years in hiding. The Souzas might be creative enough to deduce that he had followed in Pete's footsteps. Could there be a reference to Washington, D.C., in the things he had left behind? His mind fed easily on paranoia.

The humming of voices about him broke from time to time with the playful shrieks of children. Life's pleasant for the well-to-do, he thought. They did not have to run or hide from anyone. Their fortunes isolated them. They were viewed as good, productive citizens, merely enjoying the incidental wealth produced by their efforts. Unlike him, they didn't have to lie in order to survive.

But was that really true? He wasn't even sure when the lies had begun to take over his life.

A sudden need made him stand. His bladder was useless, he thought. Couldn't it even hold one cup?

The sun that came through the window cast a warm light on the table. He didn't want to lose it or share it with any- one else. He ordered another tea and placed it there with an open newspaper underneath. The shop had filled but no one would dare take a table with a steaming cup of tea.

The bathroom stalls were quiet, the kind of place in which a man could get killed and not be discovered until much later. Patrons of the Deep Black Café were mostly women. No one had any use for the men's room in this place.

The silence only spurred Martin's annoyance with himself. His busy mind needed distraction, not quiet. He agonized over the remote possibilities, over what might be in store for him—the liabilities accumulated in a lifetime of lying.

They *will* become due some day, he thought. Debtors have to pay off their balances at some point.

Lies were like loans from a loan shark, from a Souza. The interest they generated became unmanageable sooner or later, the debt *Past Due.*

A sudden bang made him jump against the stall. He had no time to panic. Two boys yelled and screamed their way into the bathroom with the exaggerated happiness of childhood. One of them flushed a urinal before he even used it, just for the noise it made, and said, "I'm going to shoot you. I'm the police."

"You can't shoot me." The other was short of breath. "The police are the good guys. They kill only the criminals. *I'm* the police."

Martin looked over the stall. A red-haired boy with large front teeth moved about the place energetically. The other had hair groomed in the feminine look of a child model. Neither seemed older than seven.

Martin checked his knee. It had hit the toilet paper dispenser with the jump. A bruise would surely develop. He even felt a trickle of blood run beneath his pants. The wound was soft to the touch. And there was more, enough to annoy anybody: with the jump he had sprayed his pants with urine. Now it would not be possible for him to walk out. He'd have to wait until they dried.

Outside the stall, the children impersonated machine guns. Sound effects were the domain of children. Wherever youngsters were, bullets ricocheted, cars crashed, bombs exploded, guns shot—all with a few movements of the tongue and lips. The sounds of crime, murder and tragedies were all in their game. But Martin could only take so much of it. He burst out of the stall as violently as the two boys had come into the bathroom. They stopped and eyed him with sudden fear.

Martin pointed at the urinal. "Are you going to pee or not?" Their eyes focused on the wet spots on his pants. "Yes. Just look at what you made me do." He looked down himself. The fabric had absorbed the moisture and the spots had grown like cultured bacteria into extended, dark areas.

"What happened?" the feminine boy said. "My mom would be very mad if I did that to *my* pants."

"I bet she would. But I don't have a mother, so I can do whatever I want." He could play a game with these boys, he thought, tell them a story—fabricate another lie. If it could take his mind away from worry, it was worth it. "I'm a police officer," he said, "a *real* police officer."

The boys jumped with excitement and let their guard down: a police officer was a stranger they could trust, a friend. The look of panic in them had moved on to the past.

"Wow! Can we see your gun?"

"No." He put his hand to his armpit as if to protect and hide a holster. "Real police don't draw their weapons unless strictly necessary." He looked down at the floor inside the stall, at the small pools of urine on the tiles. His knee smarted. "Now, listen. I'm going to have to arrest you two for making so much noise."

"We were just playing." The red-haired boy sunk his hands in his pockets as if to avoid handcuffs.

"That's the point. Whoever said a bathroom was a playground?"

He got no answer. The boys looked down meekly. It struck him that he might have shattered their ideals of what a policeman was. They would leave the bathroom, he thought, ready to worship criminals and other professionals more deserving adulation. "Now beat it—and don't let me catch you playing here again. This is my job. I live in this stall, watching out for children like you who come in to break the law." He opened the bathroom door and bade them out with a furious stare.

He still had his pants to take care of. He took them off and held them close to the hand dryer. They dried quickly. It gave him confidence to feel a sense of control again. He was no longer irritated with himself. Berating obnoxious children could distract anyone. Perhaps there was some benefit in having a large family.

He washed his hands and studied his face in the mirror. I did well, he thought. He had told another lie. As long as he could lie successfully he'd be safe. Things weren't so bleak, then. His run of good luck continued.

The tea was cold but it had saved the table. He sat down quietly and observed the faces that left and the fewer that arrived. No one paid attention to him. He ordered another cup of tea and wondered why he had chosen the Deep Black Café. On his provisional salary he could hardly afford luxuries. But there was a reason, he thought, an unconscious show of pragmatism. A Souza would never frequent a place like this. Fancy restaurants and coffee shops were safe.

He read the paper's headlines absentmindedly. The news did not interest him. Too much crime and violence. He cared more about the conversations going on around him, the detachment from the world with which the women spoke. They lived far off the mainstream, on the planet of late breakfasts, chauffeurs, maids, and beauty parlors. An endless dream of caprices.

A female voice hoarse with cigarettes said, "No one really cares anymore."

Others rushed to participate.

"Well, if the group is going to disintegrate—"

"We should form another."

"Non-profit organizations are a dime a dozen. We can hire a lawyer and have our own."

"That'll teach them. We'll be their direct competitors."

"Take their business away in a matter of months."

"No need to compete," the hoarse voice said. "There's an oversupply of people willing to contribute to the plight of the hungry, as many as there are hungry people in this world."

The power of money, Martin thought. With it, lofty plans are drawn up as easily as mundane shopping lists: hire a lawyer, take business away from the competition, feed the world's hungry—all with no more effort than that required for a simple trip to the supermarket.

Martin drew a large dollar sign on a napkin. You can do all those things with money, yes, but it won't free you from the mob. He pressed the pen against the paper. If you're marked for death, there's no amount of money that will rid you of the bull's-eye you wear wherever you go. It's indelible.

"Hi." A young female voice brought him back.

Elizabeth.

She said, "I'd never expect to find *you* here."

He looked at her with surprise. How easily an illusion of safety could crumble. He might see a Souza entering the shop at any moment. It seemed possible now.

She took the chair opposite his with a conceited smile and repeated, "Hi."

What's wrong with her? he thought, and then turned to the other tables. Patrons kept to themselves. No one had bothered to notice, even with that extravagant haircut of hers.

Elizabeth was the only student who made things difficult for him. She had shown enough disrespect in class to make him dread teaching her grade. She came in late, daily, then followed her arrivals with offhand remarks celebrated by the rest of the students. He couldn't control her, nor the others while she was present. Making trouble was her nature.

"You must have the wrong table," he said. "I came here alone."

"Sorry," she looked around, "there's nowhere else to sit."

But there was. He wished she had never made such an impression on him. To act surprised at her presence would have been easier then. He tried a lie: "Who are you?" He could be expected not to recognize her. She wore layers of silk under a sports jacket, a distant fashion from what she wore at school.

"Don't play games. My name's Elizabeth. I'm your student, and you know it."

"Oh, yes. I remember now. You are in one of my classes."

"I just said that."

"It's not as easy as you think—to remember students. I've got quite a few of you. Like verses in a long poem, it takes effort and practice to remember them all."

"Then you can think of me as the only one in the class who knew *her* poem."

"Poem?"

"On your first day as our teacher. We were to recite the poems the previous teacher had assigned—you *do* remember. I can see through you."

Martin blushed. What could one do confronted with such open sincerity? He knew she was not someone to whom he could lie. A different approach was required with *this* creature. Perhaps speaking the open truth would do. He could use truth as well as he could a lie—although he lacked the skill to coat it with tact. "So what if I do recognize you? Don't I have the right to say I don't?"

Elizabeth didn't seem fazed. She picked up his cup of tea. "You have the right to anything you want, and so do I. And if I choose to, I have the right to approach you whenever I please, and pester you to the end of the world."

"That's called harassment."

"Call it whatever you want."

They sat in silence like quarreling lovers without words left to yell.

Won't I be allowed to lead a quiet life? He stared at his cup of tea in her hands. The steam rose from it and wrapped her face. If it were possible to swim in a cup, he thought, I'd jump into it and let the tea scald me to death. He liked to imagine living in a giant's world—struggling in a whirlpool in the sink, being crushed to death by a shoe, escaping a giant cat—all nighttime childhood fantasies he had never left behind.

Elizabeth made a face tasting the tea and set the cup down. "You're very strange," she said. "A friendly man in class, talkative, helpful—but it's all a front. The moment the bell rings, you become someone else." She stared at his eyes relentlessly. It made him uneasy. Had she figured him out already? Did she know he was a man in hiding?

"You should be friendlier outside class if we're to learn anything from you."

Martin considered her words. She was right. The different voices, faces and personalities he used confused even him. But the switches were almost unconscious. A face for Tito, a different one for Pete, one for Barbara—the list was long.

She said, "We can make your life impossible, you know?"

"Hardly more than it already is."

"How's that?"

"You have no idea."

"We could force you to quit—drive you away, like that last teacher we had."

Martin felt cold. Others around him had already finished their pastries and coffee. They were leaving the shop, abandoning him to a young girl who scared him. He said, "Is this a threat? *Will* I be driven out too?"

"Not necessarily. Only if I want to."

"Why pick on me? I have much power over you. I control your grades, remember?"

"Grades don't count for much at a private school. We're the ones who pay tuition, not you. You're just an expense to them. And a liability and a burden if you become considered—immoral."

"Your words have an air of violence in them. What did I do to be threatened like this? I'm a peaceful man."

"You're not receptive to my needs."

That was not something he wanted to find out about—her needs. They would surely be many, and demanding. He said in a friendlier tone, "What was it that took place at the school, anyway? What's the scandal all about?" He hoped to draw her mind away from the threats.

Elizabeth bit her lower lip as if enjoying an inner fantasy. "A student accused the man of touching her where it feels good."

"In public?" He wanted to laugh but kept a straight face.

"No. In the girls' bathroom, of course. He went in while she was alone. Tried to fondle her."

"He deserved to be fired, then."

"None of us liked him. That's all it took. She made it all up. He never even came near that bathroom."

"Oh, I see." What a masterful idea, he thought. And others had believed *her*, of course. Liars lived in glory when accusations like these were taken seriously, with no evidence at hand. He marveled at the skill and ingenuity of the girls. He could learn a thing or two from them.

"The fool didn't have a chance," Elizabeth said. "It was his word against hers. She was a paying student. He was just a teacher."

"I suppose *you* were the student?"

"No! Of course not!" Elizabeth laughed as she tossed her head back. "Her parents sent her away to a private school in Switzerland. Her reward for being fondled."

"It isn't funny—to lose your job over a lie."

"No, I guess not. And it won't happen to you if you help me."

Suddenly there was nothing else to talk about. He turned around in search of listeners, spectators. They were always present—ready to feed on morsels of his private life. But most of the tables were now empty.

Why? he thought. Blackmail, from a child. He felt trapped. With a liar, one could at least be an ignorant victim and go on living unaware of the truth. But a blackmailer told you things straight in the face. He violated you with a simple threat, and you had to go on living with the fear.

"It's my grades," she said. "I'm not doing well in your class."

"You just said grades don't count much."

"They do with my father. I need a higher grade."

"You want me to lie?" He was relieved. "You're asking me to falsify school records?"

"No. I'm not that unfair. I want you to tutor me."

Martin relaxed. Tutoring was easy.

He studied her face: a few premature creases surrounded the eyes. They made her look older than she was, attractive—and she wanted him to tutor her, to spend time sitting at the same table, going over the same book, together. Would the class get him fired if he refused? Perhaps it's not tutoring she wants, he thought. Perhaps I'm at the mercy of her hormones. "What makes you think I want to tutor anybody?"

"You're my teacher." She yawned and stretched her torso like a lazy cat. "We'll have the first lesson at my house, Saturday." She winked at him and stood.

"I don't think so."

"It's all settled."

He thought of excuses not to go: she had forgotten to give him her address. He didn't have a car to—

"My driver will pick you up," she said suddenly.

"He'll need my—"

"I know where you live."

She was gone.

Martin stared at the empty tables. An acrid smell of over-brewed coffee had settled on them.

They all know where I live, he thought. The school principal, this girl, her driver will find out on Saturday. Soon even the Souzas.

He imagined a bright spotlight falling on him—something as bright as the sun—and a high-school girl forcing him onto a stage, in front of a large audience, despite his stage fright. What kind of a liar was he? He had failed with an adolescent girl. And now she had a grip on him.

Someone had switched on a loud vacuum cleaner behind the counter—a blunt way of telling him to leave. He was the only customer left.

"I'm not going anywhere on Saturday. I'll tell her to forget it—to eat her threats," he yelled. "The administration won't dismiss another teacher so readily over the feeble accusations of a single student, not a second time. No one's going to push me around. I'm not going anywhere on Saturday."

He talked as loud as he could. No risk of being heard by anyone. The vacuum cleaner took care of that.

2

The foreign woman circled the dining table carefully, with steady hands on both sides of a chafing dish. She set it at the center of the table and plugged it in the electrical outlet beneath it. Her uniform was impeccable and she arranged her cap as she stood. "You will need something else?" she said with a strong accent.

"I'll call you if we do." Elizabeth spread butter on a piece of bread. The woman left the room quietly.

Martin stared at the steam emanating from the covered tray. He was pensive, as if steam were a hypnotic he could not resist. "What's in it?"

"I don't know. They always surprise me." She poured a large glass of wine for him.

He had betrayed himself. To be here, at lunch, drinking wine, with a girl half his age—it showed the weakness of his determination. His decisions didn't count for much, then, he thought. Perhaps it was a sign that he had finally reached a level of comfort, an identity that suited him well, one in which he felt safe enough to let his guard down and enjoy life some. And what was so wrong about tutoring the girl anyway? Who would find out? At any rate, his intentions were good.

"You drink wine at lunchtime?" he said.

"Whenever I please." She filled her glass to the rim and uncovered the chafing dish. "Oh, it's some type of chicken and rice again." She served herself and started to eat.

"I thought I was coming here to tutor you." He tried to inject some wrath into his voice without much success.

"Can't learn on an empty stomach."

"You could have eaten before I came."

"I hate to eat alone." She dug into her food gracelessly. Her manners betrayed her. The adult features evaporated with every spoonful she shoved in her mouth. In eating, she was a girl.

"You have an answer for everything, don't you?"

"One has to in this house. My father's a know-it-all."

"Then he will object to my being here."

"He'll never know. He's never home on Saturdays."

"What if he showed up suddenly?"

"We'll rush to my bedroom. I'll hide you under my bed."

"That won't do. He'll see the table, set for two, the wine glasses. What lie could you possibly tell him to justify all this?"

"If you don't mind, I have no desire to talk about my father. He and I are not on good terms."

"That's no excuse. Fathers and daughters rarely are."

"Oh, stop it." She leaned over to check his lap. "Are you praying, or something?"

"No." His hands were still under the table.

"Why aren't you eating, then? Serve yourself."

He wasn't hungry. One can't easily eat and worry about mistakes at the same time. The lunch itself was a mistake.

I should have offered to tutor her at a park, he thought, or at the school's cafeteria—in a public place. She's in complete control here. It's her territory. I let myself fall into a trap.

He said, "What makes you so worried about not doing well in my class? I'm sure the school won't want to lose your father as a client. Whether you pass my class or any other doesn't make much of a difference, does it?"

"My dad's a proud man. Wants me to succeed on my own."

They drank the last of the wine while a clock chimed somewhere. "It's late," Martin said, still thinking of the next step—tutoring. Elizabeth rang an electric service bell at the edge of the table. His cigarettes jutted out from his breast pocket. She took the pack and lit one.

"He lets you smoke, too?"

"My father doesn't know about my sins." She held the cigarette feebly, in a fashion-magazine pose.

The maid appeared quietly to collect the dishes.

Martin watched her leave the room and said, "Doesn't she inform him?"

"Nobody likes my father in this house. They're with me. They'd even lie for me, if I asked them to."

The woman appeared again and spoke mechanically. "Dessert today?"

"No. We're going out for ice cream later, after I show him my bedroom." The answer caused no reaction on the woman's face. Martin waited until she had gone and said, "Thank you for lunch. I'm going home."

"What for? You haven't tutored me yet."

"Ice cream? Your bedroom? What do you think I am?"

"What's the big rush? You have plans for today?"

"No." He answered stupidly, he thought, before he could think of a good lie.

"And how long will you tutor me? No more than one, two hours at the most. So there's plenty of time. We have all day. Let's go."

She was out of the room before he could reply. Her steps echoed as she ran up a staircase. Now's the time, he thought, to leave while I'm still clean. Am I going to jeopardize my hard work for a thrill? Empires had fallen because of uncontrollable lust. It would take much less than that to blow his fragile cover.

He entered her bedroom with half steps—not sure he was in the right room, a space that was by itself larger than his house. It only lacked a kitchen.

"Sorry about the mess," she said. "I gave the maid the day off."

Martin recalled the women in fancy outfits at the Deep Black Café. This was what they went home to—four large closets filled with clothes; a large, comfortable bed; empty shoe boxes strewn on a thick, woolly carpet—a movie-set life.

Elizabeth paced about the room with arms extended, pointing at her possessions as if introducing them, like a model peddling products on a television show. It occurred to him she felt a thrill showing off to him—a man without the strength to tell her to stop.

She hopped on the bed and bounced on it. "Want to try the mattress?"

"No."

She poked at the eiderdown and watched the ripple effect. "It's a water bed. I float naked on it at night, like a siren in the ocean."

How much more obvious can it be? Martin thought. Am I going to wait until I'm in bed with her to tell myself it's too late? He had to leave now. It was imperative. But he felt weak at the knees. Her lips seemed suddenly wet and desirable. Her mature features had come back now that she had finished eating. He imagined the inside of her bed. He just had to see what she had to offer.

"Talking about the ocean—" She jumped up. "We'll go there now. I'll show you my dad's boat." She pulled at his arm and led him downstairs.

They rushed through the marble halls, into a study where she retrieved a set of keys, and out again.

He felt sorry for himself. Was there anything worse than this? She was playing with him. He could see it—the teasing: *Want to try the mattress? I float naked on it at night.* Tease and Withdraw. They did it to rats in laboratories to make them psychotic.

Martin recalled his mother dragging him by the hand through a shopping mall. She had misplaced a new purchase and searched for it frantically from store to store. In a sense, Elizabeth was doing the same thing.

They were about to get in the car when he recovered his senses. It's difficult for fugitives to be assertive, he thought. Assertiveness meant being loud and boisterous. A fugitive could not afford the notoriety. When he had first joined the Program, Tito had given him instructions. *The key to survival is a low profile.* Yes, a low profile. He wondered if that also meant a lowly life. And how low he had gone already—almost to the depths of a minor's water bed.

She got in the car but he didn't follow, closing the door behind her instead and rushing away on foot, toward the massive iron gate.

Elizabeth jumped through the sunroof like a hysterical jack-in-the-box. "What now?"

He ran without turning.

"You promised," she said. "Come back here! We'll tutor. Won't go to the boat. Come on!"

I'm not falling for it, he thought. A low profile, yes, but not a lowly life, not again. Study on your own.

The electric gate began to shut. He had little time to check behind him, but enough to see two Dobermans and Elizabeth rushing after him. She aimed a remote control at the gate.

Martin made a dash for it and imagined, as he ran, that he was running for his life, that it was the Souzas behind him and not the girl. They've caught up with me, he thought. The bastards. I've got to run, got to run....

3

Souza touched the dry piece of blood on the sand and then pushed it in to sink it from view. They should have been more careful, he thought. But he knew it was hard to worry about details in the darkness. They had dragged out Alfie's body during the night.

He walked on and reached the sandy footpath. Even under a bright sun the cabins appeared to him a somber sight. The memory of the murder made it so. Death sucked all color away.

The warm weather made his gloves look more the part of a costume. Business was better for him on a cold winter day, when nobody bothered twice about his hands and why they were covered.

Only the last house at the end of the compound showed signs of life. He knocked on a door marked *Administrator.* A woman wearing a black knitted shawl opened it. She had the pallor and eyes of one too sick to ever go outside.

Souza pointed at the row of cabins. "Are you in charge?"

She studied his gloves with distrust. Her ferret eyes twisted. "You the police?"

"No. My name's Bob Ford." He produced a photo identification card. "I'm looking for my younger sister. She—eloped about a year ago with the man they found dead here the other day." He strained his eyes to produce some moisture in them. A gush of wind made him stumble for a moment and cover his face from the blowing sand.

She examined him against the picture on the card. The wind forced her to step back farther behind the door.

Souza said, "I don't—we don't know where she is. The police haven't helped, either. My parents are distraught."

"I never saw a thing." She gave him back the card. "I was in the hospital with pneumonia."

A lie, Souza thought. Alfie had said a woman had taken payment from Pete and given him access to the cabin.

"It was my sister checked him in," the woman said. "But she's not here now. It's market day today. You'll have to wait."

Delays like this one always rankled him. He didn't enjoy the waiting periods, the slow process of gleaning details and clues that would eventually lead him to someone in hiding. His thrill was in what came later—making ends meet. He said, "I'll wait."

"Well, don't stand out there. You'll freeze to death. Come in."

He looked around perplexed. The day was warm. Perhaps his gloves gave her the idea that it was cold outside.

She locked the door carefully and rubbed her hands for warmth. Then he understood. The low temperature inside the house made him shiver. The bare cement floor reminded him of the cold vaults of a morgue.

"Follow me," she said.

A cat approached and coiled itself around his leg. He kicked it mildly and followed the woman.

"Excuse the mess," she said. "I've been sick, you know?"

In the living room plants greatly outnumbered the pieces of furniture. They made it difficult to move freely about the room.

"Take a seat. May I get you some tea?"

Souza considered it. It might be a long wait in this cold. "Yes. It'll keep me warm."

"Yes it will. I saw you out there, wearing those gloves, almost shivering." She left the room with the slow steps of an invalid.

The room was a converted porch. The thin walls seemed to absorb all heat and replace it with humidity. The seats were moldy at the lower ends, growing green like square plants resting on legs. The cat sniffed at them and ran its claws through the old, rent fabric as it had obviously done many times before. Then it moved closer to Souza and jumped in his lap. It had an unpleasant smell and a few spots of mange on its pelt. Souza was glad to have his gloves on and pushed the animal away.

The woman returned almost immediately with a tray and tea crockery. "It's so cold I keep water boiling all day long—ready to make a hot cup of tea." She served him with shaking hands. For a moment he thought she might be afraid of him.

"It *is* cold in here," he said.

"For sure. Would you believe the heating's on? It just doesn't reach well around the house." She gave out a sigh of anticipated pleasure before she drank her tea.

"It's not good for you, with your pneumonia. You should spend your time somewhere else in the house, where it's warm." He felt a sudden contempt for the ferret eyes and wished she would leave him alone.

"Oh, it's not the cold that gave me pneumonia. It's the suffering and depression. They weaken my body so." She gulped from the cup. "My husband died last winter. This is the room we used to spend time in."

"It's a tragedy—to lose a relative."

"Nights and days of mourning, I tell you. Bereft, not able to swallow your food or breathe properly. It's a living nightmare."

"I know what you mean."

"But one has to get over it. If it wasn't that my sister moved in soon after he—" The pain seemed to come back to her in morsels, like bites of a dish she didn't want to eat. He noticed a faint sniffle hidden under her breath. You can't get over it, he thought. The pain goes on and on, and you can't rest until you avenge your dead.

She wiped her nose swiftly. "You said *your* sister was in danger?"

"We don't really know, but think she might be. We haven't heard from her in over a year. Last time we saw her was right before she eloped with that man who's now dead."

"Apparently he was murdered."

"I wouldn't know." Souza pulled out a handkerchief and blew his nose forcefully. Nothing came out of it but a false snort of sadness.

"How awful," she said, "to elope with a fellow—then find him dead."

"Yes."

Stupid woman, he thought. Some people deserve to be found dead. He looked down at the cat. It wouldn't leave his feet alone. He pushed it away with a show of respect.

"She thinks you're my husband. Howard used to lift her up with the insteps of his shoes, like a forklift."

She turned suddenly quiet. The memory seemed to overpower her. Souza sipped tea calmly and studied the room. The furniture and curtains looked older than the house, an inheritance from relatives too far in the past to remember. The plants were limp and sullen, as if they were also mourning the dead husband. She seemed to notice his attention to them and said, "They're suffering from neglect. My sister lived in the city all her life—hates plants—and I don't have the energy to look after them the way I used to." She served more tea and gave out a sigh. "You will forgive me," she said, "but, even if the man is dead now, it's a good thing your sister eloped with him. One has to follow the emotions, do things when one's young. There's no sense in wasting your youth *not* daring to do things. She's lucky she did it at her young age." The woman pulled back her graying hair, caressing it with her hands in an effort to block her tearing eyes from his view. "Me?" she said, "Here I am, alone. Who's going to want me now—old and sick? Where am I going to find company at this stage? A new husband? He was only sixty-seven, and he died just like that."

Souza watched her sob impassively. Emotions were a sign of weakness. He didn't operate that way. Much better to suppress feelings, to turn them into actions. He had turned grief for Alfie's death into energy to pursue and kill Martin; anger caused by creditors who didn't pay into energy to harass them until they paid. He almost felt sorry for the woman. *Maybe I should do her a favor and plug her with a round in the head.*

A noise came from the front door. The woman's head cocked immediately. She could have been a ventriloquist's doll, made to change moods instantly. Souza had seen this type of reaction before, in his victims. Only fear had power to make such a sudden shift.

The woman stood. "It's my sister. She doesn't want me crying." She dried her face with her cuffs. Someone fidgeted with the doorknob before a series of knocks reached the cold waiting room. "She forgot her key again. Let me open." She rushed out into the hall.

Souza reviewed his story. Something told him the sister would be an assertive bully who would refuse to cooperate. If that were the case, he would have to abandon his display of emotions and show some force.

It doesn't pay to struggle with old hags, he thought. *If they don't want to help, I'll squeeze what I need out of them and leave no witnesses.*

He heard whispers among the rustle of plastic bags and made an effort to hear. A voice said, "Why did you let him in?" The reply was garbled by the bags.

A new set of ferret eyes stared at him from the threshold. She was overweight from sedentary city life, arched forward with the weight of her groceries.

"What do you want?" She didn't mean to be friendly. Her face, he thought, just pleaded for violence.

"I'm looking for my sister."

She set the bags on the floor and walked to him menacingly, as if dealing with him would only take a moment and she would soon go back to her things. "We haven't seen any women around here lately. Just prostitutes and male swine who come do their dirty business with them whenever they get an itch."

Souza stared at the ferret eyes with contempt. They were a duplicate set of the other's. Must be a genetic defect, he thought. "My sister was married to the man the police found dead here. You checked him in."

"I already told the police everything we know. He was a phony—refused to sign the register and offered to pay more not to sign. I said, 'I don't care if you lie. Sign whatever name you want on it.' That's all we know about the man. We're sorry about your sister but we have things to do." She took his empty cup and the tray with it.

"Could I please see the register?" He drew his hand nearer the holster under his arm. This is it, he thought, comply or die.

The woman in the shawl stepped in. "It wouldn't hurt if we show him the register. His sister has been missing for a year." The other did not move. Her heavy calves were set solidly on the floor like cement stilts under a massive water tank.

"His parents are distraught, you know," the frail one said, "very distraught." It seemed to touch a nerve in the bully's psyche—a shared childhood tragedy perhaps. She passed the tray to her frail sister with an air of contempt and disappeared into the hall.

"She'll get the book now," the frail one whispered. "I'll take this to the kitchen."

Souza was relieved. He didn't want to complicate things by adding two more bodies to the pile. Only one more person had to die, he thought, and that was Martin.

The cat continued to purr and butt at his legs. He took advantage that the women were out of sight to give it a swift kick. The animal growled and Souza stepped forward to give it another—an easy way to get back at the bully. One more kick sent the cat fleeing into the kitchen.

The bully came back. The register was an old ledger that had been in use for years. One thousand pages took many tourist seasons to fill up. More than half the pages were still blank. Souza thumbed through them until the last few entries flickered past. There it was—Pete's steady handwriting, the carefully drawn letters of a man living a fully self-conscious life.

It seemed like such an easy job in hindsight. If he had only done it himself instead of sending Alfie to his death. I could have killed Martin first, he thought. I knew where he was.

Pete had called Martin to arrange the meeting. Souza knew all about it. He had tapped Martin's telephone. It would have been an easy kill, but he had been greedy. *Why not wait until the two of them meet and then kill them together? Why not give them to Alfie? It's an easy job.*

His past decisions came back to torture him. It had been easier to deal with Alfie's mutilated leg. That had been an accident. But this—misjudgment. Why the rush to initiate the neophyte? Everything had gone wrong.

The bully said, "See it here? The police said his real name wasn't Arthur West. Bet he wasn't from Baltimore, either. That's for sure a phony address, too."

Souza looked down. "We believe my sister is in danger, where she used to live with this man, but we don't know where that is. Didn't he—?"

"I told you the police got all I know about him. They asked me all there was to ask."

"Sometimes policemen forget important details. I'm sure they were too busy with the murder and the man's corpse, trying to collect physical evidence. They overlook things they don't consider important—where the victim lived, for example, or with whom."

"I'm sorry," she said in a gentler tone. "Your sister must be very precious to you, I'm sure, but we don't know anything about her. That man's dead. We never talked much to him. We don't know a thing."

Maybe his act *was* convincing enough. The bully seemed to believe his lost-sister story. That was not the problem. She seemed truly sorry. The two women could possibly know nothing. Or the bully might have changed her tone only to get rid of him. He couldn't tell. The cat stared at him from a distance, as if also wishing to be rid of him soon. It seemed useless. He thought, It's not even worth it roughing them up. They don't know a thing. "Thank you," he said, and struggled to add, "ma'am."

The bully walked him to the entrance. The other trailed them without a word, and her silence made him wonder. Up until the bully's arrival, she had been talkative. Now a sort of fear seemed to hold her.

A breath of warm air hit his face when the bully opened the door. She looked down at his gloves and said, "You won't need those out there. It's warm."

"I wear them to protect my hands from the sun. It's tough on them—this weather." They smiled at each other for courtesy's sake. Each new what disdain each felt for the other. Souza stepped out and paced away slowly without looking back. He had nowhere else to go. Even ideas had suddenly dried up. The only thing left was that almost-faded dedication he had read inside one of Pete's books. *To Ramsey—this good book to stimulate your intellect in preparation for an arduous four-year journey at Georgetown. —Dad.* It could mean anything—that Georgetown was the university in Washington, D.C.; that Pete had purchased the book, used, in that city, the same city in which he had been hiding successfully for the last two years. Too many assumptions, Souza thought. Too much a long shot. If he only had something else to go on.

He heard hissing behind him. Maybe the cat was mocking him? He turned to look. The frail sister in the shawl hissed again as she ran toward him. She didn't seem so weak now. Even out of breath she spoke the moment she reached his side. "Sorry to have lied to you. I was afraid. I wanted my sister to be there with us, but it was a mistake. She's too inflexible." She shook her head with a gesture of disgust that was not convincing enough. "See, I wasn't in the hospital when the man came. I was feeling sick, yes, but up and about the house." She had to stop to catch her breath. "It's true the man didn't say much to us, but he made a comment about the weather—said how windy this place was compared to Washington. Then a man came later, one of the policemen—said *he* was from Washington. A heavy man, he was. He showed us some pictures as well, of another man—asked if we'd seen him." The ferret eyes rolled with self-righteousness.

Souza could not control the urge. It would be risky to ask more about the Lanes now that he knew Program officers had come to investigate. But he had to take advantage of this great opportunity. He drew out his wallet and showed her the battered photo of Martin. "Is this the man he was looking for?"

"Yes, that's him!" She was excited. "Perhaps you'll be able to find your sister in Washington now."

"I hope so." He gave an uneasy look back at the house.

"The man told us—the heavy-set fellow—to watch out for this one in the photo, or anyone else asking about the murder. He said we should report back to him any strangers who came. Gave us a toll-free phone number and all, for us to call him. I didn't like him one bit, I tell you. He was so large and intimidating. Didn't think I could trust—"

She stopped at the look of anger in Souza's face, and at the sight of the automatic. Souza held a tight grip on it. He had caught a flashbulb going off inside the house. It annoyed him that people played games with him, especially old women who had no right to meddle in his affairs. He sprinted toward the house.

The woman in the shawl panicked. "It's only my sister. The police told us to describe anyone who came. We thought a photo—please, don't hurt her!" She ran after him.

Inside the house, the bully fluttered from one room to the next. A lone hen abandoned in a burning coop, trying to find an exit. She pressed the camera tightly under her armpit.

Souza followed her into the dark living room and shot. She screamed before uttering a series of raving grunts. The plants and furniture made it difficult for him to move freely. His aim failed him and he stumbled on a chair. He missed again and again as his heavy target slid around the furniture like a giant rat in a maze. There's no time for this, he thought. He gripped a chair and lunged at her with it. The camera fell with the blow. The flashbulb went off continuously, like a strobe light. It flickered on him until he crushed it under his heel.

The one in the shawl had seen it all. She stood frozen on the threshold, staring at her sister with her ferret eyes twisted with fear.

"You lied to me," Souza said. "I don't like liars."

It took one shot. Her body collapsed as if suddenly the shawl had turned into stone. Souza went back to the bully. A simple chair blow wasn't enough to snatch life away from a mass this large. He shot her twice through the head. A man in his position had to make sure. Witnesses had the uncanny ability of showing up unexpectedly at trials later on. Her mouth spewed forth a frothy spittle. She was dead.

He suddenly felt sick with the smell. It made him think the two women had been living with death long before his arrival. He picked up what was left of the camera and put it in his pocket.

The cat seemed to be gasping for air in a corner. Animals can also feel fear. Souza hesitated. His policy was to leave no witnesses. "Sorry, puss. Your masters won't be any good to you like this. Better you accompany them." He leveled the automatic and extinguished the nine lives with a single bullet.

His work was done. He felt closer to his final goal. The information the woman in the shawl had given him was something to work on. It might someday lead to Martin. Patience is all it takes to succeed.

4

The public library was noisy as usual. Martin could never read in peace there. Young students frequented the place to socialize and flirt. The constant murmur of voices distracted him as much as the sound of chairs' legs scraping the tile floor. He could only afford enough concentration to read headlines and captions.

Martin was anxious. Being in charge of his own life had turned out to be more difficult than expected. He no longer had an excuse not to lead a normal life. But that was something to worry about later, he thought. He should be proud to have so far met every challenge his new life had placed without the help of the Program. Pete had been right all along: you *could* go solo and succeed. All you needed was imagination, and some luck.

He turned to the digital clock on the wall. It was past the hour. He took a deep breath as if to muster some patience. I hope things work out differently this time, he thought. He fingered the pages of the magazine and wondered whether he was doing the right thing. The thought left him when Elizabeth arrived.

Martin was beginning to like her. She had apologized, and he had agreed to tutor her in return, as long as they met in public places.

She took the chair in front of him and placed her books on the table. No need to greet each other with words. They had agreed to spare those formalities and use glances instead.

For a moment he worried that perhaps this *was* a mistake after all. But, no. He had to think of his sanity, to consider the loneliness of his daily life. Who else could he befriend in his position? Tutoring gave him the excuse to spend time with her. And she was perfect company. At her age, she didn't mind dishonest replies to her straight questions. No one else would do that for him.

Throughout his years in hiding he had never been able to make friends with women his age. They were too cautious, too keen, and suspected that something was wrong with his life soon after they met him. He never dared tell them the truth. As a result, every one of his past lovers had come to think of him as unfaithful. Relationships never lasted. Life had been a lonely affair since his family had defaulted on the Souza loans. Prostitutes had never managed to fill the void.

Elizabeth stared at him and waited for his next move.

He said, "We'll study in silence for an hour, and that will be all. The best way to memorize poems is by writing them. So you'll do that, one verse at a time." He drew a stack of paper slips from his pocket. This time he had prepared the lesson. "This is how it works: you take one of these slips and write a single verse on one side of it. Then I read it and write a comment about it on the other side and give it back to you. You then read my comment and write your opinion of it. And I read *that*, and so on. We go back and forth with every verse until we've discussed the whole poem—all without saying a word."

She gave him a blank stare. He got the impression she didn't care what they did, that she had come only to be with him, the way a fan might go to a dream meeting with her idolized rock star.

He bade her to start writing. She looked lost and opened her book randomly. As she wrote, he studied the long hair falling over her right temple. Her left side lay barren in contrast, plundered by her own hand in the name of fashion. She wrote slowly and paused.

Martin turned to the stacks on his left. They were gray and old and overflowing with books. He leaned forward for a look at the librarian, a short middle-aged woman seemingly engaged in busywork.

Elizabeth passed him the first slip. "Here."

"Shhh. You're not supposed to speak. Stick to the rules, please." He read it and frowned. She had written more than one verse.

From a tree I picked a flower
To which nature gave a smell.
A long day's worth its hours
If by night things turn out well.

Martin read it several times and failed to recognize it. True, he was not an expert on the subject he was teaching, but he had read enough. At least he thought he had successfully memorized the first verse of every poem in the book. But this one escaped him. He tried to buy time by writing on the back of the slip, *Only one verse at a time, please.* He gave her a quick glance. When she smirked, he added on the note, *And do one from the book, not your head.* He returned the slip to her, and she received it with a serious look. She took a new slip from the pile and began again.

Martin liked the idea of a quiet hour with Elizabeth. She seemed so much more attractive to him, as a person, when she didn't speak. Words had often driven him away from friendships. He found a kind of beauty in people who went about their lives in quiet meditation.

Scenes without sounds are the most moving in a dramatic film, he thought. Words defile what beauty's in the lips. One could even feel pity for the devil if only he were dumb. Must be the reason why Christians put words in Lucifer's mouth.

Martin rubbed his eyes and yawned. The hour had passed and he was tired. Elizabeth wrote verses with less energy and her comments no longer seemed fresh. He felt a sudden urge to hug her, to tell her to stop this boring activity and go out instead to the park.

He noticed she was writing more than one verse again, another poem from her head, probably. He snatched the slip from her hands, scaring her. Her arm knocked the heavy book off the table, and the resonant sound it made on reaching the floor played like the report of a shotgun. It made him jump with the memory of bloody bullet holes. A similar sound must have preceded Pete's death, he thought.

Elizabeth turned to the librarian's counter. The woman had stepped out from behind it to see what the noise was all about. Martin leaned back in his chair to hide from her view. Let the girl take the blame.

Elizabeth waved at the librarian—everything was fine. She picked up the book slowly and looked at Martin with eyes that seemed to ask, Did you read it?

He looked at the slip.

> *If you love your life a little*
> *God will stay with you today.*
> *If you love me at least a little*
> *I would like to hear you say.*

"Very good," he said. He didn't know what to make of it.

She dug through the pile of used slips and picked the one with the first stanza. "Read them together. They'll make more sense."

He put both slips together and read them again slowly. Nice of her, he thought, to be so romantic. But he wasn't in the mood. The shot-like sound from the book had regressed him to a state of fear. He slipped the poem in his breast pocket and stood. "I think the hour is up."

5

Souza observed the woman with impatience. He despised her type—short and near-sighted, obviously engaged in busywork and thinking herself important for it. He coughed a little to let her know he was waiting.

It took her a moment to look up from the pile of books. "Yes?" she said.

"I'm looking for my brother-in-law and a friend of—"

"You'll have to go to personnel, sir." She seemed eager not to be distracted from her work.

"Personnel won't do any good. My brother-in-law doesn't work here. He's missing and we're trying to find his whereabouts. Maybe he and his friend have been here?" He showed her two separate photographs, one of Martin and one of Pete. She strained her eyes behind her bifocals. Souza said, "They read a great deal—bookworms. Must have been here often in the last few weeks."

"Oh, yes," she said. "I saw this one yesterday." She pointed at Pete's photograph.

Useless, Souza thought. It would mean something if at least Martin and Pete resembled each other a little. But they were clearly two different men. Pete's receding hairline ran deep. Martin was handsome and youthful.

"Oh, what happened to your hand?" The librarian started.

"Nothing. Just an accident."

"My husband cut off three of his fingers once with a circular saw. So stupid! He looked so unattractive afterwards—oh, I don't mean to offend you. Your case is quite different, of course. You still have all your fingers. Perhaps if you used a cream my doctor—"

A loud bang interrupted her. "What now?" She seemed extremely annoyed and stepped around the counter with determination. "This happens so often," she said. "These kids are a nuisance."

She stood there, squinting, trying to make out who had caused the disturbance. Souza looked in the same direction. They saw a young woman with a strange haircut wave at them—everything was fine. A book lay on the floor. The young woman picked it up.

The librarian said, "These kids are so hyper sometimes. You'd think they purposely eat high-sugar snacks before coming here to spend their energies on being loud."

She returned behind the counter and resumed her work as though he were no longer with her. She had forgotten her doctor's cream, it seemed, and Souza realized he was out of luck. He wondered how long it would take him to find Martin in such a large city. I'll have to stick around books, he thought. Books are as much a refuge to intellectuals as bottles are to drunkards.

He walked outside and said a quiet prayer. If God would only give him a small clue, something to go on. He felt he deserved a divine hand to intercede in his quest. Alfie deserved it. He paced the stone sidewalk and appreciated the brightness of the day. Good thing spring weather was here. It would make his investigation much easier. Maybe God was giving him a hand already. Sunny skies were a start.

The driver would not arrive with the car until the day after tomorrow. Souza would have to depend on his feet until then. No sense in using public transportation. Taxicabs had already brought him enough bad luck.

A few of the places he could reach on foot. He took out a crumpled set of yellow pages he had torn off a phone book. Every bookseller in town was listed on them, large and small, and he hoped at least one would recognize the used book that had belonged to Pete, the one with the dedication. Book people know their books like a pervert knows his vices, he thought. Sooner or later someone will identify this one.

The glass pane on the front door at Book Fiends was cracked. Someone had made a half-hearted effort to mend it with a strip of tape. Souza had noticed that things were left to fall apart. Stores like this one seemed to sell just enough books to cover salaries. Shelves, counters, and the buildings themselves were left in a sort of intentional disrepair, as though the owners meant the places to have as worn-out a feel as the books they contained. This was the last store he meant to visit. Any others would have to wait until the car arrived.

Souza had learned much about the used-books business. The type of clientele who frequented the stores intrigued him. The average patron was a frail-looking intellectual—a failed professor or a defrocked priest, perhaps—mostly a man of a sordid sort. Like lustful boy scouts engrossed in pornography, they appropriated a corner here and there to cautiously study a page.

Souza had had no luck with any of them yet. The photographs and the book had elicited no response at the gay-and-lesbian bookstore, at the rare books shop, or the erotic literature reading room.

Maybe the tip wasn't worth the two old hags' lives, he thought.

No one stood at the counter. The pulpy smell of the old, yellowing books stacked around the cash register made him think of money. How careless, he thought. A large store like this and no attendant in sight to either help a customer or mind the merchandise.

He walked to the back end of the store. The place suffered from an oversupply of incoming material—books thrown on the shelves haphazardly, stacked on the floor to heights that forced them to lean back against the shelves. Souza had to watch where he stepped. The long rows of books were occasionally interrupted by a human form hunched secretly over a page.

He knew it was a waste of time to check every aisle. The chances of finding Martin thumbing a book here were minimal. And despite his faith in God, Souza didn't believe in coincidences or good luck. He got results with hard work alone, and that meant keeping surveillance of each library or bookstore for several weeks at a time.

Bookworms must eat about a book a week, he thought. It won't be long before Martin needs more material. If he chooses this bookstore, I'll be here, waiting for him.

Once he found Martin, the rest would be easy, enjoyable work—to follow him and find where he lived. Souza hoped anger would not overcome him and make him kill Martin too quickly. For once, even if he didn't approve of sadistic practices, he planned to let his victim's life leak slowly, drop by drop.

Dying can make a second feel like days, he thought, and Martin will be very aware of himself, fading away in a panic, for what will seem to him like centuries.

A tall anxious man tried to pass through between a stack of books and Souza. He looked pale and haggard and was in a rush to get somewhere.

Souza stopped him. "You the attendant?"

"Yes, but—"

"I need to ask you about something." He pulled out Pete's book from his pocket.

"You'll have to pay for that before you put it in your pocket, sir. Otherwise we'll think you're stealing." The man ran through toward the front counter. "Just come up here—I got someone on hold who can't wait."

Souza watched him sprint away with disdain. This was exactly the type of character who made him want to draw and shoot. But one had to be patient with people, even with pale cashiers dressed in tight, black tee-shirts and jeans, a ponytail and earrings. He followed to the counter and slammed Pete's book next to the phone while the man voiced a staccato spiel into the receiver. All this book nonsense was beginning to annoy Souza. He would have preferred Martin were a gun collector, or a devout church-goer. Those things he knew about.

When the ponytail hung up, Souza said, "First thing, this book came here with me—not from one of your shelves—understand?" He waited for a nod to continue. "I brought it because I have a question about it."

"What?" the man said bluntly, "Is it missing pages? You should have looked before you bought it. Where's your receipt, anyway?" He raised his voice and others got interested. Heads turned in his direction.

"There isn't one. I'm looking for the book's owner, the person who bought it. He's missing. I don't even know if he bought the book here at all—*that's* what I'm trying to find out. Take a look." Souza opened the book's cover, handed it to the man and placed the two photographs on the counter. A number of customers heard him and approached with curiosity. Souza said, "That's good, all of you, take a look. The more people who see this the better." It was a gamble, of course. If anyone told Martin someone was looking for him, it would ruin everything.

The ponytail examined a number written in pencil on the top-right corner of the book's flyleaf. "This looks like Jay's writing," he said, and fumbled about behind the counter through a stack of books until he found one similar in size and age to Pete's. They all drew in closer together, like a crowd of tramps to an outdoor fire in winter, and the ponytail compared the handwritten prices on both books. He said, "It's Jay's, for sure. The book's from us."

Souza could not contain the smile. "That's good, so good." He forgot all about the animosity he felt for the ponytail. "Now do me a favor. Look at these two gentlemen." He pointed to the pictures and then moved around so that everyone could take a better look. "Recognize them?"

"This guy I've seen," the ponytail said, "but not lately." He tapped on Pete's photograph with a pencil.

"Yes. I understand that he moved abroad. But it's this other one I'm really looking for."

No one said anything. Martin's face was a stranger's.

Souza sighed. But he had not failed. At least he knew where Pete had been hiding successfully for two years.

He left the bookstore shaking everyone's hand with a smile and a word of appreciation.

It doesn't do any good to get so excited so soon, he thought, but Martin could possibly be in this same city right now.

If it had worked for Pete here, there was reason for Martin to follow. A pleasant tourist destination, recommended by friends, must be given a try by any serious world traveler.

Chapter V

1

In his years of hiding in obscure small towns, Martin had forgotten how much of a hell a large city could be. Aside from the libraries and bookstores, there was not much here to interest him. It seemed difficult to view life without a future move in mind, with the idea that his stay here would be a permanent one. And that depressed him.

To clear his mind, he walked, sometimes several miles at a time. At least, in moving on his own two feet, he felt he was going somewhere, if only for part of a day. A walk was a pleasant form of distraction. He felt free.

But who am I fooling? he thought. I am really trapped here. Security turns so quickly into boredom, and a safe life can be as much a prison as one on the run.

He was painfully aware of leading a normal life, a settled existence devoid of danger. No need now to prepare a plan of action, to be ready for the next new start in life, the next new job, name, identity—the next lie. His run for survival was over and, curiously, this fact made him as anxious as the fear of sudden death at the hands of a Souza.

He crossed the street carelessly, not bothering to look both ways. If life was to be so slow, perhaps an accident could create some excitement. Days spent in a hospital bed on the verge of a coma could possibly bring about his survival instincts again. Even that seemed appealing.

As it was, his life was something to laugh about—a teacher in an all-girls school. He thought, I've joined the common masses, one more content member in a crowd of millions. My mind will soon descend into a permanent state of atrophy, and it won't be able to hold its own. I'll need things I never did before—entertainment, magazines, movies, television—all things I used to deride.

Books had always been serious material to him. They were at a higher level—not part of *entertainment*. He had read them out of intellectual interest, as a scholar. He liked to think so, at least. But now he felt he *needed* them, to keep his mind away from this insufferable routine that life had become, a routine with no end in sight.

And how ironic to think that his mind was going to waste. Perhaps I deserve to be found out and killed now. The Souzas, in contrast, will not be needing any entertainment. As long as they're looking for me—as long as there's *that* purpose in life for them—their minds will remain keen, while mine...

Martin turned the thought in his head and repeated the idea like a loop tape. Habit. Worry. Boredom. They came with a normal life. He crossed the next street and noticed some books displayed in a window. Entertainment, he thought. Good thing there were so many bookstores in town. He might find something to distract him—a book with photographs in it, perhaps.

The humidity inside disturbed his sinuses. He sneezed several times as he made his way to the back end of the store. A busy time of day. Numerous customers stood along the shelves. A man with a ponytail kept busy stacking books behind the counter.

Martin looked for the Travel section and found it at the very end, away from the street noise and the flow of browsers. He studied the books with the interest of a window shopper who covets goods for which he has no money. When he pulled one out, a hand tapped him on the shoulder. The touch gave him a second of fear that he wished had lasted longer. In it he had felt what seemed like a sweet taste of his old life.

A bright-eyed woman stared at him with a smile. She was short but gave the impression of increased strength in her old age. She said, "That's a wonderful place in the world. I've traveled a great deal and know it. I've been there."

Martin looked at the book's cover. Elephants graced it under bright words that read *Wild Safari*.

"Yes," he said without interest. "Good for you."

She drew in closer, as if what she had to tell him was something confidential. "Listen. I think you should go there, and I'll give you some tips, too. Pack some clothes, a *sombrero*, some suntan lotion, a water bottle, malaria pills, mosquito nets, mosquito repellent..." She could have been reading a Recommended Packing list from a travel book.

Martin enjoyed the intensity of her eyes. This woman lived. He could see she was not one of the masses, not one who needed entertainment in order to exist.

She patted her elbows and knees. "Make sure the clothes you take are soil-proof, too. It's not easy to do laundry in those parts of the world, you know? Water's scarce. And take your sunglasses, a small first-aid kit, diarrhea pills, your handgun and—listen, Africa is a place where you can truly escape. I know that. Remember I've been there. You can go on safari, race the animals—*live* among them. Oh, it's wonderful. Only when you're in Africa does your mind leave you alone."

She stopped to moisten her lips with a quick run of her tongue. She seemed to have much more to say. "I miss traveling, you know? My husband and I used to go about the world like two curious children on dangerous adventures. But now—" She stopped with moist eyes. Martin realized her pause was an intentional one, a request for the obligatory question.

He said, "You don't do it anymore?"

"It's my husband. He's bedridden. Some disease—"

There it was, he thought, the sign of what his life might soon be like—tied down by disease in the form of fears and lack of imagination. Restrained from the freedom to move freely or to assume a new life at will. He wondered why people sustained miserable lives for no apparent reason. He didn't know why she didn't leave her husband and go out to get a new life on her own. It was so clear that her old one had already expired.

A man walked past them and gave Martin a curious look. He said, "Don't listen to Abbey. She'll tell you a story every time."

The woman grew angry and turned to the man. "Oh, shut up, Louie!"

Louie had blown her cover.

Martin studied her clothes for the first time. They were soiled and frayed in some parts. She was one of the homeless who roamed the streets, who did time in public libraries and bookstores. "Louie!" she yelled. Her steps were like a child's, her eyes lost in a desolate stare. She had suddenly turned into someone else, a bag lady who rushed after Louie.

Martin replaced the book on the shelf. A sudden loss of interest in reading, he thought, if only a temporary one. No need to buy the book this time. Imagination would serve him better.

He continued the walk outside with his mind on Abbey. The homeless attracted him for some reason. Sometimes they seemed to be full of wisdom. *Only when you're in Africa does your mind leave you alone.* He repeated her words. *Her* mind had probably left her alone, long ago. She could now tell stories and feel as if she had actually lived them.

Martin was beginning to tire when he climbed the steps that led to the park. It had been a long walk. The flower beds on both sides of the steps bloomed in full color. He reached the first row of bright-red tulips and followed it to the other end of the garden. Parks were safe, he thought. They minimized his chances of being recognized. In an age of vehicles, few people bothered with parks. Hardly anyone used them. But he did. He used them as shortcuts and became familiar with them. The beauty of the flowers was an added benefit.

Most of the local parks were small and he crossed them quickly. Soon he was outside again on a new sidewalk, next to a busy street. A few students played lacrosse on a field. All boys, and he wondered whether it might be easier to teach to them. Teenage boys seemed less intimidating. Most of them had only one thing in mind, something he understood well. But what did girls have? Was it the same for them?

Perhaps teaching girls was better after all. Once he grew accustomed to their intimidating presence, he could enjoy feeling a sense of power over them, power without an overwhelming responsibility to go with it. In his simplified view of teaching, he had only to attend faculty meetings and go to class, not much more than was asked of a student.

This *could* be a good life, he thought. One just has to bear that grinding monotony.

After a turn onto a quieter street he heard steps behind him. He felt that common urge to turn back and look, but held it in check this time. If I'm to try to lead a normal life, the paranoia will have to stop. I can't go on distrusting everyone for no reason at all.

There came a creak from behind and habit got the better of him. He turned without thinking, and had only a second to see a short man with one leg before taking a frantic flight, not knowing where he was, not even looking ahead. He felt a pair of hard metallic bars slam against his knees before he stumbled over a human shape.

If pain was an incentive to stop human efforts, he did not pay attention to it. He tried to get up despite his knees and the pain they brought him. Soon one man after another came over, blocking his way with canes and crutches. One of them shook him violently by the shoulders and slapped him. The stranger looked like a beast, with a head half-covered in bandages. Martin felt two more slaps and someone said, "Calm down. You're okay."

It took Martin a few minutes to understand what the words meant. He looked up at the men. The short one leaned on a sturdy crutch. He was not Alfie. He was missing the right leg. Another amputee stood next to him, a man with one arm. Martin looked at another, then another. Each of them was missing something.

The man in the head bandage said, "You're fine. You was running like crazy and bumped into Bobby's wheelchair here. Fell down like a sack of potatoes." The others chuckled.

Martin stood slowly. Behind the men stood a white building. A cross projected in relief over the entrance. I'm among cripples, he thought, as he touched his knees. "What's this place?"

"Holy Christ Physical Therapy Foundation," the man in the wheelchair said as he felt for the welt Martin's buckle had made on his face.

"Didn't mean to hurt you there," Martin said, and touched the man's shoulder as a sign of apology. "I was running, and got scared." He checked his knees one last time to convince himself that they were still there. The one he had hit in the bathroom stall made him limp a little.

"That's okay—to get scared," the one-armed man said. "Children always run from me, too. They think God took my arm away because I deserved it and must be a bad man."

"Yes, I understand." Martin was confused. "My apologies again," he said, and limped away in a trance.

I was dead and came back, he thought. That's what death feels like. His hands shook uncontrollably. Was it joy? He had felt an urge to flee again, and it had been a good feeling. He looked behind one more time, hoping for more, for a Souza, for a reason to be. But he saw only a woman. She knelt down to work on a flower bed and eyed the gold-yellow tulips with pride.

2

"I've had enough of this." Elizabeth thumbed through her textbook looking for something she clearly didn't want to find. The bright glare from the sun forced her eyes away from the pages. "Let's take a break."

Martin agreed. He felt uncomfortable. The heat was strong for a spring day. "We'll stop the lesson, but only if we move to the shade. I feel like a plant here."

They left the bench and sat on the grass beneath the dense crown of a tree. Elizabeth did not seem pleased. She stretched her legs out from under the shade to expose them to the sun. "They need a good tan," she said as she lifted the tight skirt some. Martin could not help staring at the exposed thighs.

"Like them?" she said.

"You'll burn them."

"That wasn't the question."

He turned away. To spend time with her was to resist constant invitations. Sometimes he wished he could accept at least one of them.

She said, "How do you think I'm doing with my studies?"

"Just fine." His mind was somewhere else—on her legs, and his hurting knee, on the disabled and the homeless.

"Will I pass then?"

"You should."

"On my own?"

"Forget it if you expect any help from me."

"Next year you'll start tutoring me from the start. It won't be so difficult then, and we'll have more time to do other things."

Martin smiled. How easily the young built castles—without blueprints, without materials. To their naive minds everything was possible and easy. She had it all planned, and he was part of it without as much as saying a word.

He lay down and closed his eyes. He could say unpleasant things more easily while not seeing her reacting eyes. "I received a long letter from a friend in Africa not long ago."

"What did he say? Is there trouble in the tribe?" She laughed childishly.

"I might go there soon."

"This summer?" She seemed disappointed. "Summers are so long and boring. I'm tired of spending them at the beach house." She paused a moment and said, "Maybe you should go early, as soon as school's out—then come back early, too. I'd love to see your photos. Will you go on safari? My dad went on one a few years ago. Didn't take *me*, of course."

Martin spoke slowly, as a man who is hypnotized. His words flowed out continually, his mind unable to twist them into lies. He should keep his plans to himself, but he could not control the steady flow of words. The calm of the park made him do it. It made him truthful. He said, "My friend has invited me to live and teach there, to stay—for a while, anyway."

"Move away from here?"

"I can't live in two places at the same time, can I?"

"But you just got here."

He didn't hear what else she had to say. His mind had taken a sharp turn to the pleasant image of a woman in a garden. She was cultivating tulips whose petals were all of a glowing white, standing on gray stems that grew out of intensely black soil. She was a happy woman. Her cheeks glowed with a rosy tint below a pair of deep-blue eyes. She heard something and stood. It sounded like the murmur of boiling water, water she soon sprinkled on the glowing tulips from a watering can. Steam rose and laid a layer of fog over the field. The murmur grew louder and soon became a clatter. She pointed beyond the fog and said, "Look! It's the elephants!" And Martin saw them—hundreds of them—all racing toward him and her garden. He felt sorry for the woman. The animals would run over her hard work and destroy it. But nothing happened. They crossed the field disturbing not one petal. Only *he* would get hurt. The galloping legs were now over him and he felt them on his chest.

"Answer my question!" Elizabeth said. The slap she gave him on the chest woke him.

"I didn't hear it. I was falling asleep."

"Why do you want to leave?"

He was surprised at her reaction, and a little afraid of it. She wanted to know too much. He said, "It's only an idea," and wished he could unload all of his private life on her.

"You won't just disappear, will you? You'll tell me if you decide to go and when."

"It's just an idea," he repeated. "The man invited me. It's an opportunity to see something else. I never even answered his letter."

Martin regretted his words. Now she knew the possibility of his parting. No one had ever had that privilege before. He had always disappeared quietly and mysteriously. This time, someone would be watching. If he left now, he thought, it would be an imperfect departure—like going on a long trip with the knowledge that the house has been left unlocked. He could never relax.

She said, "You'll let me know before you leave. Promise?"

"Please stop—"

"Promise?"

"Promise," he said, and felt ridiculous for complying with her childish whim. "I do enjoy tutoring, and teaching at the school. I do." He pulled at the grass blades under him as if to anchor himself there and control an urge to stand and flee. He wanted to tell her that he hoped to stay, that even if life seemed slow to him at times, it was worth living it the way it was now—calm and safe.

But he went on yanking at the tufts furiously. After his paranoid reaction to the encounter with the one-legged man, he *had* to talk. There were times in life when one could not keep secrets without going insane. If Pete had been able to unload his solo experience on him, why couldn't *he* do it, too? Unfortunately, he knew no one he could trust.

It afflicted him that he didn't have a normal life. He had missed a step somewhere. But when? In his many years at religious boarding schools? Or upon the sudden death of his parents? They had fled the world early, and left him thinking, observing, analyzing every detail of life. He had turned to questioning things for which no answer lay at hand. It didn't help a normal life to question it. One soon found out it wasn't worth much.

He stood uneasily. His parents were dead, and *he* was living a ruined life. Something Elizabeth would not understand. He said, "Promise," one more time and left her there as if to never see her again.

If he could only have some type of clandestine meeting with a stranger and tell him everything. But even then, it wouldn't help much. Who would that stranger be? A psychiatrist? A Priest? Not even a priest could absolve him of all the mistakes he had made so far. He tried to convince himself instead that there was really nothing to regret about his life. *This* is my life and I should be happy with it, at least, if I can't be proud.

3

It always made Martin anxious to be put on hold for too long. He imagined people at the other end of the line discussing him or making fun of his voice while he waited.

He checked outside the telephone booth: the bar was dim and empty in the early afternoon. Even drunks stayed away from drinking at this time of day. He wondered why the owner even bothered to open the place.

As he waited, Martin went over what he wanted to say to Tito. Not much. He had called just to clear his mind, to tell Tito he was doing fine on his own. Calls to the Program's office could become a form of therapy. He should contact Tito more often, he thought, if only to keep the Program thinking that he might return to it someday.

He waited. Perhaps Tito had given orders to the operator to give him the runaround, or to trace the call. But that couldn't be. Martin had taken care not to give out his file number.

Tito's voice came on the line with the usual din. His words always sounded as though spoken through an iron pipe. "I was waiting for your call. It was foolish of you to hang up the last time. I hadn't finished telling you details."

"I didn't call for lectures, Tito. Just—had a scare the other day and wanted to talk to someone. You know how lonely it gets."

"A scare? Already? You're not safe on your own, see? I told you. You don't have the resources we—"

"It was just a scare, a trick my mind played on me, nothing else. I was never in any danger." Martin disliked being on the defensive.

"Well, forget all that. We need you to come in. There are two more bodies unaccounted for. Two old ladies. They used to manage the resort where we found Pete. Similar deaths, too. Shot between the eyes, one of them pointblank. Pretty disgusting, if you ask me. Their cat was shot, too. Do you know anything about this?"

No answer. Tito's labored breath played alone on the line.

Martin tried to remember. Pete had mentioned his diffi-culties in renting the cabin, dealing with some disagreeable woman.

Tito said, "I'm sorry to tell you this but—if you don't come forward, we're looking into pinning the two old ladies on you. I didn't tell you last time we talked—you didn't give me a chance—but we know you were in Pete's cabin. We found evidence."

"He was already dead when I got there." Martin noticed the bartender outside, a stout man who could surely bounce rowdy patrons from the bar as easily as he could mix drinks. He was peering from behind the counter with menacing eyes.

It occurred to Martin his conversation with Tito could be heard outside the booth and at a distance. Perhaps the word *dead* had caught the barman's attention. It always did. People were fascinated by it.

"Tell us all you know about Pete's death," Tito said.

"I only know he's dead."

"What was the blood all about? It wasn't Pete's. You wouldn't be talking to me if it had been yours. Whose blood was it? You know it. Who were all those people walking in and out of the place? We got enough footprints to start a museum."

"Then you know it wasn't me."

"That's why we need you out here—to help us determine that."

Martin didn't like Tito's deceptive tone, the lying. They could prove very easily that Pete had been killed by someone else. Tito was saying things for the sake of saying them. He had never been so talkative before. Something was wrong. They were tracing the call.

"Where are you, anyway? Just let me know and we'll go pick you up."

"I'll call you later." Martin thought for a moment and added feebly, "I'll want back into the Program—soon."

"Wait a minute. You—"

Another unsatisfying phone call, Martin thought. He made a move to exit the booth but the sudden ring made him jump. He hesitated before he picked up and listened.

"This is a good tracing system we got here. We know where you are." Tito chuckled.

Martin slammed the receiver in the cradle and struggled with the booth's door. His hands were shaking. He couldn't believe it. Even those who were supposed to be of help were now hunting him, trying to find him. The phone rang again as he rushed out of the booth.

The bartender had come over with an unfriendly face, his fists tight and ready to inflict pain.

Martin evaded his grip. He stumbled on tables as he ran and yelled, "Don't answer that!" Then as an afterthought he added, "Tell him I'm leaving town," as if he hoped the man would convey the message to Tito and his men when they arrived, and that they would believe it.

Running cleared his mind. He gained confidence the farther away he got from the bar. Panic gave way to impudence.

I don't have to run, he thought. All they know is a phone number. Surely they don't expect me to stay here?

He had only to hide at home, take a taxi to and from school, and keep away from overly crowded places. It would never occur to them to look under Pete's name. Everything he now had belonged to a man they knew was dead.

He stopped to mop the sweat off his forehead. He was only two blocks from home, on a quiet street where a vegetarian restaurant shared a corner building with a flower shop. On the wall someone had sprayed a warning: *Hitler was a vegetarian, too.*

4

The warehouse was large and poorly lit. This late at night, he could only see shadows made out by a narrow shaft of light that came from outside. He advanced slowly and with care. If anyone else was around, he didn't want to be seen or heard by them.

Someone's muffled sounds of panic reached him first, then additional noises joined in—the clink of chains, the rustle of clothes, and the panting of animals. He imagined hyenas salivating over a newly-found heap of carrion. The sounds of a sadistic sort of pleasure.

He turned the corner and ran his hand along a stack of cardboard boxes in order to guide himself in the darkness. The cardboard felt damp and cold, and it sank under the pressure of his hand. He stepped ahead until he reached the large section of the building, an abandoned theater in which the seats had been torn off in a fit of violence. Piles of refuse stood in various places. Behind them rose the stage. Garbage heaps cluttered it like bad actors frozen in an act of mime. The sounds were coming from there, but he could not see a thing.

He advanced stealthily, from behind one heap of rubble to the next, like a weary soldier on a congested battlefield. Only when he reached a vantage point did he realize that they could not see him. They were too busy with their game.

Five of them played—five filthy, vicious hoodlums—with a very pale woman. Their intention was to rape her. She kicked and wriggled any way she could. The rapists seemed inept. They could barely manage to subdue her and were having a difficult time ripping off her clothes.

He observed quietly as he thought. Five of them, against one of me. I'd like to help her but—

He would have to show his face in order to come to her aid, and he didn't want to do that, not yet. At any rate, there might not be any need to help. She could possibly free herself and run away before they hurt her.

The hoodlums were ravenous, as if on a rut call that was to be the last in their lives. They were certainly going to hurt her, perhaps even kill her after their pleasure was over. They were murderers, too. He saw the knives they carried hanging from black thongs tied around their waists. Their pointed black boots were also a weapon. With them, they could kick their victim's life away. And then there were the clubs and the bottles.

Still, he would confront it all to save her—if only he didn't have to show his face.

Her thighs swung back and forth as she tried to free her ankles from the grip of her tormentors. The hoodlums tried in vain to undress her. Her clothes were like the skins of an onion. One peeled off after another, but she was still fully dressed.

It wouldn't take long, Martin thought. An onion had only so many skins. Her pale thighs would finally appear, and he would have to make a decision then.

She had begun to cry. The gang was overpowering her. He could now see her bare body under the twisted smirks of the five men. They were ready.

Martin leaped out from his hiding place and yelled, "Leave her alone!"

A complete silence came, as if someone had abruptly cut off the electricity on some infernal machine. The men dropped the woman's legs and turned to him with interest. As she crawled away unnoticed, they picked up their clubs. One with a beard stepped forward—he seemed to be the leader—and pointed with his club. "Get *him*!" he yelled, and the gang followed orders without delay. Martin took flight.

He did his best but tripped, falling on the floor under a shower of blows before he could yell. There was no point in defending himself, though he tried. He lifted his arms to block the blows and to try to see who they were—these men who wanted to hurt him. He got a better look at the one with the beard. It was Christ. Of the others he could only see their coming blows, the tips of their clubs. Christ was the most savage. He wore a neon chaplet like a glowing halo that had fallen from grace. With every blow he gave, and through his sadistic grin, he said, "We won't leave you alone. We won't leave you alone. We won't..."

Two old women arrived with their clubs to join in the beating. They had bullet holes through their heads.

Martin tried to free himself from the lynching mob but only hurt his wrist as he knocked it against the floor. The pain woke him.

Sometimes the terrors of a nightmare are more frightening once the sleeper awakes. Martin relived every blow of the beating as he gasped for air. He wondered what should have made him so confused as to endanger his life for the sake of a woman, one he had never even met. He got out of bed unable to control the fear that had taken over him. If panic was induced by shock, he thought, perhaps it could be treated by it. He stood under a cold jet of water in the shower and concentrated on the jabs the drops made at his skin.

Soon his doubts reemerged with renewed intensity. As a marked man, I have no right to live within the range of those who hunt me, unless I want to get caught. He knew it wouldn't take long before he ran into the face of a Souza. The Souzas had contacts. They could find whomever they wished.

To be a rat in a hole, he thought, with a perennial cat waiting outside for a chance to paw him—that wasn't a life. Even a rat had a need to venture out of its hole regularly for food and fresh air.

Maybe the time had come to move again. The idea excited him tremendously.

He dried himself energetically and got back in bed with a lucid mind. Nothing could boost the spirit like a new resolution. Things were finally in order once more, and his next step was as clear as it was sound. If only he could share it with someone.

5

Martin waited for her with anxious anticipation. He had never asked her to meet him anywhere before. Elizabeth had always been the one requesting meetings, tutorial sessions he had often tried to evade. But this time he needed the company, and he only hoped she would not get the wrong idea. Sometimes people confused the need of companionship with desire or lust.

He studied the wine list. *Concord grape wine. Made in our kitchen. No sulfites.* The restaurant was busy. Vegetarian food grew more and more popular, despite Hitler.

Martin felt safe between the gaudy-green wallpaper and purple-covered tables. Patrons were like old acquaintances he knew by sight but never bothered to engage in conversation. They sat there minding their own lives, sharing the room the way strangers share the cozy, dark space of a movie house.

He opened the paper and studied the headlines. It seemed ridiculous to be reading a morning paper this late at night. The news couldn't really hold his interest, and he looked up from the pages every time a headlight shone through the window.

Elizabeth arrived with an obvious air of confidence, with the proud look of someone who has just won something—a contest, a coveted job, or the adulation of a man she has intensely desired.

Martin felt something else—fear instead of devotion. Though, he thought, for most couples they were often the same thing.

He had come to tell her about his departure not because of his promise to do so but because he had no one else to tell. Tito was no longer trustworthy.

She sat with her eyes on the rest of the room and said, "We should have met somewhere else." The small restaurant was obviously beneath her.

"It's a modest place, but I like it because I can afford it." He reached for her hand under the table and held it for what he hoped would be a sign of emotional support. Do I really expect her to be so crushed by my departure? Her feelings for him, though immature in his opinion, had been obvious. He was afraid to tell her, as if he owed her an excuse for leaving so soon.

She pulled his hand to her thigh and smiled. "Finally," she said.

Martin felt a fleeting desire to take the offer, to leave the restaurant now and rush home with her to his bed. There was no longer a reason not to accept the invitation. He would depart soon.

"No," he said, and quickly drew back his hand. "You're getting the wrong idea."

"You held my hand first."

"Yes, but it doesn't mean what you think."

She thrust her elbows on the table with visible anger.

A waitress came wearing a bright-green skirt ruffled to resemble a head of lettuce. Martin gave her a serious look. She seemed to understand this was not the right moment to take an order and left.

Elizabeth played with the salt shaker making a bored face. One might think she was at school, at a lecture on a subject for which she had little interest. It seemed to Martin that she knew what was coming.

He said, "I know you've made an effort to be more than my student, and that I be more than a teacher and tutor to you. Don't think I haven't noticed. The notes in class, the poems, your calls. I understand your feelings and appreciate them, but am not interested—not because I don't find you attractive. I just have my share of problems right now. There's no room for you to fit in."

"But you led me on." She was perfectly calm. He could tell that she had rehearsed her words. She said, "You made me believe—"

"I'm going to leave soon, Elizabeth, in a few days, perhaps weeks. Something has come up. I really can't stay much longer. It's unfortunate because I really enjoyed teaching the class, and tutoring you." He forced a smile and said, "You're a good student. You'll do well on your own."

Elizabeth did not seem to care for his speech. She had prepared her own—with lines so fluent that they seemed natural. "You made me believe you loved me."

Something in the way she spoke scared him. She underscored her lines with too much seriousness on her face, and he wondered how far she would take this effort to make him feel guilty. She said, "I poured my love to you."

Martin laughed. How silly this is, he thought, repeating lines from all the mindless entertainment—the cheap romance novels and soap operas she's put into her head.

"Stop this," he said. "You're making a fool of yourself. You can't *pour* love in real life. That's just poetry." He could see his words hurt her. The lines on her face were set on the verge of crying. "Elizabeth, get rid of this fixation. I'm not interested in you. I'm a teacher, you a student. And that's that."

"It's no fixation. You raped me and you're going to pay for it."

Somehow it didn't surprise him. Rejection often turned people into liars.

This lie created a new problem, though, another mountain to climb on his way to freedom. He had gone soft on her and it could ruin him.

What did that other teacher do once accused? he thought. The man never had a chance to defend himself.

"Don't think it's going to work again," he said. "The school will investigate thoroughly this time. Besides, what threat can this be to my job? I'm leaving anyway."

"I don't care about your job. You're going to lose your freedom. Jail. That's where rapists end up spending their filthy days."

"Even that is not much of a threat to me." His freedom had been lost long ago. One found no freedom in a life in hiding, and little opportunity to defend one's name.

Was he to go on collecting responsibility for crimes he had never committed? The murder of the two elderly women, a rape? Didn't he have any pride left?

The system was not really fair, and he could not trust it. Liars could never defend themselves, even when they were innocent. Their past lies always emerged in court, timely and with a built-in bent on discrediting any current testimony no matter how true. A jury would never believe a former liar.

He said, "Listen. This type of thing may hurt you, mark *you* as a liar for life. They have tests that can prove no one touched you."

"I can take care of that. Dad won't need more than a few bruises to believe me, and—"

"You wouldn't dare."

"Dare me."

"Why? Public humiliation, for no reason at all?"

"Why not? I'm bored. That's reason enough. And it would hurt *you*, for leading me on, and—"

"I didn't."

"And it would be a challenge—a good performance. You know I almost failed my acting class? That bitch, Mrs. Livermore, had the nerve to say I needed more character. Well, this is my chance to show her I can act. It's fun."

The waitress came back. Rushing customers was to her advantage. "We're not ready," Martin said almost showing his annoyance. He placed a small bill in the woman's hand and whispered in her ear. He wanted a bread basket and to be left alone.

When she was gone, he hastened to say to Elizabeth, "It's *not* fun. You're talking about ruining my life on a lie, like your classmate ruined that poor teacher's. Where do you think the man is now? Do you think they allowed him to teach again? That he's happy?"

"That's *his* problem." She hardened her face as though she were slowly falling into a planned role, one that called for a look of insurmountable despair, for teary eyes and quivering lips.

From a distance and without the benefit of hearing their conversation, the two of them could easily pass for a disaffected couple on the verge of separation. By her expression, he was telling her he had been having an affair and was leaving her for another woman.

Martin began to understand her true nature. It had come out with her last words.

Her wealth allows it, he thought. It insulates her from reality. All her problems are forever patched with money, so she assumes everyone else does the same with theirs.

"It is *not* his problem," he said. "The man has nowhere to go. He's being persecuted by a lie, and he has *no* money to make things easier for him." He realized he was talking about himself. This was more than he could take. Christ's words resounded in his head. *We won't leave you alone. We won't...*

She raised her voice. "You raped me!"

"You're crazy. Stop this!"

"I am not. From now on my act begins. You raped me and you're going to pay for it." She cleared her throat and yelled, "You raped me and you're going to pay for it!" and she repeated it again, much louder, and again.

The words echoed on the thin walls of the restaurant. Like an avalanche, they commanded attention. And like worried skiers, those around them turned to see where it all came from.

Martin was in the spotlight once more, forced there by a child. A nightmare—one even more terrifying than that of an evil Christ and a gang of rapists beating him to death. This nightmare was real. This was the woman he had saved from the hoodlums, the young woman yelling in front of him. He saw her well now. She was paying him back for having saved her.

Elizabeth yelled at the top of her lungs. She had obviously rehearsed her act. And there was more to it than words. She snatched the table cover off the table. "He raped me! He raped me!" The ashtray and cruet set crashed on the floor. Then she reached a peak, a shrill that amazed him. She made it seem so easy—to lie like that, to add a performance *to* the lie. She was hysterical yet he saw her as so untroubled, so much in command. It was admirable.

A man in a white shirt and tie approached him. He was the manager, he said, but his words were lost behind Elizabeth's. Martin knew the man would have no choice but to call the police if she continued. He tried to explain, but the manager only stared at him. Everyone did. They expected him to do something about the girl, now.

When Martin finally slapped her, the blow left her tears on his fingers.

Elizabeth was suddenly quiet and did not bother to even feign a sniffle. She said, one more time, quietly, as she looked at her audience, "He raped me." With her head leaning to one side, she gave the impression of begging for understanding. Then she ran outside like a frightened actress who had lost her confidence upon forgetting her lines.

Martin relaxed. He could better justify her actions in the absence of her unpredictable behavior. He counted a few bills and placed them on the table next to the manager. "To pay for the damages," he said. Then, by way of explanation, he turned around to everyone else and said, "She's just a girl. She's lying."

How unsophisticated and stupid he felt at trying to lie effectively after her flawless performance. He just couldn't compete.

Outside he walked quickly, far enough, until no one could see him. Then he ran home. He didn't even bother to check if Elizabeth was waiting for him somewhere. All he wanted was the safety of his home, and a cold shower. God, he thought, how many mistakes I've made lately. He had to go over them, analyze them, consider what they meant. Would they require an immediate departure? Or even merit changing his identity again?

He pushed his pace and felt his lungs puff like tireless bellows. If he got arrested for rape, he thought, it would be the end. If convicted and sentenced, he would have no refuge in jail. His name and photo would be all over—another public scandal at the school. The Souzas would hear about it, and a mere payment from them to an inmate's family would suffice to have him killed in jail.

Martin could hear the soothing sound inside his skull as the cold water drummed upon his head. In his mind, he went over every inch of the house. The windows were locked, so were the doors—even the one to the bathroom where he was. And he had turned all the lights off. He was safe. It occurred to him that if anyone came in to kill him now he would never know it. Death would come muffled by a noisy shower, and the running water would wash his blood away.

If only I had not panicked with that dream, he thought. A hoodlum Christ. How ridiculous. Without that dream, I would have never told Elizabeth I was leaving.

Her reaction made sense after all—a bad case of teenage infatuation, a girl upset by bad news. A word from him would be enough to soothe and bring her to her senses. He planned to ask her to forgive him: There's no need for you to act like this. I'm not really going anywhere. I'm staying.

Words he wanted to believe himself.

Words were never any good at convincing a stubborn young woman, Martin thought. Elizabeth had attended his class in the last week but not participated at all. Now she sat there again, in the same fashion—a monolithic threat that distracted him from his lecture.

He had tried in vain to get her to say something by asking her questions, by telling her to read a poem or write something on the board. But she never moved.

How he regretted not having gone to Barbara with the problem earlier. How stupid of him to have let it fester to this hopeless stage. A regular teacher would have gone to the principal for help. As unprofessional as Barbara was, she usually dealt effectively with troublesome students. But Martin feared the worst. Going to Barbara could trigger Elizabeth's performance into its dramatic climax. He had no wish for that.

Her classmates had adapted quickly to the new Elizabeth. They ignored her completely.

It's easy for them, he thought. They have nothing to fear, while I'm at permanent risk.

As a teacher Martin felt like a failure. His lectures were boring. Those in the back of the room turned to their own personal discussions. It exasperated him that only a few students showed him any respect. He could just as well have been openly accused of rape already. They acted as if that were the case.

He caught two of the girls writing notes to each other. It gave him a good excuse to stop the class, to show some anger.

"Bring that piece of paper up here and read it aloud to the rest of the class." He knew the girl wouldn't do it, which would justify his next move. The girl blushed. He tried to press her by going for the note himself, but she put it in her mouth and chewed. Her classmates laughed.

Martin turned quickly to catch Elizabeth joining in the laughter, but she was as serious as ever. It filled him with anxiety. Why, she was barely breathing. Was this also part of her act? He wondered how far she would take it, and for how long.

He returned to his desk preparing his own performance. If Elizabeth could act, so could he. His acting ability knew no limit. He had been at it for years. "I won't tolerate this." He addressed the class as a whole but used Elizabeth for inspiration. "You come here to learn, not to chat or warm a seat or exchange notes."

They faced him with the glassy stare of famished children. For a second, they all looked like Elizabeth.

"That's it," he said. "We're having a pop-quiz." He had done it often in class. Quizzes freed him from teaching.

He heard a few complaining grunts but soon every student had a blank sheet in front of her, except Elizabeth. She remained as still and serious as she had throughout the week.

No one in the staff room had said a word to him about her. Was she doing this only in his class? He had already cornered her outside the school once and begged her to say something, without results. Her eyes grew more vacant every day. She was torturing him and he didn't know why. He couldn't tell by her expression. There wasn't one. If she enjoyed herself by doing this to him, one did not see it. She appeared to be suffering a genuine trauma, as if she had really been raped and were keeping the tragedy to herself.

Every morning on his way to school, he feared it would be his last. He imagined a police car, waiting, with Elizabeth standing next to it and pointing at him.

When will that happen, he thought, if at all? When will she speak?

His students had begun to despise him. He could tell. His contract would probably not be renewed for the next school year. So what was the point in staying? Why expose himself needlessly to this quiet threat? Why risk a scandal?

He had no answers. Barbara had given him no indication of what she thought of his teaching, even after having sat through some of his lectures, quietly, with the same blank stare Elizabeth had now.

I should stay but also be ready to leave, he thought. I should be prudent and prepare my exit, a quiet one, just in case.

But he didn't even have the funds for that yet. If anything happened before the next pay day, his departure would be a miserable effort on a trail of poverty. No one is free from the need of money, not even a hunted soul on the run.

6

The streets grew darker as Rufus drove farther into the core of the inner city. He turned the radio on and looked at Elizabeth in the rear-view mirror. She did not seem concerned with how he felt about driving her father's car in this neighborhood. But it was her quietness that worried him most. It contrasted with her usual expressiveness and insolence. Now she was no more than an unobtrusive passenger, mesmerized with the rows of shoddy red-lit bars and nightclubs along both sides of the street.

He wondered what was on her mind, why she had told him to bring her here. He had once worked for a family with two teenage boys who often asked him to drive them to seedy brothels for a taste of life. But a girl? He couldn't imagine Elizabeth's intentions.

He stared at her—an insecure adolescent girl full of nervous anticipation, quiet within herself, making some sort of decision, perhaps.

"Stop here." She pressed her face against the window and observed the corner building across the street. It held her attention like a strange animal would a child's. "This looks like a safe place, doesn't it?"

"Nothing does around here. I would—"

"It's large enough to have private rooms inside. What do you think, Rufus?"

She turned suddenly talkative. Something seemed to have excited her vocal chords.

Rufus turned to the building. It housed a nightclub. Two bouncers in white suits guarded the entrance. They were there to give the club an air of respectability, to cull patrons from a constant stream of arrivals. Those who were rejected walked on into a dark alley—men in search of an affordable thrill.

"The women must have a different entrance," Elizabeth said. "And those men look tough—the customers, I mean. Do you think if I went in there and found one drunk enough he might hurt me?"

Rufus noticed how little her clothes covered her, how she constantly checked them as though they were the wrong outfit for the occasion. Her legs and shoulders were exposed, and she shook with a quick shiver.

"This is a dangerous place, miss. Please, let's go home."

"No. I'm going through with this, if only to teach them a lesson. I'm sick of assholes, you know? They make my life miserable, and I'm going to punish them for it."

"You'll only punish yourself, miss. These aren't people you play with. These men don't come here to sit and chat. They—"

"Oh, shut up. I want more than just sit and chat, obviously. And what do *you* know about life, anyway? If you knew anything, you'd be more than just a driver."

He turned back and challenged her with a furious look. But what could he say? Her commands, like her insults, were things he took quietly and obediently, like a trained dog who performed well and never talked back—the perfect servant.

"Rufus. You know these places. Where do the women go in?" She seemed desperate to get an answer, to learn quickly about this somber neighborhood so that she could finish her business with it soon. "If only I had more experience doing this type of thing. Sex with boys my own age definitely hasn't prepared me for life."

"Whatever it is you have in mind, miss, I don't think you should go through with it. I feel responsible."

"You *are* responsible. You already got me here. You're hooked."

"Let's go, please."

"It's my life. Just answer my question. Where do the women go in?"

"I don't know."

She clenched her fists. "The last thing I need is a lowly driver trying to make me feel guilty! You just let me do what I want—and not a word of this to my father, ever, understand?"

She got out of the car and the bouncers across the street paid her immediate attention. In the realm of sexual pleasure, it was always exciting to see a new face.

She turned to Rufus and said, "Go. I'll get home on my own."

"Miss—" But it was too late to persuade her. She had already slammed the door and was talking to the men in white.

Rufus didn't move. There was not much he could do, but at least he would wait to see her enter the building.

Immediately those in line to go in the club took a passionate interest in her. A heavy older man held her hand and begged her to follow him into the alley. She refused and pointed at the club's entrance instead.

But there was a problem. One of the bouncers shook his head and denied her entry.

A mob of men began to gather around her. Desperate bidders in a disorganized auction. They approached her with bills in their hands—each offering more than the next—starting a bidding war. She played the auctioneer and the desired collection piece all at once. The men wanted her. They knew a fresh flower when they saw one. This was not a sick-looking prostitute with years of service on her back. She was clean and safe, and they were willing to compete violently for her. They argued little before the first push was followed by a shove and a scuffle.

Elizabeth moved out of the way and made a forceful effort to enter the club. The bouncer grabbed her with one arm and pressed her against the wall. She fought him and yelled. Rufus felt his heart race and made a move to open the car's door. But the man released her and told her to leave, so loudly, that even Rufus heard him. She yelled back unintelligible curses while eager customers pleaded with her. They formed a moving mass around her from which she tried to retreat unsuccessfully. Soon they had carried her away into the darkness of the alley.

Rufus took deep breaths. There was so little he could do against a mob of lusty men.

He leaned on the horn and switched the car's alarm on. The blare of the siren commanded the attention of those who were still on the sidewalk. The car's lights flashed on the men's faces intermittently and in rhythm with the screeching noise. One of the bouncers made an obscene gesture at him and threatened him with a fist.

Seconds later Elizabeth ran out of the alley and back to the car. Those who followed her stopped the moment they saw her get in the black sedan. Such a car meant a powerful customer, someone with money. They knew they couldn't compete.

Rufus locked the doors and sped away leaving the alarm on until he felt safe. The quiet audience of hustlers and drunks disappeared behind them in a soft tone of neon signs. Elizabeth looked back at the men as if they were already deep in her past.

"So that didn't work," she said with little concern. "But never mind. The trick for actors is not to experience trauma, but to play it out. It's called acting for a reason."

Rufus studied her determined face. She sat quietly and with the confidence of someone who never fails. Her words were as convincing as they were naive. She made a fist and began to punch softly on her breasts. Then she said, "Do you think my father loves me?"

7

When the bell finally rang it seemed to Martin he had waited a lifetime for it. The stress of being in the classroom grew more intense. Elizabeth had not come to class on three consecutive days. And not only his class. She had disappeared from the school altogether. No one mentioned her absence, and he didn't dare bring it up for fear of being associated with her in any way.

The students rushed out of the room with the efficiency expected in a fire drill. He meant nothing to them, he thought. The moment the bell rang they cleared out of his way. He was not their friend. In case of another scandal, he knew they would stand behind Elizabeth, not him. Schoolgirls could reinforce their lies and corroborate any of their fantasies into an acceptable reality. Their parents kept the school going and they knew it.

When he left the classroom, the halls were already empty. The new period had begun. Students had switched classes with the haste of players in a game of musical chairs. He stood alone in the middle of the hall. The music had stopped and all participants had taken their seats. He was the loser.

On a turn he ran into Barbara. Her sudden appearance stunned him.

"I just heard some gossip." She was joyous. Her face shone with an unusually radiant smile. "Apparently, Rosmell Girls' has decided not to open next year—financial difficulties. One of our board members was approached about transferring all their girls here. Isn't that news? That would be *some* infusion. It would keep us afloat at least for the next two years. Your check's in your box, by the way. It's pay day, remember?"

Martin wanted to say something about Elizabeth. His duty was to incriminate himself by telling Barbara about the girl. "Have you—?" he said. "Do you know what happened to—?" But Barbara had already left him.

Why should I worry about incrimination? I'm innocent. I didn't do it. They have DNA tests to prove who has raped whom.

His interest in Elizabeth was now based mostly on curiosity. He wanted to know what she was doing, where she was. It seemed natural to him to want to hear about her. But he also felt a touch of jealousy. She had offered herself to him after all. Sexual offers, even if refused, brought on a sense of possessiveness that could not be explained. The possibility of her being with another man bothered him.

He entered the teachers' room and pulled the check from his box.

At least, he thought, I have enough to go now.

On his way home he stopped at the bookstore. It was quieter than usual. He studied two books, one with only pictures of Africa and one with only text. He tried to make a decision. A reader with no imagination needed a little of both, he thought, and he sat down to review the books and reconsider the need to purchase them. Whatever their price, it might be worth paying it if the material took his mind away from Elizabeth.

Elizabeth. The moment he thought of her his mind turned to worry.

At what point in her performance is she now? What if I called her? Her phone may be tapped already, maybe by the FBI.

His fears escalated. She might direct agents to the school. They would find Pete's name in the records. A quick computer search would tell them that Pete was dead. The FBI agents would then ask questions within the Justice Department, since Pete had once been under its protection. Tito would hear of it, and so would the leak in his office. Shortly the news would reach the Souzas.

He stood and slapped the books against his thigh nervously. How ridiculous of him to ponder all these things. Why on earth would the FBI come in on a rape accusation? Even if Elizabeth's father was a powerful man with connections, no police department would arrest a teacher on rape charges without some form of evidence. They would want to examine her first.

He placed the two books on the counter between a stack of old receipts and the cash register. The cashier said, "Africa!" as he opened the cover in search of a handwritten price. Martin observed him quietly. The man wore an earring, a ponytail, a black shirt and black pants. Everything black. The color reminded Martin of his aunts and uncles—all people he despised—and the formal dress they had worn at his parents' funeral. They had not allowed him to cremate his own parents. Instead, they had arranged for what he felt had been a morbid open-casket funeral. A complicated funeral. Martin despised black.

The ponytail said, "Have you ever been to Africa?" and looked up at Martin. He immediately frowned at the face, as if questioning his memory.

Martin handed him a bill. "No, not yet. Maybe someday."

The ponytail pointed at him bluntly. "Wait a minute. I know you. Some guy came asking about you the other day. He showed us a picture and—"

The phone had been ringing and the ponytail answered it. Martin took the books. He was not about to wait for the change.

The experiment was clearly over. He didn't need any more incentives. The time had come to abandon his first solo attempt at hiding.

Chapter VI

1

The doctor entered the room quietly, carrying his worn leather briefcase with an air of respectability. At his advanced age, his reputation preceded him wherever he went. The old briefcase, like his gray hair, was as much a testament to his experience as the professional degrees that hung in his office. He took it with him on house calls only as a lucky charm. Most of what it contained he never needed.

The room paled in comparison to the luxury he had seen downstairs. He studied the furniture—almost abstract pieces that resembled the ones he had bought years ago for his practice. He smiled at the thought that some people still called them modern. His younger patients referred to them as uncomfortable and obsolete.

The soft light of a lamp aimed at the ceiling gave the room an innocuous atmosphere. A perfect environment for talking to a disturbed patient, he thought. Light should be a standard required by all building codes—more light, more space, and more air. As the abused animals we humans are, we need compassionate surroundings.

He stared at the white walls and wavered.

Why? What was it that I came here to do?

His mind had begun to play tricks again. It often did these days. He made efforts to keep focused on his work.

I was thinking of the house, he thought, and...

A man in a sports jacket approached him extending a hand. "Thank you for coming, doctor," he whispered.

"Came as soon as I could."

They moved to the far end of the room. There, the furniture lay hidden under white sheets as though someone had been painting the ceiling. The man in the sports jacket said, "She likes white. We've been trying to please her."

The doctor turned to her. She sat in a large couch, still and sullen. Her lips had little color in them and almost matched the tone of her pale face. The usual, he thought. He had seen her type many times. Surely she had nothing new or challenging to offer.

The man in the jacket positioned two chairs facing the girl. He seemed eager to participate.

The doctor said, "You *are* her father, aren't you?"

"Yes, of course."

"I thought you said she wasn't talking to you."

"She will now, doctor. This isn't a father-daughter conflict. She hasn't been talking to anyone, not just me. We get along well." He took her hand as an example.

"Perhaps we should go outside first and discuss this before I—"

"I already told you everything you need to know, doctor. Her mother and I are divorced. We—"

"Then leave me alone with the girl."

"I must be here," the girl's father insisted.

"It would be better if you weren't. We may have more luck that way."

Another inflexible man, the doctor thought. Wealthy families and their recognizable patterns. They're all the same. Overly ambitious parents always drive their normal teenagers into psychological traps.

He studied the father's face. The man looked the type, alright—clearly successful, powerful, without an ounce of understanding in him. A man who must have the last word every time.

"Where's the girl's mother?"

"Not available, if that's what you mean. The girl lives with me—my custody." The father stretched his shoulders upwards as if to try to get an edge on the doctor. "As her father, I have a duty to witness this process, doctor. I want to be the first one to know what's causing her pain—what's made her lose her speech—so that I can remedy and take care of it at once."

They sat and the doctor considered the request. He took a notepad from the briefcase and placed it in his lap.

Sometimes, he thought, it is better to allow monkeys to watch their own circus show. They stay distracted that way and bother the trainer with fewer requests for peanuts. "As you please," he said, and noted his observations on the pad. "I'm writing what you told me on the phone yesterday. Preliminaries." He wrote in code and in large letters and poked at the paper to mark a final period. Then he turned to the girl.

She appeared to be in a comatose state. Her chest heaved mildly with her breathing. Her eyes were void of movement except for an occasional blink.

"What is your name?" He enunciated each word as if talking to someone twice his age. He repeated the question several times while the girl's father shifted impatiently in his chair. The doctor gave him a quick glance and thought, There he goes, looking at his watch. He expects immediate results, eager to close this matter quickly so that he can go on to his next corporate meeting, as though his daughter were one more business decision and nothing else.

The father said, "Shouldn't you ask her something else?"

The doctor put his hands down forcibly. It exasperated him to have to deal with people like this. What a misfortune that only they could afford his services. "I'm afraid I'll have to ask you to leave."

"I'll remain quiet from now on, doctor. I apologize."

"This may take weeks. She may never talk with you in here." He gave his voice an authoritative inflection.

"I'll take my chances. I know my daughter better than you do, doctor. Don't forget that. I know this is nothing serious. I've read about these things—losing one's voice because of shock and what-have-you. I just need you to give me a hand here. Get her going with a word or two, then I'll take over." He turned to the girl and said, "Honey, you know I'll do whatever is necessary to make you feel safe and normal again. Just—work with the doctor." Then he looked at the doctor. "I'm willing to cooperate. Just ignore me, and make her talk, please."

The doctor wanted to yell, to curse the man. But with what purpose? After all, he had come here to help a young woman. As her doctor, he should only be concerned with her, and work with whatever tools or difficulties were at hand. He turned to her again and said, "What is your name? Mine is Marcus."

While he waited for an answer he examined her pupils. They were dilated, possibly from something she had taken. But what? He couldn't tell. These days street drugs mutated faster than the medical community could identify them. Just a few years ago the popular choice with school girls had been diazepam. Girls used to steal it from their mothers' medicine cabinets. Today choices were overwhelming, and mothers were no longer the unwitting suppliers. He often wondered how and where young people got the latest trend, and who made it.

"Your name is beautiful and very easy," he said. "Do you remember it?"

The question had to be modified as many times as necessary. In some other cases, it had taken him hours, days, even weeks to get an answer. The only skill he needed was patience. Eventually, he would construct the question in a way that might elicit a response. That was the reward, and he cherished it.

He had been accused by colleagues of using unorthodox methods, obsolete and old-fashioned theories. But he never bothered with criticism. The only correct approach in his practice was the one that got him results. "My name is Marcus," he said, "and yours is—"

"Leave me alone."

Her voice startled him. He turned to her father with a questioning look. You claim to know your daughter? he thought. She's obviously not in shock. This is just an act.

He found no answer in the father's complacent grin. Another ignorant man manipulated by his child's whims.

The doctor put the pad aside and stood behind the girl. He would expose her lie. "Why have you been so quiet lately?"

"The school," she said.

"You don't like your school?"

She shook her head.

Her father sighed, and his hands moved with anxious energy, as though he were ready to interrupt the session to ask a few questions of his own. He seemed disturbed by the doctor's slow pace.

The doctor remained quiet, with his hands in his pockets, thinking of a strategy. The difficulty was not in letting the girl know that he was familiar with her type of behavior. It was more in getting the gullible father to realize that hers was only an act.

"What's wrong, doctor?" the man said impatiently.

"Nothing." He leaned closer to the girl and whispered, "Why? What's bad at school?"

"My teacher."

"What's bad about your teacher? She gave you a bad grade?" The doctor knew where the girl was taking him. Why not make it easier for her? He said, "She's not a good teacher? Expects you to study? Picks on you?"

"He—"

"Oh, it's a *he*."

"Yes. He hurt me."

"He hurt you? How?"

The girl began to weep softly and moved her arms for the first time to cover her face. Her father drew near her and said, "That's enough, doctor. You've done your job. Let me handle this now."

The doctor said angrily, "I haven't even started to do my job."

The father did not seem to care. He comforted the girl with caresses and soothing words. "How did that teacher hurt you, honey? Who is he? I'll switch you to another school. Or we'll get him fired."

Nothing wrong with a teenager who lies, the doctor thought, but for a parent to believe? He observed the father and saw a man who could hardly hold his emotions, a man desperate to satisfy, to amend mistakes.

"What did that teacher do to you?" the frantic man asked his daughter. "When did he hurt you?"

"He—" She took in a deep breath, inhaled all her courage, and wailed the words out: "He raped me!"

"Where!" He shook her. Emotions no longer drove him. He had found out what he wanted and, like an expert manager, now he needed facts to act on. He said, "Where did he rape you! At school?"

"At the boat." The words were almost lost among her sniffles and cries, but clear enough for an enraged father.

"What is his name? I'm going to deal with this man today."

The doctor tried to pull him back. "Please. Let's step outside for a moment. Let's not jump to conclusions or retaliatory actions without—" He turned quickly to the girl. She had already stopped her sobbing and was listening carefully to his words. "Please," he said to the father, "let's step outside."

They stood at the edge of the terrace. The doctor said, "This may be just a fabrication of hers. It happens often. Maybe she got a bad grade, or was infatuated with her teacher and he paid no attention to her. Such things happen. This could be no more than a lie, an act on her part to get even. There are ways to find out whether she was in fact—"

"Doctor, you're a stupid, naive man. My daughter is suffering, and you take me out here to tell me that those aren't real tears? That what I witnessed in there is just an act?" He seemed to have no desire to listen and, with agitated rashness, he ran back in the house.

The doctor did not feel offended. He had been called worse things and dealt with more impossible people.

You can't force an animal to do something it isn't capable of, he thought. A bat is as blind to its cave as an empire-building businessman is to the lives of his wife and children. And there's nothing anyone can do about it.

He prided himself on being a good doctor. He knew when to stop his services. In cases like these, there wasn't much more he could do. He would not even charge for the visit, as a form of protest.

When he walked back inside through the swaying curtains, the girl was sitting alone, scratching the grotesquely shaved half of her head.

He pitied her. What an awful waste of wealth, he thought. So much in the hands of a father and daughter with no wits.

He replaced the notepad in the leather briefcase and approached the door. When he looked back one last time, he found the girl staring at him.

He said, "Aren't you ashamed of yourself?—playing on your father's weakness like this?"

She did not answer. At her age one wasn't ashamed of anything. She still had years ahead to live free of remorse.

"You take me for a stupid old man, don't you? Why are you lying?"

"Leave me alone. I didn't call you here."

"You'll be found out. The police will need evidence. They'll have you checked."

The father came back with a man and a woman. He led them in and addressed the doctor. "These are my driver and my cook." He seemed to have completely forgotten that only minutes ago he had insulted the doctor. He was calm and amiable. "Please stay, doctor. We'll find out more from them. They were witnesses, apparently. They've met the man."

The doctor felt a sting of curiosity. It might be enjoyable to watch the girl self-destruct. What could these two servants say to support her claim? He watched the driver carefully. The man moved uneasily, holding his cap like a useless prop in a role he had been forced to play.

The father said, "Doctor, I have not said a word to them about what my daughter told us. So they don't know, and they couldn't be biased as I obviously could—that's why they're useful." He turned to his employees with an air of urgency. "I asked you about a man who came here. Please repeat for the doctor exactly what you told me."

After a pause the cook said with a strong accent, "He eat here a few times. I never ask him, but many times he say to me he was here to teach. He is the teacher, he say." She looked at the girl once before turning her eyes to the floor.

The driver was overly demure. It took much effort for him to speak. He said, "Likewise, sir. I drove the two of them together a few times—to the marina, from the library, here—and the man alone, too, to his house. They talked about school a lot. He seemed interested in her—as a teacher, I mean. He wanted her to learn—"

"I think he hurt her, sir," the cook said. "She now act like this since he stop coming here."

"That's enough," the father said.

The doctor stared at the girl. These statements, he thought, can only help her, unless... He said to the father, "I strongly urge you to report the incident to the police, sir. They are well equipped to deal with this type of accusation."

"Accusation?" The driver came to with alarmed eyes.

"No, no, no, no." The father moved in quickly to allay his fears. "There will be no police involved here. I'll take care of it myself." He had turned into a different man, relaxed and composed. He opened the door and said, "Thank you for your help, doctor. I won't be needing you again."

The doctor turned back to the girl one last time. "Maybe she will," he said, and left.

2

Martin entered the Petit French Café with determination. With the usual unpredictability of spring, the weather had turned unpleasant. The humidity of sporadic rains and the drop in temperature had brought in a large number of customers. A bowl of soup was a small price to pay for a cozy room and the unobtrusive company of strangers.

It pleased Martin that he did not have to eat alone or hurriedly this time. His departures had always been frantic last-minute escapes. In the past, he had only had time to swallow a quick cup of coffee at some convenience store on his way out of town. In contrast, he thought, this meal would be as soothing as the remainder of a Sunday service after the ordeal of confession.

Martin had decided not to rush his departure. In his earlier state of anxiety, he had exaggerated the actual risk he was in. The man asking about him at the bookstore must have been Tito, who knew that he was not responsible for the murder of the two old ladies. And no one at the bookstore knew where he lived, either.

All that mattered now was that he was ready to leave. It gave him a sense of accomplishment to have his books, clothes, and few personal belongings waiting at home, ready for packing.

The waitress brought him a bowl of beet bisque and a bread basket.

My last American meal, he thought. What a relief.

It would be some time before he returned, hopefully long enough that Tito and Elizabeth would forget about him, and the Souzas give up on their search.

But that was far off in the future. For now, he had only freedom to look forward to, and a new world to imagine—life in Africa, in an exotic capital city, in a comfortable home and with a meaningful job.

Moving to Africa would not be the same as moving from one American city to another. Life in America had always meant convenience stores two or three blocks from whatever new home he chose. That franchised environment made escape only a physical experience. The mind hardly ever noticed a change. Martin had often felt cheated fleeing that way, leaving no more than people and a set of coordinates behind.

New customers arrived. A young couple sat at a table at the end of his row. An elderly woman and her granddaughter ordered the moment they walked in—a large piece of pie for the girl. A reward for still being young and happy, Martin thought. They took the last empty table next to his and waited for their order.

The girl began to mock him maliciously, sticking her tongue out every time her grandmother wasn't looking. One could never tell with children. Perhaps she wasn't so happy after all.

Martin thought of Mudoga's children, of how many there were. It would be appropriate to take something to them—a gift or memento. They might cherish an object from a faraway place. He should buy some liquor for Mudoga, and jewelry for his wife, too. The least he could do. He had sent a fax to Mudoga at the last moment to announce his arrival. A few gifts would offset the inconvenience of the sudden visit.

Two large men in badly-cut suits came in. They had the appearance of retired football players, not French food lovers.

Martin decided to leave when he heard them ask for the manager. He waved at the waitress for the check.

The two men talked to the manager in whispers. They were not here for a meal, they seemed to be saying. Their gestures were unfriendly, like those of dissatisfied customers in the midst of a passionate complaint. The manager listened attentively as he studied a photograph one of them showed him.

Martin took the bowl to his lips in an effort to hide his face. He got the feeling the trio was discussing him. And when the manager pointed briefly at him, he knew.

The waitresses also looked his way with a mixture of awe, fear and hatred—as if this were the moment of capture of the most dangerous, nationally-known criminal.

Martin set the bowl down inadvertently, spilling what was left of the soup in his lap. The heat made him stand abruptly while the girl with the pie laughed insolently at him. Her high-pitched voice blended with the football player's, who had approached to ask, "Are you Pete Lane?"

The man showed Martin a photograph Elizabeth had taken of him at the marina. How ridiculous he looked in those Bermuda shorts of her father's that she had let him borrow. Why had he ever allowed her to take pictures of him? The scar on his chest stood out like a bright sign of violence over the pale skin.

The girl laughed louder and pointed at his crotch, highly amused with the red stain on the white fabric. Hers was the voice of a younger Elizabeth, and she mocked him with the same intensity that he would expect from the older girl. *You raped me and you're going to pay for it.* She laughed as her grandmother tried in vain to quiet her.

Martin looked down embarrassed. The stain grew larger and gave the impression of unrestrained bleeding, of a wound he could not stanch in public because it would entail holding his private parts.

The football player said, "Please step outside, sir. We need to talk to you."

No point in resisting his fate now, in lying his way out of their hands. The stain humbled him into submission. He looked up quickly at everyone—a new audience, witnessing another of his acts.

The football players were strikingly similar, trained in the same academy, almost twin-like. They stopped him in front of a plain sedan with missing hubcaps.

This is it, Martin thought. The arrest, the beginning of the end.

Only one of the men spoke. He put on sunglasses though night had already fallen. "You're being accused of raping Elizabeth Fraser, a minor. We want to—"

"She tried to seduce me, but I never touched—" He stopped too late, and realized how stupid his words always were. He looked back at the restaurant. Behind the glass stood the laughing girl and the adults—all of them gloating at him shamelessly. How fun to watch other people's punishments from the safe cocoon of self-righteousness.

The man with the sunglasses said, "We want to ask you a few questions."

"What about?"

"Just come with us."

They made him get in the car with threats and warnings of what would happen to him if he did not cooperate. The idea that police detectives were polite and respectful of citizens' rights amused Martin. He had always known it would be like this—brutal treatment and neglect, and no rights mentioned whatsoever.

The car screeched away from the curb. Inside, it smelled strongly of aftershave and plastic. It nauseated him. He opened his shirt collar and said, "May I roll down the window?"

"Yes. But don't try anything." The man raised an automatic to eye level.

Martin felt the cold spring air numb his face. It would make him feel better soon, he thought. But nothing happened. His nausea had a different source—maybe the man's driving; he seemed to be going in circles, turning at every available corner. Martin was not yet familiar with the city and could not tell the difference. The turns only made him feel worse. His hand fell on the cold, wet spot the soup had left on his pants. The smell of beet reached him and added to his nausea. His head turned with the car and the streets, and he knew he couldn't take much more of this.

"What's the matter?" The driver glanced at him.

"I think I'm going to be sick."

"Don't! Put your head down between your knees."

Martin tried it and got some relief, but his knees could not hide him from the fear and anger he felt. Fear was causing him nausea, more so than the continuous turns of the vehicle.

He thought of a cell, of a cold room with an iron bedstead and a thin mattress. A room he shared with someone, a criminal, a man who tried to stab him to death with a blunt piece of metal. He heard the criminal's voice say, *This is from the Souzas. What do you know? Their old man is rotting in this very same jail. He asked me to give you this.* And Martin felt the imaginary stabs pierce him in the abdomen.

He was angry with himself for not leaving earlier. I could be in Africa, where my mind... He tried to remember the homeless woman's words, but the motion sickness impaired his memory. His brain had no other purpose but that of making him feel ill.

He turned to the window for air. The streets were empty. The abandoned buildings that seemed to flash past him led to the bright lights of a busy street far ahead.

The man in sunglasses took another turn, and another. It seemed to Martin that they had been driving long enough, slowly getting away from the city, away from the safety of people. Only a lost driver could justify so many turns. He looked out at the street signs and tried to recognize the names. But they were either all new to him or their letters blurred more and more with every turn. "Where are we going?"

"You just shut up and sit tight. And don't mess up the car."

They turned again, onto a busy street. Martin felt a final urge and leaned over the window. His vomit washed the side of the car while the driver cursed him and brought the sedan to a stop.

"That's right," the man in the passenger seat said. "Get all that crap out of you. We don't want it in the office."

Martin sucked a glob of saliva from his tongue and used it to rinse his mouth. Then he spat.

What's next? he thought. After soup on my pants and vomit on my sleeve?

He sat back exhausted.

"Finished?" the driver said.

"No. Wait." He talked with bated breath, as if he expected a miracle at any moment, one that he wanted to be able to hear as it came.

The man at the wheel lit a cigarette and shut off the engine. He seemed impatient, eager to get his work done and go on to something else. The other put on a black baseball cap and turned on the radio.

Martin checked his pockets several times as he would when coming out of a busy train station, feeling for his wallet, fearing theft. All he had was money, all the cash he owned in the world. His plane ticket and forged documents were at home. His whole life waited at home. He couldn't be of much use to the two men without identification. What would they do? Take fingerprints? Photograph him? Line him up with other rapists so that Elizabeth could point him out? They could do nothing if Elizabeth was not there to identify him. He wasn't even Pete Lane. They didn't know who he was.

He looked across the street. Business boomed here despite the dangerous appearance of the neighborhood. Two police officers stopped their squad car to disperse a group of hookers. A man slept on cardboard sheets on the side-walk—a body swathed in old rags. Cold turned street people into miserable wretches. It made them lose their sensitivity to temperature, and they ended up wearing winter coats and wool caps year-round, regardless of the weather.

Martin thought of the homeless woman. What had she said to him? She had given him some packing tips for his trip to Africa. And he had actually bought most of what she had told him to.

He still had almost a day left before the flight, a day to make it to the plane and go on with his life. And why not? The football players didn't really have him if they didn't know who he was. They had nobody.

He leaned out of the window as if to throw up again, and let the impulse carry him through to the other side. His hands landed on the puddle of vomit, but he had no time to mind it.

He ran from behind the sedan and across the street, dodging the slow-passing vehicles whose drivers had eyes more for the sidewalk than for the wheel. Their cruising slowed down traffic. The longer they took to find pleasure, the better for Martin.

Pedestrians also helped by moving out of his way: only a dangerous man would be running like this so early in the evening, with a blood-like stain on his crotch.

He ran past busy bars and clubs, across the street, into an alley and then out of it. Soon the slow-moving vehicles and prostitutes lay behind him. He came upon an idling taxi, yanked open its door, and threw himself in. The driver stared at him.

"Let's go," Martin said.

"I have customer! I wait for him." The man was furious. His mild Ethiopian features belied his character. "Out!"

"Damn you. Let's go." Martin looked back. Two tall figures approached rapidly from far behind.

"Get hell out! I have customer."

"*I'm* a customer! Come on!" Martin groped frantically in his pocket for money.

The cab driver took him by the shirt collar. He was about to ram his head against the side window when Martin waved a hundred-dollar bill in his face.

"I'm your customer," he said. "Let's go now—please."

The man took the bill hurriedly and stepped on the accelerator without another word. He seemed to have noticed the two looming figures almost abreast with his cab. After a while, he said, "I don't have the change."

"That's fine. Keep it."

At home, Martin undressed and rushed through the house in the dark, like an animal familiar with its cave. He wanted to pack, to turn the lights on and be able to see the documents and things he was quickly stuffing into the duffel bag. But he only gave himself a minute to do it all and counted every second, even faster than a stopwatch. The books would have to stay.

After putting on fresh clothes, he rinsed the stale taste of vomit from his mouth.

He was nearly out of the house when he thought of Pete's address book. It contained only obsolete information, perhaps, but it wouldn't hurt to take it.

He went back for the book and recalled with panic that he did need it after all. He had copied Mudoga's address in it from the blue envelope. What other mistakes was he making in his rush to leave?

On his way out, he kicked a glass he had lazily left on the floor days ago. It rolled across the room and crashed upon hitting the front door. He cursed as he stepped carefully over the slivers.

As he ran from the house he wondered whether he would make the flight after all. He had enough time, but someone might be at the airport, by the airline counter, waiting to foil his race to the plane.

3

Souza had missed his father's funeral for this—for nothing. He pushed the door open as calmly as his anger allowed. Alfie and his father had died because of a man called Martin, the man who had until recently lived in this very house, the man who had gotten away from him *again*.

"We should've done him earlier, boss," the driver said.

"Shut up." Souza stamped his feet on the floor to lose the broken pieces of glass that had stuck to his soles.

Why didn't I kill him when I had the chance? he thought. So much planning—it doesn't do anyone any good.

Souza and the driver had spent days keeping an eye on the house, figuring out Martin's routine: out early in the morning, away at school, and back home in the early afternoon. They had found out where he lived by following him from the bookstore. Souza had wanted a perfect plan, an enjoyable vengeance. The pleasure of watching Martin, knowing that Martin had no clue that he was being watched, had made him postpone the execution foolishly. Now there was no one to kill. Martin had slipped away unexpectedly during one of the last two nights.

How did he know we were here? Souza could only wonder.

A day after Martin had failed to follow the routine, a middle-aged woman had come in a Cadillac. A nosy creature, Souza thought. She had banged on all doors and windows and walked around the house in vain.

Then a tall girl with a strange haircut and a chauffeur in uniform. They had had as much luck as the middle-aged woman.

Souza turned to the driver. "Don't turn the lights on. We better work in the dark."

The driver trod over the broken glass.

"We'll take it all," Souza went on, "except the furniture. Don't leave one thing behind. We'll even use the garbage."

The process had to begin again. Souza had to study the evidence, find a clue in it that showed where Martin had gone. It did not bother him anymore that his prey had escaped. With Alfie and his father dead, the hunt for their killer had become his profession. Eventually, he knew, the chase would end—and it would be *his* turn to kill.

Part Two

Chapter I

1

The light bulb on the ceiling burned for no reason. In the midafternoon the room was bright with daylight. Martin stared at the bare fixture as though it were a deity to which he prayed.

"You don't have a reason to exist, either, do you?—giving off light when you should be extinguished, like the rest of us." It made him feel better to speak to inanimate objects, to know he was not the only one spending useless hours in this gloomy hotel room.

He had kept the bulb burning through days and nights for almost a week, like a candle lit in church to honor a saint. It just might fulfill a wish.

The music started again and he got up. He had a good view of the park from his third-floor room. The heat of the day bothered him but the stridency of the music forced him to keep the windows shut.

The lead singer fidgeted with a tape player. The music stopped momentarily, then blared through the speaker columns again and filled the park. No one had an instrument in sight. Recorded music alone accompanied the performers. Two men and four women approached their microphones and began in a whisper:

Leave me, leave me, Devil, leave me NOW
Leave me, leave me, Devil, leave me NOW.

They repeated the chorus in a crescendo until their voices matched the loudness of the music.

Martin had heard the same performance every afternoon since his arrival. He felt the songs were directed at him. They were telling him to leave the country, to stop trying, to give up his wait for Mudoga.

> *Leave me, leave me, Devil, leave me NOW*
> *You just don't belong in my life.*
> *I despise you, GO AWAY!*
> *I despise you, GO AWAY!*

The lead singer was also the officiating preacher in charge of the daily performances and oratory. The only one dressed in a sweater and suit. It made him look more reverential, despite the glistening sweat on his forehead, a product of the calisthenics he performed during the routine.

To Martin, the preacher looked like Mudoga—as much as did any other man in the park. After a week here, faces still seemed all the same.

Martin's friendship with Mudoga had suffered. He had not met with his host yet. Their limited contact had come through the telephone, and mostly through Mudoga's secretary. She had apologized to Martin for her boss' busy schedule. Martin waited in the meantime in this decaying fourth-class hotel room.

He thought bitterly of the tone in Mudoga's last letter. *Welcome to my country any time you come. We welcome you to our home with open arms.* That had been the Mudoga on paper. The one in Africa was an unfriendly man, one who reneged on his offers with curt pleas for more time. He was doing his best, he had said, to get Martin a job and a place to live.

I despise you, GO AWAY!
I despise you, GO AWAY!

The singers stopped the music and cleared the stage. The preacher mopped his forehead with a handkerchief as he positioned a stand at the center of the set. He cleared his throat and tapped on the microphone in an effort to silence a vexing shrill of feedback.

An assistant brought him a Bible and he began to preach in the local language. Martin understood only the words *Jesus*, *Hallelujah*, and *Amen*, which the man uttered repeatedly. The assistant interpreted the sermon in English at intervals. But even this Martin could not understand—a type of English to which one had to grow accustomed.

A quiet prayer followed. The preacher invited those present to bow their heads, close their eyes, and hold hands. The group of office workers and vagrants stood and obeyed. They remained still among the jacarandas and the noise of traffic from the busy streets.

The same scene replayed itself every afternoon.

I wonder if their prayers are ever answered, Martin thought. I would pray, too, if I felt it would do any good.

He turned to the room and switched the light off. Perhaps he would have better luck if the wishing candle were put out, if there were no wishing at all. Sometimes it worked better to ignore hope until there was no need for it.

The change of light modified the contrast of colors in the room. The gray on two of the walls stood gloomier now against the pink and green of the remaining two walls. The black concrete floor seemed colder against the cream colored ceiling.

Martin kicked a pair of plastic thongs someone had left there for his use. He studied them with critical eyes. They were filthy and worn. How could they expect him to use any of the squalid items they had put here for him? The towel was moldy. The sheets had rents that let him see the stained mattress. The pillowcase was frayed. He despised this temporary home, the only one he could afford.

He had often heard that a difficult life was more bearable when one had no choice but to live it—when there were no other options. It was not true. He had no options now, nowhere else to go—yet it didn't make the waiting any easier. Life now was as bad as ever, if not worse. With the threats from the Souzas and Elizabeth completely out of his mind, he became less tolerant, more demanding—a man disgruntled with the world.

The chorus started again with lyrics he knew too well.

> *Jesus, Lord, my Jesus, I love YOU!*
> *You're the best*
> *You're my World...*

Enough to drive even a believer to madness, Martin thought. Religious parrots spend their lives in a cage. If they were truly as free as they claim, they would shut up. Only the captive have a right to complain.

Martin felt in confinement himself, so he still had the right to clamor and demand. Only he lacked an audience. He had nothing at all. His work, income, and living conditions depended on someone who was too busy to talk to him.

He thumped the room's plywood partition with his fist, thinking of the face he had not seen in years. A long-absent friend can be hated as easily as he can be missed.

Martin moved about the room restlessly. Not even self-imposed chores served to distract him. He tried the tap. In the heat and dust of the city he often felt the need to wash his face. But the water had been cut again. It only made him kick the sink. He didn't have any words left to damn the things that surrounded him. Words were no longer enough.

The sermon and music faded only once he had walked more than four blocks away from the park and hotel. The bustling sounds of traffic and street vendors gradually drowned the loudspeakers. More than half of the pedestrians in sight were peddlers selling trinkets made at home with recycled trash. Men and women moved about like ants, offering their wares to disinterested passersby. Some sold plastic sandals that would surely tear the buyer's feet after no more than a block of wear.

"Look the magazines!" a man called out to him. He had stacks of old issues of American and European magazines for sale—all of them discolored with age.

Martin had little patience for street vendors. He pushed them aside every time they approached him. But it happened less and less now. They had already begun to recognize him and stepped out of his way. He knew he was no longer a tourist passing through downtown—only a white face twisted with anger and no money to spend.

Martin didn't want to make any friends, and he advertised it well. As long as Mudoga kept him waiting, he thought, he would maintain a negative attitude to everything and everyone that surrounded him.

  A.R. Eguiguren

He strongly disliked walking in the city, but did it out of necessity. To have to spend more than a few hours in the hotel room was torture.

Mudoga, he thought, you better come up with a good position in a good school soon. I won't put up with this urban filth much longer. This is not what you promised me. Where are the clean suburbs? And the international schools where diplomats send their children? Where *is* everyone?

Someone ahead of him stopped abruptly to shake hands with two different men. Martin cursed him under his breath. The man stood in his way. The rest of the sidewalk was blocked by a crowd of men clinging to the iron bars of an electronics store. They seemed stupefied by a television set on display, their eyes fixed on the appliance as though it were an object of utmost desire. The image on the screen never changed—a talking head—someone they recognized, perhaps a politician. It didn't seem to bother them that there was no audio to go with the image. Their eyes stared at the set in a fixed, longing gaze.

The Hindu store owner, a woman in a sari, noticed Martin among the frame of black faces and rushed outside to address him. "We have good prices for tourists. Discounts."

"I don't have any money," Martin said. For once he didn't have to lie, though he wished he were lying.

The men around him turned and stared at his clothes.

"No money?" a voice said.

A nice shirt and pair of pants seemed to be a sign of wealth to them.

The men turned back to the Hindu woman with eyes full of hate. She stood two steps up from the sidewalk, and the height allowed her to look down on them. Some of the men grumbled, then everyone moved on.

Martin followed them past additional old-magazine stands, hand-made jewelry, leather purses, ebony figurines—the sidewalks seemed to go on forever with their display of gaudy glitter.

2

Dusk often caught Martin outdoors. He dreaded the coming of the evening in the hotel room, when mosquitoes came out for their blood meal. It didn't matter if he kept the windows closed all day. The moment the sun set, they droned out of their hiding places to jab at his unappetizingly pale skin. On the streets he was at least moving. The insects did not bother him then.

Store owners in downtown closed early and hurriedly. They locked and barred their merchandise with what seemed exaggerated precaution. Emaciated watchmen then guarded the padlocks and bars. They sat on wooden stools outside, wearing tattered orange uniforms with blue stripes around the cuffs and on the breast pockets. Some of them were already asleep on the job, still holding their nightsticks tightly.

The street vendors had left and most side streets were silent and deserted. Martin frequented the busier avenues, where many deformed beggars plied their trade.

I don't have any money, he thought whenever a grotesque human form dragged itself to him on a tangled mass of feet. With some, one could imagine an angry god nipping at their clay limbs with mighty fingers. Whatever was left of their bodies and minds did not seem enough to make life worthwhile. But here they were—alive. And begging was a trade like any other. Panhandlers put full hours into it, and usually got some results. Children were the most professional.

They followed their potential benefactor with determination, their hands extended to the tune of pestering chants that begged for change. Martin ignored them, and only after several blocks did they give up on him.

He entered a fish-and-chips restaurant and immediately smelled the frying vats of used and reused shortening. A sign on the door announced *No Alcoholic Drinks Served*. He wanted a beer.

"Across the street," a man told him.

The *African Fellowship* was the only bar near the hotel, a room filled with smoke and murmurs. Martin took a stool at the counter. A presidential portrait stared down at him sternly from the wall. Two men played darts in a back room. One of them stopped playing for a second to stare at Martin with a contemptuous grin.

"Don't look trouble with those people," the bartender said. She was short and burly. Her arms, Martin noticed, were the diameter of his neck. She said, "Only women here are safe to you. The men come to drink and fight."

She was the only woman present, and the men seemed to know her well. They called her Grace.

Martin ordered a beer, and she placed two midget bottles of ale in front of him.

"Only one," he said with a touch of annoyance.

She opened one of them. "Just you drink one, then. If you're thirsty some more, there's another ready for you here. You just tell me. I open it."

"Grace!" a man yelled from the other end of the counter. It seemed understood: she rushed to him with another bottle. The man had assembled a collection of empty ones around him. He had come here to drink.

Martin looked behind his back. He had almost finished his third beer but still did not feel safe. The bar seemed too quiet. The murmurs had stopped. No one spoke except to order the next drink. It felt as if every man had come alone, with the exclusive purpose of quietly choosing an adversary. As soon as the alcohol gave them the courage, a fight would begin.

Martin was not pleased that many of them had their eyes set on him. This is too much like a wake, he thought. Everyone mourns his own sorrows while getting ready to bury someone else.

The irregular tapping the darts made on the wall played like the ticking of a defective clock. It counted down the minutes to an event eagerly awaited by all.

An attractive woman took the stool next to Martin's. Her long, bare legs ended with a pair of cheap plastic sandals.

A prostitute, he thought. She must be as sexually worn out as she is pretty.

No one else bothered to look at her. She had chosen him as her client and the men seemed to respect her pick.

"Don't you buy me a drink?" she said.

Martin looked at her. Her purse hung half-open, stuffed with newspaper balls. Her polyester dress barely covered her thighs. "I don't have any money," he said.

"You must be lying." She laughed with uninhibited pleasure. "All white men have money. You are rich."

Grace came with a beer for the woman. "This is Emily," she said. "She's working for you."

Martin smiled. "No, thanks. I already have a permanent, full-time employee in that department."

Grace and Emily frowned. They didn't seem to understand what he meant.

"I'm married," he said.

"Oh, please!" Emily laughed. "That doesn't count!"

The men playing darts grew louder and more noticeable. A third one joined them and they argued about whose turn it was to play next. Martin tried to ignore them while Emily encouraged a fight, like a lovely cheerleader urging suitors to vie for her.

Grace locked the cash box and took it away. A few men stood and paid closer attention to the dart players.

Emily said, "They're like boys, fighting about who gets to play and who doesn't."

Martin finished his bottle quickly. Something told him it was time to leave.

"Your wife—where is she?"

"Far away, in America."

"She'll never know, then. You can have some fun with me."

Grace came back and uncapped another bottle for him.

"I didn't ask you to—"

"Take," she said. "You drink this one free." She went on to open more bottles along the counter and collected all bills. Bar owners never knew what could happen during a fight.

"What's your name?" Emily said. "Your wife has a name, too?" She licked her artificial red lips with every query. The questions were no more than a plot. They came in quick succession, too fast for him to even try to answer them. Her only purpose seemed to be to try to get him involved in her world, to keep him hearing her voice.

His curiosity in her dwindled quickly. He wished she would give up on him and go, in the same way the begging children had done out in the street.

Did one walk out on a prostitute? Was it safe? The men might get the wrong idea—turning down a woman. It might give them an excuse to beat him up.

Emily drew closer to him. "You don't want to talk to me now? Don't worry. Men usually tell me *everything* after sex."

Martin laughed but no one heard him. The dart players had begun to yell. A fight was about to break out. Customers focused their jaundiced, blood-shot eyes on the two men with anticipation. Soon the insults would turn into slaps.

Martin looked back at the entrance. A drunk man leaned on it, unaware of the world around him.

Emily said with a malicious tone, "You are scared because they're going to fight now and it's dangerous for you." She rotated her seat to face him with her legs wide apart. "Don't you want to go to my room? You'll be safe there."

"Leave me alone, will you—? I'm a priest."

"A priest?" Her cackling laughter almost drowned the dart players' scuffle. She held her purse tightly against her belly. "Your wife in America—liar," she said with a serious face. "Priests are all liars and homosexuals. You're no use to me."

The dart players shoved each other into the bar's main room—two sweaty bodies stumbling with the fill of alcohol that ran through their veins. Their menacing faces flashed with anger. The shorter man brandished a dart. He babbled his threats noisily at anyone who made the mistake of setting eyes on him. When he could not babble, he hissed.

The other man was tall, standing erect, closer in shape to a fit athlete. A wide scar ran down his long neck. He had been in fights before.

They moved in circles, approaching the bar, then reaching a corner. Everyone moved out of their way, even cleared the floor by pushing tables and chairs against the walls. The tall one spat and studied the crowd as if he were looking for something on the horizon. When he found Martin he said, "You, English!"

Martin stood uneasily—all eyes were on him.

The tall man pointed at the babbler disdainfully. "Tell this black dirt who was next in the game." Then he turned to the drunk faces around him and said, "We'll let the white man decide what I'll do with this dirt—this useless nigger. The white man knows justice. He'll say."

Grace stepped near Martin and whispered, "Pay no attention. They want to push you in the fight so they all can hit you. You're the only white one here. Leave before—"

Martin had stopped listening. His attention turned to the violence, to the sight of the hissing babbler sinking the dart repeatedly into the tall man's chest. The vicious little frame thrust the pointed piece into the flesh with a passion. He continued until the weapon got stuck inside the victim. Only a bit of the plastic fins remained outside.

The tall man lay on the floor in agony. The scar on his neck turned pink as he strained his vocal chords in uttering frightful shrieks. Emily was already kneeling next to him, with her hand covering the wound and the blood that gushed from it.

Her pimp, Martin thought, always near his girl, supervising her work.

She would have to get a new pimp now. The tall man would not make it, not bleeding like that. Martin was glad to have turned her down.

Nobody helped the wounded man. Emily pulled him away to the back room while a mob of drunks fell on the hissing little man with a battery of blows and kicks until blood splattered.

How effective it all seemed. No long trials, no lawyers, no boring depositions, and no waste of taxpayers' money. Mob justice was as swift as it was deadly. They kicked and punched until justice was made.

Grace came over and urged Martin to leave.

He moved toward the partition between the mob and the bar's entrance. What if someone pointed at him now? What if Elizabeth had accused him of rape here, in this country? Mob judgement would have surely fallen on him already, before he could explain.

He ran up to the entrance of the hotel before he looked back. The bar's neon sign reflected on the wet roof of an arriving police car. It had started to rain. He felt the warm, heavy drops wash his face.

I forget this is the tropics, he thought. Law of the jungle.

African Fellowship was just a bar's name. Violence lived everywhere.

3

Martin had been waiting for nearly an hour at the Beef-o-teque when Mudoga arrived.

He stood to greet a man he barely recognized. With the years, Mudoga had gained more than weight. Time had shaped a mocking twist on his prematurely aged face. Numerous gold chains adorned him. Martin had never seen

     A.R. Eguiguren

so much jewelry on a man. The solid gold rings pressed against his palm with the handshake.

By way of introduction Mudoga said, "How do you like this carnivore's paradise? Did you try the burgers?"

"Haven't eaten yet."

"They have the greatest meats here. Any animal. Try the zebra steak. It's dry and tasty. Waiter, service please." Mudoga sat quickly, as if this were a minor business lunch for which he had no more than thirty minutes.

"So what have you been doing with yourself, Martin?"

"Walking the streets of downtown, avoiding the beggars—"

"We'll talk about that later. I meant in *your* country, in these years since we last saw each other."

"Not much. I haven't been doing very well, actually. Not as you have."

"Well, it's different in the States. Quarter of a billion people. Racial problems. The economy. Yes, the U.S. is definitely on its way down. But me, I'm well regarded here. People respect me and my work, what I do for them. Besides, my firstborn will be circumcised in two years. I'll become an elder."

Mudoga's receding hairline made his head appear elongated, as though a flourishing intellect had stretched the skull out of shape. He moved his hands enthusiastically as he spoke. A perfect orator. His suit was impeccable—dark, tailored, adorned with a flag pin on the lapel. A Party button next to the pin showed the same presidential face Martin had seen everywhere.

Mudoga caught him looking at it. "This is our president," he said, and touched the button with affection. "A good man."

"Yes—"

"Tell me. In your letters, you never mentioned children. Have you any?"

"Can't afford them."

"Ah, yes. It's different in the States."

Martin clenched a fist under the table. He had waited long enough for this meeting to waste it on talk of children and cultural differences.

How long will I have to take this posturing? he thought. What gives him the right to amuse himself with my condition? He hasn't even asked me where I'm staying.

The Mudoga he remembered was a man who savored giving others good news. Perhaps the new Mudoga had already secured a teaching position for him? Was he just postponing the announcement for sheer pleasure? Martin played with the dream: an international school, a comfortable house in an expatriate neighborhood, a vehicle and a live-in maid.

They finished dessert quickly and Mudoga lit a cigar. The coffee in his cup was as dark as his face, and he stared and blew at it as he waited impatiently for it to cool down.

"We export better coffee than this," he said. "All the good stuff goes out to foreigners. We're left with foods of inferior quality for our national consumption."

"I'm sure it doesn't affect *you*. You must have the export coffee at home."

Mudoga flashed a wide row of white teeth. "Of course. But coffee is nothing. It's the tea I have that counts, the same batch we export to England—which reminds me. Let's talk about the wonderful job I got for you. You'll be living and teaching in the midst of the most beautiful tea plantations in this country."

Martin listened with interest. Had Mudoga failed him already? What would an international school be doing near tea plantations?

"It's the best job for you because my brother-in-law is the schoolmaster there. I'm glad I thought of him. I tried hard to get you something near the city, but I had problems."

Martin knew he had not tried hard enough, maybe not at all. A high government official, with connections, having problems? Inconceivable in a system that seemed to work by graft alone. After all, had not his own uncle awarded Mudoga the scholarship to study in the U.S.? Had not Mudoga inherited his present high-level government position from that very same uncle? What was a mere school job after that?

"You don't seem excited by this news," Mudoga said.

"In your letter you mentioned something about the best school in the country."

"But I tried. Believe me. I just don't have much access to hiring there. It's a private institution, run by Americans. You know how strict your people are. The fact that my children attend it doesn't give me any influence."

He had not tried at all. Martin could easily tell inexperienced liars. All politicians belonged to that group. They could lie to the masses, at a distance, but not in the quiet sphere of a personal chat.

Mudoga said, "Besides, you don't have teaching credentials to speak of. Major schools don't overlook that. I'm sure you're a good teacher, but—"

"That's fine. Don't bother to explain. I appreciate your efforts."

"You'll like it out there in the reserve. You'll feel fulfilled, accomplished. Rural schools need teachers. The pay is low, the turnover high. Rest assured, though, I'll ask them to pay you a city salary. Free housing, too. You'll get it all, especially the slow pace. How many times didn't you tell me in your letters how tired you were of your fast living, always on the move, working hard? This is your chance to get away from all that. You'll be isolated."

Isolation was a key word. Martin had nearly forgotten why he had traveled to Africa in the first place. In a rural school, he wouldn't have to explain things to anyone.

Mudoga reassured him, "You'll be treated like a god, with much respect. They seldom get to experience a white man living in their community. It's an honor to them. Rural folks are ignorant. Most of them think whites are superior. Why, they even believe in God, or at least fear Him. And don't tell anyone I said this—my brother-in-law, especially. He's one of those religious types—but if your loins are aching for female company, just buy yourself a bride. Most parents will be honored to give their young daughters away to a white man, as long as you pay the bride price, of course."

Government projects kept him on the move, Mudoga said. He would not have time to meet with Martin again. "So ask me any questions now. I won't be available later."

Martin felt he could be talking to Tito about a new assignment. Little had changed.

They talked at length until the afternoon closing time. Toward the end, Mudoga rushed his words with obvious eagerness to part. He acted like a businessman dissatisfied with a meeting that had gone bad, with a client he never wanted to meet again.

"I'll have my driver take you tomorrow morning. He's going in your direction to deliver documents for me. Won't take you all the way to your village, but close enough."

"What about a resident visa? You said you'd help." Martin placed an envelope on the table.

"Oh," Mudoga said with displeasure. "Okay. I'll take care of it." He took the envelope and pulled out Martin's passport.

"There's one thing," Martin said. "I've changed my name."

Mudoga chuckled as he studied the photograph. "You Americans are so funny. You all think you're movie stars." He read the name. "Okay, Mr. Pete Bloom. I'll get this back to you with an official stamp."

4

Martin gripped the door handle whenever Joseph, the driver, pressed on the accelerator. Joseph seemed to have a nervous tick, an anxiety about staying behind other vehicles. He had to pass them, even at the dangerous turns that came often on the narrow road.

Martin said, "Do you know where we're going?"

Joseph merely nodded. His hairless arms were too busy maneuvering the gears.

"Is it far?"

"Yes. We must hurry." Joseph pressed on the horn. A truck in front of them climbed the hill slowly, in a cloud of burnt diesel that blocked the view on all sides. Joseph honked again to warn possible oncoming vehicles as he prepared to overtake the truck. The maneuver seemed to last a lifetime.

Martin turned to the truck to avoid looking ahead. One didn't stare death in the face.

But death was everywhere. He saw it in the remnants of a passenger bus that flashed past his side—an upside-down skeleton, partly burnt, partly cannibalized. Many must have perished with it. He knew its driver had tried a similar stunt: the odds were not favorable when overtaking a smoking diesel truck.

Savannas and escarpments alternated. The scenery slid along the horizon like the backdrop of a boring film. Martin had seen it before. Nothing in it excited his senses. He was waiting for the elephants and lions, the elands and zebras, the scenes Africa was supposed to be. Blue gums and grass were hardly exotic. And the few scrawny heads of cattle that grazed on the side of the road only made him think of fatal accidents. One of the animals might suddenly get in the way.

"That never happens," Joseph said. "The children take care."

The young boys who drove the animals hardly seemed capable of such control. They were as malnourished as the animals themselves.

To a tourist, Martin thought, all this might be picturesque, a ten-day exotic adventure.

But he already felt a gloomy sense of captivity in this trip. His was not a vacation but a long-term stay. If he disliked the views, the food or the accommodations, there was no travel agent to whom he could complain.

Joseph crossed the double line on the center of the road to overtake a long line of vehicles. "These people too slow," he said, and sped ahead until a roadblock appeared abruptly.

He was signaled to stop by police officers dressed in khaki uniforms and thick navy-blue sweaters. Two-way radios and machine guns hung from their shoulders like accessories in a war-flavored fashion show.

They had blocked the road with spiked cement blocks to discourage runaways. Joseph drove slowly around them and brought the car to a stop.

A policeman approached and circled the car twice, slowly, as though immersed in a careful study of details. He stood next to Joseph's window and took notes on a pad. Then he looked inside again and stared at Martin. Joseph seemed calm. It appeared to be all routine to him.

"Documents," the policeman said.

"In there." Joseph indicated the glove compartment.

"Take them out."

A cassette player sat inside the compartment. It had played continuously since their departure. Joseph retrieved a fat plastic pouch that lay next to it.

The policeman stepped aside. "Out of the car."

Joseph obeyed. Martin made a move to open his door, too, but was stopped. "You stay in there," the officer said.

The two men walked back away from the car.

Martin watched them discuss the contents of the pouch, then he turned to the line of tarpaulin-covered military trucks parked on the berm across the road.

Violence, he thought. These people are armed to the teeth—a small army for a mere roadblock.

There were policemen and soldiers. He could not understand the heavy navy-blue sweaters in that heat.

The cassette player clicked in its hiding place as it switched sides automatically and began again, the same melody he had heard twice already in the last hour.

I've never felt so filled with life and joy
And if I saw you
I wouldn't know just how to thank you,
For I've never seen your face
So if you hear me
Then hear my gratitude.

He ejected the tape. A pirate copy. Someone had written *Christian Country* on it with a felt-tip pen. He put it back in and looked behind him. The men in uniform were stopping additional vehicles.

Joseph walked back briskly. He got in the car with the empty pouch in his hand and began to search in his pockets. "Expensive!" he said, as he pulled out bills of large denomination. Martin wondered how a simple driver could be carrying so much cash on him. He envied his wealth.

Joseph stuffed the bills in the pouch carelessly. "I crossed a double line," he said. "That is an offense." Then he replaced the pouch in the glove compartment and gave it a pat as though it were a faithful dog. "This one for the next roadblock."

When he tried the ignition nothing happened. The car failed to start, and he was out looking under the hood before Martin could ask what was wrong. The same policeman approached again and fumbled with the carburetor and battery cables. He and Joseph moved about the engine like two children playing with a complex toy. But nothing worked, and Joseph was soon out talking to other drivers in the inspection line. He pointed back at the car, then at the road.

Martin had no time to lose. He emptied the pouch and packed his pockets with the crumpled notes. And why not? Had not Mudoga cheated him? There was no guarantee that his salary would really match an urban one, as Mudoga had said. In the face of a politician's promises, one had to look after oneself.

Joseph returned with a malicious smile. "You're going with those white people now." He pointed at a Land Rover parked across the road. "This car is finished. Those are nice church people, American missionaries. They take you up-country."

Martin stared at the dog. It shared the back seat of the Land Rover with him.

It's easy to tell when people are happy to see you go, he thought. Joseph was as eager and effective at getting rid of me as Mudoga. But—the fool. It cost him much.

"Her name is Humanity," the woman in the front seat said. She patted the dog with a loving hand. Her light brown hair—long on the sides and short in the back—partly covered her face. Her husband looked back occasionally from the wheel to offer a smile.

"Yes. Humanity. I read her collar," Martin said. "Beautiful name."

"She's great company, like a child. You should see how locals laugh at us for how we care for her. They say we treat her better than a baby."

Martin wondered whether he should be talkative and friendly with the couple. He had come all this way to hide among Africans, not to befriend American missionaries. They might start meddling in his affairs. Missionaries often did. He had met their type—busybodies bent on saving other people's souls, as they claimed.

The husband said, "So you'll be living up-country for a while?" He struggled with the gears. The car was old and powerless, and he drove it at a snail's pace, perhaps in the belief that doing so would help the engine survive a few more years. "Life up-country is no picnic," he went on, "especially when you're used to the luxuries we have in America." He seemed to know: the fine watch on his wrist—with its silver casing and leather fob—was the sign of a pampered life.

Martin patted the animal. "I'm not interested in fine living."

"Good," the woman said. "Don't expect it. The only extras we have are this decrepit car and a fourth-hand kerosene refrigerator. The car we could possibly do without. Public transportation in this country is generally good. But—" She stopped at the sight of her husband's shaking his head. "Actually," she said, "in our line of work the car is essential."

Martin caressed the animal and watched the road. Other cars passed them, taking foolish risks with the buses that continually approached from the opposite direction. Like charging beasts, the buses lurched to one side as though eager to crash head-on with the Rover. Martin felt the draft they caused as they passed. He got the feeling they were trying to suck his life into a collision.

The husband said, "What type of work will you do here?"

Martin hesitated. What does one tell people? What *am* I doing here?

"Are you a missionary?"

"No. I—volunteered to teach English in a village school."

"With a development agency?"

"On my own."

 A.R. Eguiguren

"Oh, just like us." The woman seemed happy. Her earrings chinked every time her head bobbed with a bump on the road.

"I thought you were missionaries."

"Yes. Independent ones."

"We raised money locally, in our home town," the husband said, "at our church. They support us while we do our work—four or five years." His arms were strong, like a logger's. The left one yanked and pushed at the gearshift lever. "We didn't come here to proselytize. Our interest lies chiefly in immunizations."

"I'm a nurse," the woman added.

Martin had seen two young children walking alone on the edge of the highway. They couldn't have been more than five or six years old. He looked back expecting to see an adult join them, but none did.

"That's a common sight here." the woman said. "Children put in danger unnecessarily. You will learn how different these people are from us. Life seems to have less value in these parts of the world."

"That's only because of the size of their families," the husband argued. "The most recent census counted eight and one-half children as the average family size. It doesn't matter much then if your child is run over by a truck. You just have another."

"Don't be so crude, honey."

"It's a fact."

They left the paved road when the last spark of sun lay on the horizon. Martin looked at the clouds of dust the vehicle left in its wake. The highway, like the sun, disappeared in a few seconds.

That's the end of it, he thought. Civilization stays behind—with all its marvels and problems, and with the violence that it extracts from all of us.

He wondered how long he would last severed from modern life, immersed in a culture that had no more to offer him than a good hiding place.

The rows of pine trees that flanked them soon became shadows. The car rattled over deep ruts of hardened mud. When the woman saw Martin take his hand to his forehead, she seemed excited, as though she had finally found a long-lost friend. "You suffer from motion sickness, too?" she said.

"I'm fine."

"I always carry some Dramamine with me. The first two months here were wretched. I couldn't go anywhere by car. Now I've gone into the chronic little fevers, almost every day. They're a nuisance."

Her husband laughed and motioned to her to help their passenger. She turned the dome light on, opened the window, and fanned Martin's face with a copy of *Demographics Magazine*. Martin noticed the starving faces of children on the cover as the magazine swung by. "I'm fine," he said. "Don't bother."

"The road is not usually this bad. It just hasn't rained in a few weeks and the mud turns into rock. The locals call it a drought, but they exaggerate. They're used to daily rains, so they never save water. When it doesn't rain for a week, it's a drought. They have to go to the creeks for a drink."

Martin retched. "No. Keep on going," he insisted. "I need to learn how to live with this."

When the complete darkness of the night had taken over, they arrived at the *Happy Hotel*, a small hovel of corrugated iron walls, roof and door. Somewhere dogs were yapping, but no one was in sight.

The husband said, "Are you sure you want to stay here? We're not even near your village yet. Go on with us and spend the night. We'll bring you back tomorrow."

Martin declined the invitation. Mudoga had arranged it this way. A man called Francis would come for him early tomorrow morning at the *Happy Hotel*. They were to walk together to the village, and Francis would help him get settled.

The woman said, "You know, a hotel here is not the same *we* would call a hotel. This is just a filthy little restaurant. That's what villagers mean by a hotel."

A frail black man came out of the structure swinging a kerosene lamp next to his face. It gave him the effect of an emaciated ghost.

As if to put an end to an aggravating situation, the husband extended a hand to Martin and said, "We're the Bakers. Sam, and my wife Megan. Come visit us when you're settled. We live in Kipchibet. The house with the old pine tree."

Their village was an hour away on foot from Martin's, Sam said. But that was through a short cut. It took over ninety minutes to get there by car.

Martin liked that. The farther away they lived from him the better. He would surely never see them again.

5

The cold woke him early in the morning. The *Happy Hotel* offered no comforts. The frail man had left him a moldy old blanket that was not warm enough.

Martin sat on the bed and drew his legs up beneath him. He turned the blanket into a poncho—passing his head through a large rent—and sat quietly to study the room in the semidarkness.

Finally alone and in peace, he thought.

The bed and the table next to it gradually acquired perspective with the slow arrival of light. Near the equator the sun rose late, long after the inhabitants. In contrast, animals got up very early. A donkey brayed loudly outside. A sound that seemed human—much like a protracted moan of pleasure. Martin peered through the window expecting to see a stud mounted on a mare. But only the shadow of one animal stood next to the fence. Perhaps animals suffered from solitude in these parts of the world. What did donkeys do for company? Or was company to them the same as sex? He thought of Megan Baker, the missionary, the only white woman he knew in Africa so far. One could easily imagine a love affair with anyone when the choices were so scant.

He dressed with the intention of leaving the room before daylight exposed its filth. Someone turned on a radio in another room. The sheet-iron walls were no barrier to the monotonous arpeggios of popular African songs. The quick succession of notes made every tune sound alike.

Martin packed his few belongings in the duffel bag and tried the door. Someone had locked it from the outside. He banged on it until the old, cadaverous man came.

Francis arrived late. Martin had been waiting for him outside, watching the hens peck at the hardened ground. The sun was already high and the morning no longer crisp. A group of children had gathered to stare at Martin from a distance. They didn't say a word but giggled occasionally, especially when he spoke to them.

Francis was another similar face, but one that rested higher than the rest. He was tall. "How are you?" he said, and held out a hand.

The children gained confidence by seeing Francis shake hands with the stranger. They approached Martin offering sweaty little palms as they called out "Howar*you*. Howar*you*. Howar*you*." Martin obliged them but Francis shooed them away as if addressing a pack of pestering dogs. The man seemed to be able to switch personalities at will—the nasty martinet to the youngsters, the meek man to the foreigner.

Francis treated Martin with exaggerated deference, at times even bowing his head like a priest consecrating a loaf of bread.

It made Martin feel awkward. He would have to grow accustomed to this. Just to make conversation he said, "You came on foot?"

"Yes. We walk to the village. It is not far."

Francis started on the hard clay at a brisk pace. Martin followed and studied the other's suit as he tried to keep up with him. The cuffs had begun to fray. The elbows were patched and some buttons were missing—a far cry from the elegant clothes Mudoga owned. But Francis wore his with more dignity than his brother-in-law. This was surely the best suit he owned. And he had donned it with pride for the special occasion of meeting the white man.

Francis said, "We thank God that you have come here to help us. When my brother-in-law told me you were coming, we were very very happy."

"I'm glad." Martin got the impression Mudoga had told them too many wonders about him, too many lies. By the way Francis spoke, he felt that perhaps too much was expected of him.

"I think," Francis said, "you're a very good African history teacher."

"I'm not." Martin enjoyed disappointing him. "I don't know the first thing about African history. Mudoga said I'd be teaching English."

"Oh, but we have one English teacher already." Francis kept his eyes on the road and said with humility, "I think you will enjoy history. You read the books and then you teach. The students cannot tell. They do not know anything. They will learn from you."

The road steepened. The grooves in it, dry and fallow, had been carved out by torrential rains. Inaccessibility was as evident as the indelible postmark on a used stamp. Martin could imagine no vehicle driving through this.

Vast slopes of emerald green appeared in the distance. Francis pointed at them with a long fingernail. "That is tea. It is very green—the leaves. And it smells good."

"Will I be the only white man in the village?"

"Yes. There are others, but they're few and live far."

Martin exulted quietly. Mudoga was right. The villagers would treat him well.

They left the road for a narrow footpath that descended between poorly erected wire fences and parched vegetable gardens. Lumps of dung littered the way. Most of it was dry and coming apart. Martin could not smell much more than the fresh scent of tea. And he wondered where it came from now that the tea fields were already out of sight.

The house stood on a clearing past a row of silky oaks. Mud and wattle sides topped by an iron roof. Martin studied it. The floor inside was not covered. The windows were too small. Wooden furniture painted blue cluttered the living room. A placard on the wall read *Jesus Christ is the ruler of this home.* He strongly disliked what he saw.

Francis said, "This is my home."

"Oh." Martin was relieved.

"God has blessed us with a good home."

"I hope mine will be even more blessed than this one."

Christianity, Martin thought, had reached the most remote corners of the globe. It had been a clever move by missionaries to convert masses of rural dwellers. These people were now the guardians of the faith. They kept a balance against the millions who had lost it in the urban hells of the earth.

"My wife and children are not here now. Let us go."

"How many children do you have?"

"Eleven—ten. One died last week."

Martin paused as he looked at the empty food cans someone had perched upside down on the fence poles. "It must be painful to lose a child. I'm very sorry."

"No need. God took him. We're very happy."

They walked along the house to a round thatched hut. Francis went in quickly, not giving Martin time to follow. From inside he said, "This is our kitchen." Martin peered inside. It was dark. There were no appliances or counters. A mud wall divided the interior. Behind it, he could see a pot cooking on top of a grate made out of stones. Francis emerged with a whiff of smoke. He carried a load of pineapples and avocados. "These are for you."

"I don't even have a kitchen yet."

"You will soon. We go to the school now."

They packed the fruits in the duffel bag and Francis insisted on carrying the heavy load uphill on their way back to the main road.

Martin lit a cigarette and smoked it with pleasure until he noticed his host's disapproving glance. He put it out and replaced it in the pack.

They walked quietly as Martin considered what type of personality he should adopt here. He had always been forced to be quiet and withdrawn in order to remain inconspicuous. But it would matter little what type of man he became in this remote world. As the only white man, he would always stand out anyway. He could be as assertive as he pleased.

To hell with it, he thought, and lit the cigarette again. He exhaled the smoke forcefully ahead so that Francis could see it.

They encountered a small herd of Friesian cows foraging on the side of the road. The young children in charge of them passed the time switching stones with long tufts of grass. But they quickly dropped the pastime when Martin walked by. Their supple limbs turned rigid with fear. Martin smiled but got no response. He stuck his tongue out at them and made faces. The youngest boy began to cry but the others laughed. "How*aryou*." They followed him with enthusiasm. "How*aryou*. How*aryou*."

"How are *you*?" Martin answered.

It seemed to annoy Francis that the children made friends with the stranger so easily. He yelled at them in the vernacular as he flung his arm menacingly at the sky. Martin continued to walk, faster, if only to force Francis to leave the boys alone.

When Francis caught up with him, Martin said, "They're only children amusing themselves."

"No matter. You will find there are people in the village who have evil vices. These are their children, reared in sin. Their parents smoke cigarettes, drink alcohol, circumcise the girls—"

"Circumcise girls?" Martin smiled. "Girls? How do you do *that*?"

Francis struggled for an answer. His protruding brows strained with effort. "They—do something evil to the girls. We Christians don't circumcise girls. Boys, yes. But not girls." He seemed satisfied with the explanation and added, "I am a Christian."

No doubt about that, Martin thought.

They reached the school when afternoon classes were about to begin. Part of the village lay downhill, on the other side of a thicket on which cows grazed. A few bars, stores, and small restaurants lined what seemed to be the only street.

Martin got the feeling every villager had come to welcome him. The number of people intimidated him. They grew quiet as he and Francis approached. Some of the younger students had the courage to walk up to him and follow. But no one else crossed his path. They even moved out of his way, as though keeping a distance from a rabid dog.

Two men emerged from the crowd. One wore nothing but a blanket. He stumbled forward and offered a hand as he stooped in reverence.

Francis said, "This is Soi, the school watchman."

Martin shook hands with him. The blanket smelled strongly of alcohol.

Soi assented and held hands possessively. "Welcome, welcome," he said. "This is your home."

Francis pushed him aside subtly to make way for the other man. "And this is our Division Chief."

The Chief wore an old colonial uniform and a battered pith helmet. On his lapel shone the same presidential button Martin had seen on Mudoga's.

The Chief said, "I am honored, sir, to have *you* in my Division." He spoke slowly for the sake of perfect enunciation. "We have waited for you with anxiety since the news came, and made all the preparations. This is your school." He pointed extravagantly at the cinder-block buildings surrounding them. "They are new buildings. We built them just for you only one year ago with the help of charity from America, your wonderful country. The best in the world. And now the last building there belongs to me."

Martin immediately disliked the man. The thin mustache, the ring, the baton he held in his hands—all played like the weak props of a powerless politician, one who had, unlike Mudoga, started too late in life and with too few family connections.

"Yes. That building belongs to me," the Chief said, "and I now allow you to use it as your home. You can live in it as long as you stay here. All your life, if you wish. It is my building. The school is mine. The Division is mine. You are welcome here."

The students clapped.

Martin tried to see the house through the crowd. It seemed small next to the large water tank that flanked it. Young bushes surrounded it and a narrow dirt path led to its blue front door.

A group of youngsters brought out a table and the Chief climbed on it. He clapped to demand everyone's attention.

A boy with large scars on both forearms drew next to Martin. "You are from America?" he said. Martin nodded. "I'm Benjamin." The boy offered a hand.

The Chief cleared his throat. "Let us all welcome to Keptembei our friend from America, blessed a million times by our Lord, Jesus Christ. This wonderful man has come to help us, and we love him. The *students* love him. He is going to be the best mathematics teacher they ever had."

Martin turned to Francis. "Didn't you say African History?"

Francis shrugged. "The Chief wants mathematics."

The Chief said, "Welcome him with an applause," and the young hands obeyed without delay.

Before the ovation subsided, he asked Martin to join him on the table. "Tell them how glad you are to be here," he said.

The excited faces looked up with anticipation. The girls wore their hair as short as the boys, with no make-up or jewelry. Only their bright blue dresses indicated their sex.

The villagers' enthusiasm was contagious. Martin felt a need to match it with a pompous speech of his own, with words of happiness and hope. His new role, he thought, was about to begin. It required intensity and he gave it his best. No pleasure matched that of developing a new personality.

"I know," he said as loudly and boisterously as he could, "that you are the most intelligent students in the world! Teaching you won't be difficult because, I know, you can teach yourselves, and maybe even teach *me* something!"

The Chief laughed, and the students—who had missed the point entirely—followed suit.

Martin nodded in appreciation. "I love you, every one of you. I love this school and I love Keptembei. I love the people here and—most of all—the Chief. Today, I want everyone to know I thank our Lord, Jesus Christ, for having sent me here. I love Him, this is His home, and I'm blessed to be here."

Chapter II

1

I have all the time in the world, Souza thought. He looked at the group of singers from the window of his hotel room. They were getting ready to repeat their performance for the fifth time today. He almost cringed at the sound of the music. I have all the time in the world—but not the patience to listen to this again.

The choir began.

Leave me, leave me, Devil, leave me NOW.

And a preacher dressed in a wool suit responded enthusiastically, "Yes! He will leave!"

Souza left the room and the building. He walked away as fast as possible, trying to avoid the wave of hawkers and pedestrians that seemed intent on blocking his way. He felt a strong urge to act violently, to strike back. Mudoga, a man he had never met, had mocked him long enough, had made him wait unnecessarily for a simple piece of information that could take but a minute to convey over the phone.

He walked with his fist ready to strike, closed and tight. The heat annoyed him, and the dust, and the smell of humanity and overpopulation that lingered everywhere in this strange place. Two or three more days of this and he would lose his mind. Then he would have no choice but to pay a threatening visit to Mudoga. Maybe, he thought, it was the only way one could get the friendly cooperation of a smug African—with the threat of a gun.

He walked and observed. Everything he could learn about the culture during these days of waiting might be useful soon. Whenever another white man walked or drove by, he studied the face. That was his only reassuring thought: in this vast wave of black faces, a white one stood out as easily as tar on fresh snow. It wouldn't take long to find the one he was looking for.

Souza had last talked to Mudoga's secretary almost an hour ago. A few more minutes remained before he would try again. He entered tourist shops to waste time, handling cheap African souvenirs as though he had intentions of buying, haggling endlessly with merchants, forcing them to lower their rates. When he easily got them to go as low as a tenth of the original price, he said, "I never really wanted it," and left the seller in a confused state.

The general attitude toward white foreigners was already apparent to him. Locals betrayed their spite for tourists even as they rushed to please and serve them.

He checked his wristwatch for what seemed to him one time too many. Not much longer, he thought. Two or three additional loops around the block.

The entrance to the open market sucked shoppers in like the receding tide of an angry sea. A marquee above it warned everyone that spitting was strictly forbidden. But judging by the globs of phlegm on the concrete floor, it was obviously in a language that few had learned.

An endless line of carts passed him, burdened with fruits, on their way to the stands. He followed them in order to waste some more time.

From the blue envelope, Souza pulled the letter Mudoga had mailed to Martin long ago. He dialed the number in it as he studied the colorful butterflies on the stamps.

To his surprise, a male voice answered the call immediately. He crossed his fingers and said, "Mudoga, isn't it? Am I so lucky to have you answer your own phone?"

After a long pause, Mudoga spoke with the temper of a politician in distress. "Who is this?"

"I've left several messages with your secretary concerning my brother-in-law. I have waited several days for your answer—sir." Souza forced a polite tone.

Mudoga clicked his tongue as if upset at himself for having answered the call. "Your calls were not returned deliberately. I have no desire to have any more to do with Mr. Bloom, Mr. Lane, or whatever name he may be using now. He's a thief and a liar."

Souza hesitated. He had not expected to find an enemy of Martin's in the only local contact he had to lead him to his prey. "I'm his brother-in-law. He's in trouble back home. His wife—"

"I bet he is. He never told me he was married."

"Won't you just tell me where he is, sir?"

"I'm an important political figure in this country and don't need damaging connections with shady characters. If you want to help him, tell him he must leave the country at once, or suffer the consequences."

"Don't you worry. It's what I'm here for—to take him home."

"He's up-country, in the tea plantations. The name of the village is Keptembei. Now don't you call me again, ever." Mudoga hung up with force.

"Keptembei," Souza repeated to himself several times while a group of men fought for the receiver he had just replaced. "Keptembei."

In the hotel room he assembled the hard-plastic handgun he had smuggled into the country. It handled cheaply, like a toy. But it had saved him trouble with the x-ray equipment and customs personnel. He played with it and took aim. It seemed harmless—a white piece of hard plastic shaped into a crude butt, barrel, and trigger. But it was all he needed. A throwaway.

2

The village's slaughtering pen stood too close to the house. Martin had already experienced and learned a butcher's job from his window. The pungent smell of blood stayed with him long after the animals had been killed and the butchers washed off the slab. Killing for meat was a daily operation, and they were at it again.

Martin tried to keep his mind on a game of solitaire but the voices disturbed him. By the sounds, he knew the butchers had already tied the cow upside down and were about to begin their work. They placed a bucket under the animal's head before slitting its throat. And then came the sound that made him uneasy—the gasping for air as blood and life flowed out from the neck and into the bucket.

Martin imagined the bathtub. It filled with the blood that never ceased to flow from Alfie. He wanted to stanch it. He had not meant such a deep cut, so much blood lost. But too late. Blood was like indelible ink: you didn't need much of it to stain the rest of your life.

Time goes by so slowly in this village, he thought. He had nothing exciting to do. Teaching local children had turned out to be a dull affair. He had problems with their diffidence. Personality, not mathematics, was what they really needed. A change in beliefs and lifestyles.

He fanned the flies off his face. Perhaps it wasn't people but noises that annoyed him—cows lowing, dogs barking, birds chirping, even the din of the flour mill, which stopped only during the night. One could no longer expect a quiet life in the countryside. The noise of technology had reached everywhere.

Curious children gathered outside his window every time he looked. They stood watch, as if in a vigil for a sick sibling, and cheered at once whenever they saw the white man.

Martin could not leave the house without being followed. He had lost all privacy outside the building and was a slave to boredom inside of it. He needed a pastime. A distraction. A lover. Mudoga had mentioned the possibilities—a young woman from the village at little cost. Why not? Would it give him pleasure to have one of those bald, frail-looking girls under him? Hard to imagine.

Village women were frail only in appearance. They seemed to do all the work, all the cooking, the farming and laundering. He had seen them plodding, bent under loads of firewood and water pails. He could not imagine what type of intimate relationship those same abused figures could have with their mates.

A knock came from the door.

My first visitor, Martin thought. Someone had finally dared. Would it be a girl with a smile on her face and an offer?

It was Benjamin.

Martin recalled the boy only from the large scars on his arms. He still relied on scars and physical defects as a guide to remembering names.

Benjamin handed him a folded piece of paper—a note from Francis.

Martin read with disappointment. He had hoped to receive news from other people, from those who could understand him better—the Bakers. The missionaries were not the ideal company, but he already longed to see them. Who would believe? he thought. He had hoped never to see the couple again after that night. But now...

Francis had written the note hastily and in pencil. Martin could not decipher what seemed a collection of careless strokes.

"He invites you to his house to eat," Benjamin said without looking at the note.

Martin tried to find those same words on the piece of paper without success. "Tell him I'll be there."

"He knows."

Benjamin did not move. He seemed eager to be a friend, to stay and absorb every detail in the house that was foreign to the village—Martin's clothes, shoes, watch, even the smells. The boy sniffed. "What is that?"

"Deodorant—a major requirement for acceptance in Western societies."

The boy paid no attention to answers. He only wanted to ask. He was already inside, pacing the room, taking in every unfamiliar object. The pocket knife with the magnifying glass seemed to mesmerize him.

Martin recalled his childhood visits to the *Toy Palace*, the store to which his parents took him but where they never bought him a thing. All that remained was the memory of the simple pleasure of pacing the aisles, staring at colors and shapes that would never go home with him.

This place, though, was no toy store. Only a small, dark building. The somber blue walls were already stained. Construction had stopped long before workers were done. Even a later attempt at wiring the building for electricity had been abandoned. Holes in the walls once meant for outlets had filled with cobwebs and dust.

Martin said, "Want to see the bedroom?"

The boy reacted. He shook his head and headed for the front door. Martin knew why. Soi, the school's watchman, had done the same thing. *Bedrooms are private places*, Soi had said. *Dirty things can happen in them.*

Martin stopped the boy by the shoulder. "There's nothing wrong with bedrooms, Benjamin. You people consider them taboo, don't you?"

The boy did not seem to understand. He stood by the door with a frozen gaze.

They were quiet for a moment. Martin collected the playing cards and shuffled them while Benjamin observed him. The boy was motionless and cautious, like a zoo patron watching a lion whose cage is known to be open.

"So what are you going to do? Stand there all day?"

"I brought a gift for the outside of your house." Benjamin approached the table with a crumpled piece of newspaper and unwrapped a collection of seeds. "These are yellow flowers," he said pointing at a cluster of small berries. "These ones are vegetables. We can plant them and you can have your own garden. I help you."

"Be my guest. There's a hoe in that corner."

Benjamin took it eagerly and retrieved the seeds from the table.

"But I can't help you," Martin said. "I must go to the headmaster's in a minute. You know that."

"No matter. I like the garden. I work alone." The boy ran outside.

Martin locked all windows, the door, and followed Benjamin to a small plot facing the back side of the house, uphill from the privy.

The boy set to work. He moved with exaggerated enthusiasm and speed, grubbing the soil with his hands, fetching topsoil from a mound nearby. He patted over the covered seeds gently, as though his hands were a shovel on the fresh grave of a loved one.

Martin said, "Who's that there?" and pointed at a man in a thick red sweater who stumbled toward the nearest hut.

"That's Mutai. He's a bad man. Always drunk. He hits his wife every day. He drinks too much."

Martin studied Benjamin's arms. "Were you beaten as a child, too? Your father, stepfather? Did he drink?"

Benjamin twisted his face in apparent confusion.

"Those," Martin said pointing at the scars.

"I made this. The sign of a man. When you are little, your friends dare you to place burning coal on your skin. It burns you. If you cry, you're not a man." He resumed burying the rest of the seeds.

"Did you cry?"

"No. That is why the scars are big. More large scars, more man."

Benjamin took a discarded cooking pot with him to the water tank on the other side of the house.

Martin tried to imagine a red-hot coal searing the skin of his own arm. Some cultures demand too much from their people, he thought. Much easier to wear deodorant.

"The water tank has a lock," Benjamin said from a distance. He turned the empty pot over to show Martin. "I can't get water for your garden."

"Yes you can. I put the lock there." He approached the boy and handed him a key. "The Chief said I should lock it. It's an annoyance to have people coming for water at all hours of the day."

"Why?" Benjamin seemed disappointed.

"They can go to the river from now on."

While the boy ran back and forth for more water, Martin played with the soil. He crumbled a few dry lumps between his fingers and watched the resulting dust fall on two short sticks that lay there, one over the other, casually shaping a cross. They made him think of Francis.

The idea of having lunch in a religious home appealed little to him. He had to make sure they would never invite him again. An insult might do the trick. He patted his breast pocket and smiled. The pack of cigarettes was ready.

3

They had set the radio right on the table. Music blared through the two small speakers and made it impossible to have a conversation.

Martin punctured the bloated goat intestines they had served him, and a putrid smell burst from within. He could not eat it.

A voice said, "You don't like?"

"It's very good." Martin forced a bite, and Francis' wife did not take her eyes off his jaws until he swallowed.

She said, "You eat this in America?"

"Yes. It's very good." Martin took another bite.

She sat on a bench next to the table with her hands in her lap. Only Francis and Martin sat at the table and ate. A large group of others watched.

"And your wife in America cooks it just like this?"

"Yes."

Everyone in the room laughed. They were amused every time he confirmed the existence in his country of something they knew locally. He said, "We eat everything in America, even cats, *and* dogs."

Only the children laughed now. The adults became somber, especially Francis. He seemed a bitter man. Martin liked that, and he lit a cigarette thinking it was the appropriate time to get a violent reaction from his host.

Francis' face twisted with anger but protocol surely forbade him to reproach his guest. He did not say a word.

And how Martin enjoyed exhaling the smoke.

The more they avoid offending me, he thought, the less I'll respect them.

Was it a direct result of colonialism—to allow a white man to insult them so? Or had colonial brutality actually been the product of such meek and submissive behavior? They called themselves a free and independent nation now, but their lives were still ill with timidity.

Francis snapped his fingers angrily at his wife. The woman went in the kitchen without saying a word and came back with a home-made salt shaker. Francis shook it repeatedly over his plate.

Martin filled his lungs with as much smoke he could fit in them, then exhaled. The cloud covered the room gradually, like fog moving in with the dawn. He looked at the others—a large extended family, most of them women with children. One couldn't tell who was related to whom. He got the impression that they had only come to see him. Every mother wanted to show the white man to her child.

"Where are *your* ten children?" he said to Francis' wife.

"These young ones," she pointed at three of them. "The others are not here. They went to see my sister today."

"You have too many."

"Yes."

"I thought Christians practiced abstention." Martin smiled at the thought that he had achieved his goal: Francis left the room with what looked like annoyed determination. The others seemed to know that he would not be back until Martin left.

"Francis is a busy man," Martin said, and put out the cigarette with a smile. Women were a lot more interesting to him than men. Wives tended to relax when their husbands were not around. On their own, he could ask them what he pleased.

"Our children are good children," she said. "We're Christians. If we have more children, there will be more Christians in the world—more good people." She was demure, the only woman without a child in her arms. Her hands were busy knitting a doily.

Two of the other young mothers nursed their infants. Another woman dandled her child to keep it from crying. The room had the feeling of a post-natal pavilion.

"Where are your children?" one of them asked him.

"I don't have any. In America, one has to pay the government for every child one has. It's very expensive. I don't have the money."

They seemed distressed by these facts and remained quiet. Only the infants made their presence heard.

This is a heaven for liars, Martin thought. I can tell these people anything and they'll believe it.

He enjoyed the prospect of creating new, outrageous facts about America and its culture. It didn't really matter what he told them now. He was sure Francis would never invite him again either way. "The police come to your house in America." He sat straight in his chair to depict, even mock, the tall stance of the law. "If they find out that you have extra children and that you are hiding them, you have to be punished."

"You can't pay them?"

"No. It's too late. You pay for your children *before* they're born."

Perhaps lying to these people was not right. The women were sure to tell Francis about the American atrocities later. Francis would probably laugh at them—he seemed more educated—and soon the village would know Martin was a liar.

"How do they punish you?"

"First of all, they kill all the children."

Too late to go back now. With the smoking and these lies, he had already alienated the only family he knew in the village, his only link to Mudoga in the capital.

Locals had been kind to him. It seemed stupid to mock their ignorance. But he could not control the urge to retaliate in some way. He had begun to resent their kindness, their overbearing interest in him. Old men constantly staring. Children pointing and laughing. All eyes focused on him, the visiting circus, the white clown in town. It made him uneasy. He had spent years of his life diverting attention.

These people have no idea about privacy, he thought. They live so many to a house. They never have a chance to be alone.

If he did not entertain and distract himself more with their rural ignorance, he feared their disrespect for his privacy would end up driving him away too soon. He had to stay here long enough to make it safe for him to return to his world. Years, perhaps. He dreaded the idea.

"After killing the children," he said, "they—castrate you."

The women shook their heads at the word. They didn't know it. Martin made a cutting motion with his hand against his crotch.

"Oh, circumcision!" Francis' wife said.

"No. All of it—out! No more children."

She understood with a trace of terror on her face. "And what do they do to the wife?" Her hands let go of the ball of yarn as she braced herself for the answer.

"Nothing. The *police* are women. They want to control everything. They don't want babies for themselves so they make it difficult for everyone else to have babies. And they hate men, so they cut them." Martin motioned again. "And they kill all the babies."

She winced at the last words. They made her look around for her children, as if afraid they were in danger of meeting the American police he described. She said, "There are bad people in America."

"Yes."

"It is a bad country."

"That's why I left it."

Chapter III

1

The Land Rover struggled on its way up the dirt road. It seemed so long since Martin had last seen a vehicle with a careful driver in it. The daily vans that zoomed through the village had shown him how little consideration local motorists had for pedestrians. Only paying passengers deserved respect.

Martin waived, but the Bakers either missed him or chose to look the other way. Had they heard already? He wondered. Perhaps they would soon come to complain. As missionaries, they taught respect for human life and were here as the enemy of sin.

Martin, the walking sin, had already smoked in front of children, lied about America, and promoted contraception and women's rights. If the news was already out, it surprised him that the couple had not come to condemn him.

He would gladly hear and argue any of their sermons, if only to spend time with them. He needed their company and would tolerate anything to have it.

I'm sick and tired of strangers knocking at my door at all hours of the day, he thought. Tired of children following me everywhere.

A private man could take no more living in a fish bowl than a fish could in dry sand.

The Bakers' home was not far from where he was. Why not visit them? Why not go in their house and free himself of this incurable file of children that trailed him everywhere he went?

"Howar*you*. Howar*you*," they repeated endlessly.

He threw rocks at them, but they took it as an invitation to play.

"Howar*you*. Howar*you*."

It would never end.

Humanity, the Bakers' dog, came out to greet him. Animals know their friends. She sniffed and seemed to recognize him at once. Like Martin, she was an import. Healthy dogs were as rare in Africa as were cars without a scratch. He patted her head and considered a hug. He felt closer to Humanity than to any of the village fawners who were constantly telling him what an extraordinary gift from God he was.

She guided him to the front door like a friendly hostess. The Land Rover was parked behind the old pine tree. White shirts hung from a clothesline above a row of flower pots blooming with zinnias. They made for a colorful sight—a bright garden next to a cozy home. Martin hoped the Bakers would be as welcoming as their dog.

Someone opened the door for him before he knocked. He stepped inside to find himself alone.

"Make yourself at home." Megan's voice came from another room.

Martin took his shoes off. "Did you get my message? One I sent about a week ago?"

"Yes. A cute little boy brought it. But I think he also brought germs." She entered the room in a bathrobe. Her face was swollen and covered with rashes. "Don't be scared. It's just an allergic reaction. They come and go like this. I'll be well in a day or two. That boy you—"

"I'm sorry. I should have sent someone else."

"It's not your fault. It wouldn't have made much of a difference. They're all filthy, these kids."

From another room came the loud sound of someone clearing his throat.

Megan said, "That's Sam." She lowered her voice. "He's working in there. Doesn't like to be disturbed."

Martin leaned forward to get a better view of the room. Sam was sitting at the desk with his head buried in books. The room looked clean and organized. A few colorful charts covered the wall and a portable computer sat below them.

"What's he working on?"

"Records—for our church. We keep careful track of the immunizations we give. The numbers are used later by international health organizations."

Martin nodded. "Very advanced."

"Even the Church has to keep up with technology."

"That's right," Sam said as he came out from the room. He had been listening. "Adjust to our changing times or sink." He shook hands with Martin while Megan cleared the coffee table.

"I'll make some tea," she said.

The Bakers' movements seemed premeditated and mechanical—a husband and wife team, working, sharing duties like a professional duo of entertainers in the presence of an unwanted guest.

"How do you like your new place?" Sam said.

"The place is fine. It's the people—"

"How many people in your village?"

"I don't know. A few."

"Young? Old?"

Martin shrugged. "I spend most of my time among students. There must be over eight hundred of them, even from neighboring villages. They all look alike, and I can't tell their ages. Most of them are young, I guess."

"You'll get used to it. Will start distinguishing features in no time. Make a point of calling everyone by their Christian name. It's easier than uttering those tongue trippers they use."

Megan returned with porcelain cups and saucers—a very different set from the enameled tin cups locals used. She moved quickly back and forth from the kitchen, bringing additional items with every trip.

Martin could tell they did not want him here. He was in their way, keeping Sam from his work and Megan from her rest. But he needed their company. This was a comfortable home, a livable space. The Bakers had brought the West with them, the luxury and gadgets of civilization. They spent their days in the familiar, in the company of their loving selves.

But what do I have? he thought. Days filled with students who seem to enjoy mistreatment as naturally as a mule allows a burden; somber evenings trying to communicate with a mixture of sign language and pidgin English with the school's drunken watchman; nights of endless loneliness on a cold mattress on a concrete floor.

He could not go on like that and not lose something on the way—his sanity or the ability to communicate with people of his own culture and race. He had to make the Bakers his friends, get them to be open and welcoming to him whenever he needed them.

He thought, Perhaps if I were more openly religious they might feel some affinity for me.

He had to do something to make the couple enjoy his company. Their home could be his refuge from Africa. It had everything his lacked.

Martin crossed his hands as if in quiet prayer while Megan served tea. Her hair fell over her forehead and covered her eyes. Martin stared at the allergic flares that spread over her cheeks. They bore a likeness to welts inflicted by a whip. He said, "Those could be simply a sign of stress."

"They are," Sam said. "She worries too much."

"You would think one could lead a more relaxed life here. These people don't ever seem to be in a hurry, except of course when they're driving those damned mini-buses."

"Easy for you men to say. I'm the one in the kitchen, worrying about all the diseases we can contract from the market's produce, from the water, from insects. I'm the one who has to boil everything we eat and wear."

Sam looked at Martin with a grin. "She boils our laundry."

Megan handed Martin a cup. "Who does *your* laundry?"

"I pay some woman."

"See?" She turned to her husband. "That shows you how foreign men quickly adopt local ways. They soon become as condescending to women as locals are. They treat women like animals. How much do you pay the woman to do your laundry, Pete?"

"Not much," Martin said. "It works out to about a dollar."

"And how long does it take her?"

"A few hours."

"Half a day, probably. If that isn't exploitation—"

"You can't pay these people wages that match those of an industrialized nation," Sam said. His expression had changed. This seemed to be a topic that interested him. He grew more amiable and talkative. His burly frame and boyish face gave him the look of a happy farm boy. But as much as he appeared eager to feed the discussion, he stopped.

Martin perceived a subtle air of conjugal discord. With no more than a glance, Megan had warned her husband to end the conversation now or suffer the consequences later. She was clearly the master. It would make more sense to gain her support, then, to sympathize with her views.

Martin said, "Feminists have a hard time in this country, don't they?"

"Not feminists. Humanists!" She stood and left the room without faltering. From the controlled manner with which she shut the bedroom door, Martin got the impression she was more likely on her way to compose an essay on the inferiority of men than to cry herself to sleep on a pillow.

Sam shrugged. "It's happened before."

A quick succession of knocks came from the front door before a tall figure opened it from outside.

Sam turned to Martin and whispered, "This is Father Reeves. We're not at all associated with him." Then he stood and called out, "Come in, Father. Welcome."

Father Reeves had spent years in Africa. Bouts of dysentery had left his large frame looking emaciated and weak. He offered a freckled hand to Sam and Martin. Some of his fingers were red and swollen, like bloated sausages someone had overcooked in suet. He said, "I came to visit a few members of the parish in the village and thought to come by for that lamp you promised us."

"Want some brandy, Father?" Sam produced a bottle.

"Yes, yes. I'm parched. This heat is brutal, especially on those who refuse to drive a vehicle, like me." He let himself fall in a chair and became immobile, as if in a conscious effort to save energy. Only his large eyes moved under fuzzy eyebrows. He looked spent. Martin pictured a threadbare stuffed animal abandoned on a garbage pile.

Sam served the liquor in fine crystal glasses. "Father Reeves is a veteran in these parts of the world," he said. "He knows the culture and customs better than the locals themselves. He's very useful to us relative newcomers. Ask him anything you want."

"No, no. Don't exaggerate my skills, Baker. I'm just an observer for the Lord."

"He's also full of profitable business ideas to bring the Church revenue. He started the only apiary around and sells the honey to a tourist shop in town, at premium prices. They call it *African Wild Honey*. And—"

"Please, please," Father Reeves begged with a whisper. He was a modest man.

"And," Sam insisted with a mocking tone, "he came up with an ingenious experiment to try to ferment honey—to make wine. The Mead Master, you called it, didn't you, Father? The villagers were very excited about it. Still are."

Father Reeves drank his brandy ceremoniously, as if from a chalice. His face had blushed lightly with what might have been the shame of having to admit illicit activities to a stranger. He seemed a humble and pious man, a man too satisfied with his African benefice to ever complain about anything. The Bakers were made to look like amoral lay people next to his ecclesiastical grace.

Sam's tone showed more than a disrespectful attitude toward the priest. And Martin saw in it an opportunity to show loyalty to the Bakers. He said, "I thought heavy drinking was considered a sin, Father. God knows there's more than enough drunks around here. Teaching them how to make another type of alcoholic drink doesn't help things, does it?"

"No," Sam said.

"The experiment failed," Father Reeves said, "even though the villagers are still talking about it. It was just an idea. It kept them busy for some time. No harm was done."

They were quiet while Sam served a second round of brandy. Father Reeves wet his lips at the sight of the drink flowing from the bottle. He looked up at Sam coyly, as if asking permission to drink it right away. Sam made it easy for him by emptying his own glass in one gulp.

Father Reeves followed suit, then turned to Martin. "Aren't you that new fellow in Keptembei everyone's been talking about?"

"I suppose. What have you heard?"

"Bad things. You better watch out. Not that any of it is your fault. I'm sure you're quite innocent, but we all make mistakes in a new culture when we're not yet familiar with the running standards and mores."

"Let's hear the gossip, Father," Sam said eagerly.

"The word is that a local woman has been having a sexual relationship with you." Father Reeves placed his wizened hand on Martin.

"That's absurd," Martin said.

"It may be. But you're not aware of village customs. Right now they may seem all vagaries to you, but they're not. Someone saw a woman go into your house for whatever reason. When such a thing happens here, you're automatically linked to that woman—sexually, no less."

"But no woman has gone in my house—except for the one who does my laundry."

"See! That's her." Father Reeves seemed excited, like a busy investigator who has finally found the clue to a crime. He said, "That's her. You must get rid of her services."

Martin had to laugh. How could anyone construct a sexual affair between him and a woman he considered immeasurably ugly? "I can't get rid of her, Father. I need her to do my laundry."

"Then get a boy to wash your clothes. Or next time she comes, make her work *outside* the house, in full view to everyone in the village."

"I never even shook hands with the woman."

"No matter. The villagers believe whatever they want to believe."

The bedroom door creaked ajar. Megan did not want to be seen, but she seemed to want to listen.

"Have you seen," the priest said to Martin, "any husband and wife holding hands or displaying affection for each other in any way, in public, around here?"

"I haven't paid much attention, Father."

"That's because such practice is not part of the culture. Therefore, in public, it isn't possible to tell who's married to whom or who has a sexual relationship or not. You see? Even if you *were* married to the woman and were making babies together, your public disposition with her would be exactly the same as it is now. So everyone assumes."

Sam had gone into his study and seemed to be taking notes on Father Reeves' lecture. Martin leaned forward to get a better view of the study and stopped listening to the priest. But he didn't get to see much. Sam had noticed his curiosity and pushed the door to block his view.

Martin turned back to the priest and said, "That's very interesting. I'll keep it in mind." He opened the bottle and offered some more to Father Reeves. They emptied their glasses in tandem with their eyes on the study door.

Martin had had enough to drink. His head swam with ideas. If it made no difference to the people in the village, then why not get a young concubine? A full-service companion would do him good—sex, laundry, cooking, housekeeping. The arrangement might keep his mind away from boredom. Others could gossip all they wanted. He would not give it a thought.

He said, "Father, what is it they do to women? What do they mean by female circumcision?"

The priest chuckled. "*That* you will have to find out by yourself." He turned to the partially-closed doors. "I'm leaving, Baker. Should I take that lamp with me next time I visit?"

Sam's voice came out faintly. "It's in the car, Father. I'll take it to you tomorrow morning. And sorry about this. I've got work to do."

Father Reeves shrugged and looked at Martin. "That comment's meant for you, too," he said and lowered his voice. "Sometimes these people can be very strange. It's this new breed of missionaries I can't understand. They work too hard, too worried about numbers and accountability. God's house is no bank, you know? There's no need for all this computing." As he spoke, he fashioned a cup out of the cover of a magazine and filled it with what was left of the brandy. Then he opened the door and said, "Have to go now. Go back to my bees. They're like a wife to me. I take care of their hives, they give me my sweets." He winked and laughed heartily as the screen door slammed shut behind him. It seemed the alcohol had brought him back to life. Humanity accompanied him away from the house until Martin lost sight of them.

The Bakers were silent in their respective rooms. The perfect hosts, Martin thought. They left you alone the moment their company reached a saturation point.

He walked outside. The day was breezy and warm. Perhaps it was the flowers, or the brandy, but he thought he heard a growing buzz of bees. Amused, he said to himself, "I want my sweets, too."

2

Dear Elizabeth, Martin wrote and then stopped.

A letter shouldn't be a cry of desperation, he thought. Much less one to an immature girl. She'll just laugh at me.

He knew that even if he finished writing it, he might not mail it in the end. Sometimes letters were written only as an exercise, as an effort to distract the mind or free one's chest from anger.

The last few days had all been as bad as this one. Life in Africa was not easy. He envied Father Reeves' complacent approach to living in all this isolation. Martin had nothing comparable to the priest's apiary to keep him occupied. His search for sexual distraction had come to nothing yet. The women looked grotesque to him—almost bald, with bruised or scarred limbs, and those crooked, stained teeth. Utterly unappetizing, even in the dark. The only two he had found attractive enough he had discovered to be married.

He thought of Emily at the *African Fellowship* bar in the capital. She had been attractive. Urban prostitutes knew how to groom themselves to the taste of a white man. Rural women knew of no beauty aid other than the Vaseline they daubed all over themselves. But it was the lack of hair on their heads that worked the most against them.

Tell your father the truth, he wrote, and folded the piece of paper four times, as if to make the message seem small and unimportant. Then he unfolded it and wrote *Please* in front of the sentence.

He knew adolescents had a short attention span. Elizabeth would soon abandon her acting efforts and go on to something else, if she had not done so already. Such a short, desperate note should be enough then to arouse pity in her.

What purpose the note had he wasn't sure. As much as he wished to leave Africa, he was not ready to go back to the dangers of America. After all, it should take less effort to overcome boredom in this village than to escape the Souzas' hunger for vengeance back home. He only needed a few petty distractions, even a hobby, like collecting dead insects, or rocks. Things would fall into place once he took that first step.

All the same, he wanted to keep doors open, options available. A letter to Elizabeth might do that. If there was ever any need to go back, it would be better not to be arrested upon arrival.

The sound of a motorcycle approached outside. The rider revved the engine in neutral gear and then let it die out among sputters and chokes. Martin looked through the window to find the Chief, who immediately took off his helmet and sunglasses with a grin. The Chief carried himself with unjustifiable pomp. He seemed to think he had the right to pester foreigners any time he pleased.

He had already approached Martin several times with subtle petitions. Could his son be sponsored by Martin so that he could afford an education in America? Could Martin contact large American corporations to fund his local pet project, the social services building he wanted built on *his* property?

Martin opened the door abruptly and rushed outside. Better to be impersonal with such impudent characters. He made sure the Chief noticed the envelope with the letter to Elizabeth in his hand. "You arrive at a bad moment, Chief. I'm on my way to the post office."

"I am not to disturb you for long. Only wanted to ask you about the money. Have you heard from America?"

"Yes. They're getting ready to wire the funds, soon." It seemed the best response to all requests for money. But Martin had already used it too many times. It wasn't convincing anymore. Lies, like pleasure, had to be renewed periodically if they were to remain effective.

The Chief could see through it. He said, "But how soon? They told you when? A date? I have a calendar here." He pulled a worn pocket calendar from inside his jacket that was three years out of date.

"No dates yet, Chief."

"Yes. And the sponsor money for my son? You said maybe this week."

"Not yet, Chief. The economy in America isn't good now. You know that. We have a very bad president. He's stealing all the money. There are problems. It may take much longer than I thought."

Martin showed his impatience. He made an effort to start off to the post office, but the Chief insisted and held him intimately by the sleeve. Martin could smell the alcohol on his breath. He was tired of being wheedled by drunks. The situation required a stronger lie, perhaps even an accusation.

"Please," the Chief said. "We must talk about this."

"No. Not now." Martin pulled the sleeve free from the Chief's grip. "I'm furious with the people of this village. I have come here to help them and someone breaks into my house and steals my things!"

"A thief?"

"Yes." Martin was glad to have taken the step. Now he would be considered a victim. The Chief and everyone in the village would be on the defensive. They would finally leave him alone, at least for a while. Victims were not usually asked to do any favors. People felt awkward around them.

The Chief put on his helmet and sunglasses hastily, as though he were on his way to find, prosecute, and sentence the thief all at once. He said, "Good Lord Christ the Almighty. This cannot be. What did the thief take?"

Martin thought quickly—something useful, coveted and expensive. "A short-wave radio—and a photographic camera, and—"

"God. God. God."

"That's right. Invoke Him. Many things were taken."

"That is not good—to steal from a visitor."

"Why don't you go talk to that man over there?" Martin pointed at the stumbling figure in the red sweater. "I think his name is Mutai."

"No, no. He would never steal anything. Always too drunk. He is my brother-in-law. He cannot steal."

"Then why don't you have him arrested for abuse? He comes here repeatedly to bang on my door during the night, and to vomit on my flowers."

The Chief had taken off his sunglasses and was now pointing behind Martin as if he had seen a ghost there. "Maybe *she* took—?"

Martin turned. It was Megan. How pleased he was to see her. She smiled.

The Chief said teasingly, "You did not tell me your wife was coming."

"She's not my wife. Only a friend. She's the wife of a missionary in—" He could not remember the name of the Bakers' village and pointed instead. "That way."

Megan said, "Kipchibet."

"Yes, Chief. This is Megan Baker. She's a missionary."

"Oh, yes," the Chief said and chuckled. He winked at Martin so clumsily that even Megan could see. He started the motorcycle and said over the din, "I will find the thief. She will be dealt with the full measure of the law. I will not tolerate thieves in this village or in any other one under my command. I will crush them like rats."

Martin knew those were not the Chief's words. He had heard them uttered many times in the capital, by higher-ups in the government when referring to outlawed political opponents.

The Chief put the sunglasses back on and maneuvered between Martin and Megan. "Meantime," he said, "I will do some things good for you until we find the thief and your stolen goods." He smiled a row of decaying teeth and moved on in a cloud of noise.

"What happened?" Megan said.

Martin didn't care about lying to her, either. "Someone stole various items from me." If you lie to one, he thought, you lie to all. "The Chief has promised to find who did it. But I know he's just all talk. He'll never find anybody or do anything about it."

Martin walked back to make sure he had locked the door.

I guess now I have friends, he thought, if Megan has come to visit. Sam must have told her I was suitable company.

She waited by the water tank. "You should be very careful with whom you accuse of being a thief here."

"I didn't accuse anybody." Martin turned to see if Mutai was still there but didn't see the red sweater bobbing in the field.

"You don't need to accuse anyone. Just by saying that something has been stolen from you, the Chief may make up a thief in order to please you. You have to consider whether what was stolen is worth a person's life before you broadcast the news."

"What are you talking about?" Martin began to walk. The erratic post office hours made it necessary to get there long before the posted closing time.

"Theft is not accepted here," Megan said. "You call out, *Thief!* and a mob will fall on the man *you* have designated, and beat him to death."

"Don't worry about it. The things stolen were small and unimportant. They'll never catch the thief. Let's close the matter. I must get to the post office."

"May I go with you?"

"It's far. And I want to walk."

"I know. A long walk will do me good. My sinuses are getting better. They need air."

She followed him around the house as he checked every window. All of them were locked. "About an hour's walk, each way," he said.

They passed through the center of the village. Martin noticed people's eyes falling immediately on them, following their steps, judging Megan. He knew the gossip they would start soon—that he was sleeping with the missionary's wife. He enjoyed feeding their imagination, giving them new material.

He turned to Megan. The allergic blotches on her face had almost disappeared and she looked much better. If what the villagers believed in were only true, he thought. If he were actually her lover....

She said, "I'm sorry about the other day at our house."

"Forget it. Friends have the right to be rude to each other every once in a while."

"No. Actually, the rash on my face was really itching. I had to leave you to do something about it."

A white lie, Martin thought. That was acceptable. He offered to carry her bag and made sure to touch her shoulder as he took it from her. Behind them, he saw the women and men of the village turn heads and comment. What a pleasure.

3

Martin left the classroom disappointed. Teaching to the village's children was not much more than an eternal monologue. The impassive stare of his students never changed. Not one of them seemed interested in learning or participating. He tried to elicit contributions with an informal approach, encouraging them to raise their voices, forcing them to shout their names from the far end of the room. But they were too timid and only managed to open their mouths wider, failing to increase the volume. What a lost cause. Martin was ready to stop trying.

When he reached the house, he found Benjamin already working at the garden. The boy had a curious zeal for flowers and plants, and his enthusiasm for nature was visibly rewarded. The flower beds had sprouted already. Perhaps the dung patties Benjamin had crumbled and meticulously blended into the soil had something to do with it. At any rate, the boy was now ready to sow another furrow.

Martin said, "You don't have to work on this every day of Creation, you know, or infringe on my privacy by constantly pounding the soil right outside my walls."

"I promised to work your garden and flowers."

"I won't think any less of you if you don't do any more work. Do you understand?"

The boy did not pay any attention. He was busy covering seeds, pressing the soil on them lightly with his hands.

"I'm being honest with you, Benjamin. I don't want you to spend all your free time around my house. An occasional visit is enough."

As Benjamin didn't react to his words, he gripped the boy's thin, scarred arms by the wrists and said, "Listen. In America, people are open and honest. They tell you things as they are, straight to your face. It's not like here, where people utter pleasantries when they mean an insult. Now, this is the last time I'm saying this. I want you to stop this work and leave it. I mean it."

The boy had stopped working only because his hands were captive. Martin had the feeling they would go back to the seeds as soon as he released them.

But he forgot all about the boy's arms and hands—all about the classroom, the garden, the seeds, and privacy. He had seen a girl standing a few feet away in the shade under the eaves.

At first he felt annoyed by her presence—another villager who had come to violate his space, another gadfly eager to pester him. But soon he realized the difference between her and the rest of the women in the village. This one, despite the lack of hair on her head, was attractive. No scratches or scabs spoiled her beautiful legs. Her dress was not faded. And her eyes, hiding below thick, bushy brows, really captivated him.

"Who are you?" he said.

Benjamin answered for her immediately. "She is my cousin."

"What's your name?"

"Rebecca," Benjamin said, not paying much attention. He was busy again with the flower bed.

This must be the gift from the Chief, Martin thought. He recalled the imaginary short-wave radio and photographic camera the Chief had promised to recover and make up for. And this was it—Rebecca, part payment for the stolen goods, a favor and a present. The Chief had understood the needs of a man surrounded by a culture not his own. Only intimate physical contact could ultimately make a stranger feel at home. The rest—friendship, brotherhood, collaboration—was all idealistic nonsense.

He approached her with the attention one gives a museum piece, almost expecting a warning whistle for standing too close to the priceless work of art. At close range, her eyebrows grew wider and more unusual. Her complexion was clear.

"Where do you come from? I haven't seen you before." He would have remembered her beauty among all the other faces. "Can you cook?"

She giggled. A shy girl like all the others. But that hardly mattered. Shyness was no more than a stage in life. It could be overcome, and Martin knew just the things to teach the girl to help her become the assertive, independent woman he had in mind. Was not this the grand opportunity that a true teacher awaited all his life? He could make it his project to groom the girl into a local controversy.

"Come," he said, and took her hand. "Teach me how to make that corn cake you people eat here."

"No, no," she said with a giggle. It only made her look frivolous and more desirable.

Martin gripped her arm. He had to openly show everyone that he accepted the Chief's gift. He waved at the red speckle of Mutai far away in the corn field. "Come on. Let's cook that cake. I have all the ingredients."

He led her to the door and noticed how quickly Benjamin sprang up to follow. "You stay outside with your flowers, Benjamin. The girl and I are going to cook inside."

"She cannot be with you in the house. She is my cousin."

"So she is. We're only going to cook. It's about time you people started trusting me. Go back to your flowers and leave me alone. And lock that water tank. I'm tired of your letting others come to steal water from me."

Martin walked the girl back and forth along the path before going in. The exposure would make things easier, he thought. The sooner the village gossip started about his affair with the girl, the sooner he could begin to change her.

He gently pushed her against the kitchen counter the carpentry students had built for him. All the utensils were on it.

Rebecca had replaced her giggling with modest smiles. She got busy. Martin brought down the ingredients from a basket he had suspended from the ceiling. The cornmeal, millet, and salt kept dry and fresh there, out of the reach of rats. He moved about like an eager kitchen helper trying to impress the chef. Anything to please her.

Rebecca looked down at her feet and around the floor. "Fire?"

"I don't use an open fire to cook." Martin unveiled a small kerosene stove he kept protected under a cover.

"I do not know that one."

"It's easy. I'll show you." He lit the wick and demonstrated how to lower the flame by turning the knob. She turned it herself with a smile, then placed the pan, half-filled with water, over the flame.

They waited in silence. She kept her eyes fixed on the small bubbles that began to churn with the heat on the bottom of the pan. Martin admired her slender neck. There were no creases on it. It seemed so delicate, he touched it with fear—afraid it might snap in his hands. He slid his fingers under her jawbone and caressed her from the ear to the chin. The closer he got to her, the more he appreciated her beauty.

Every woman is a goddess, he thought, when you look at her from this short a distance.

He stood behind her to kiss her nape. Rebecca did not move. Only her chest heaved mildly with every breath.

The water boiled and she poured a mound of cornmeal and millet into the pan. Her arms worked independently from the rest of her body, which Martin held from behind in a tight embrace. He kissed her nape and she giggled as she tried to blend the ingredients into a thick mass. Whiffs of steam emerged from under the compound as though the pan were a volcano's fumarole. Martin stopped kissing her and stood still—with his arms around her—to watch her cook. She seemed to have years of experience making this dish. Her bare fingers held the handleless pan without a sign of pain.

"Don't you burn?"

She shook her head. All her concentration rested on stirring the mass, which became thicker as it lost water through vapor. Her temples were beaded with sweat.

Martin waited anxiously, wondering how much thicker the mass would have to get, how much longer it would take before he could lie in bed with her.

A column of ants headed toward a crack on the wall behind the stove. Their formic march showed determination. They knew their goal in life and were headed in that direction. He had to do the same, he thought. He knew what he wanted right now, and had only to get there. Impatiently, he turned the wick down to extinguish the stove.

"Not ready yet!" Rebecca protested.

"It doesn't matter." He kissed her. "Leave it. We'll finish later."

Benjamin burst into the house with the hoe in his hands. He gave the impression of a disheveled fireman holding an old-fashioned ax, one that had already fallen to pieces from overuse. "We go now," he said to the girl. Then he spoke to her in the vernacular.

The two of them argued back and forth until Martin pointed at Benjamin and said aloud, "Listen, you little creep. You may do all the work you want in my garden, but you have no right to meddle in my personal life. It's my business when I decide to—" He stopped at the sight of Father Reeves standing on the threshold.

Benjamin did not seem upset anymore. He led Rebecca away and said, "I will come tomorrow to work more on the garden," as if nothing had ever happened. It showed Martin how unfamiliar he still was with local body language, with the meaning of a twitch on someone's face. In a simple squint he saw anger and rage, emotions that perhaps had nothing to do with what the person felt.

He watched with regret as the girl disappeared behind the priest's large frame.

"Students?" Father Reeves said.

"Teachers. They were teaching me about flowers."

"Oh. I wish I knew more about flowers. It would help me direct my bees into the production of even better honey." He brought forth a paper sack from behind him. "I can't stay. There's a meeting with members of the parish half a kilometer away in ten minutes. Not that people keep tight schedules here, but I always like to keep my end. Even after many years of life in Africa, I still like to be punctual." He handed the sack to Martin. "I brought you some honey, to sweeten your life."

"Thank you, Father." Martin looked inside the sack with false appreciation.

"And if you ever have some extra time, why not come help our church with the handicapped children?"

Martin suppressed a laugh. "Thanks. It's frustrating enough to work with *able* children here. I just don't have the patience."

"Well, think about it. But I do have to go now. We can discuss it later."

Martin watched the priest rush down the slope toward the village. He felt a sour lump in his throat—so sour no amount of honey could sweeten it. Father Reeves had intrusively replaced his sweets.

Chapter IV

1

"You, English," the youth called out to Souza from a distance. He approached with what seemed to be a baby in his arms.

Souza recognized the wool cap on the youth's head and decided to ignore him. His name was Zacharias.

So many of the villagers seemed to have the same name. Souza had memorized each one with an accompanying physical trait. Zacharias One had a scar on his cheek. Zacharias Two had a limp. This one, Zacharias Three, wore the wool cap without fail, no matter how the sun baked the day.

This Zacharias was also useless to Souza. They had already discussed Martin's whereabouts and the youth had not been able to help.

Zacharias scuffed the dirt road with plodding feet. "You got the money?" The baby in his arms turned out to be a radio set. "The money? You got?"

"I've already told you. There's no money for you." Souza walked on.

"You won't sponsor me? I will study in England. You sponsor me with scholarship, yes? I was the best student in my school—very bright."

Souza smiled. "Listen, Very Bright, I've told you I'm from America, not England. Get lost."

"But no money?" Zacharias lowered the volume of the radio set with a snap of his fingers, as though blaming the music for his lack of success.

They walked together in silence on the rich-red dirt road, through a tea plantation, and by a number of weighing sheds, where tea pickers arrived continually with their loads to get paid.

Chepchibei, Souza thought. He was in the wrong village. No one had heard of Martin here. Mudoga had either given him the wrong name on purpose or he had forgotten the correct one. So many of the villages in the district ended in *bei*. Chepchibei came closest to what he remembered Mudoga telling him. And it was the wrong place. He wondered how long it would take now to find his prey.

"No money?" Zacharias said again.

Money is the only language these people seem to understand, Souza thought. They might be more helpful if I offered some in exchange for information. He said, "Remember that photograph I showed you?"

"Your brother?"

"My brother-in-law."

"Yes, yes."

"If you help me find him, then you'll get your scholarship."

Zacharias seemed so eager he almost dropped the radio. "I already helped you! White men everywhere. One in Kipbei, one in Sochipbei—"

"They were not the one I'm looking for. You have to find the right village and the right man, quietly. I don't want to scare my brother-in-law away. You find where he is, tell me without telling anyone else, and then you get your money. Much money."

Souza doubted that the youth, or any other villager, could come up with a lead. Their genuine urge to help strangers was visibly hindered by their lack of determination.

They were always working on some large project, they claimed. But the projects seemed to never be completed. He had seen the school buildings someone had begun and abandoned before the cinder blocks reached waist level. Even the room he had rented was missing its windows. His landlady had said the builder had forgotten to install them, four years ago. Somehow, things never got done.

They turned onto a footpath flanked by tall pines. A sickly cow with docked ears moved out of their way. Without saying a word, Zacharias went his own way. Souza had noticed how locals always followed him for only a few minutes, like stray dogs. They stopped as soon as it became clear he had no money to give them.

Souza crossed under a barbed-wire fence. A clothesline flew the same shirts and pants he had seen earlier, on his first attempt at meeting the division's Sub-Chief. The large woman who received him signaled with her hands that her husband was not in again. She asked Souza to come in and wait.

Souza sat in the cool, dark room. The sofa and the coffee table almost pinned his legs. The room was crammed with furniture. He stood and paced back and forth on a narrow strip of bare floor—four steps to the window, four steps to the wall. Someone had covered the dirt walls with pages from an old Dutch magazine—wallpaper from a foreign land.

The Sub-Chief's wife brought out a tray laden with warm sodas and a plate of food she placed on the coffee table. He noticed the foul smell from the stewed pluck that rested on a mound of rice.

"Eat," she said.

He sat and tried a few bites while she watched. She made him uneasy. He might have to eat it all.

"You like?" she said.

He nodded. "The reason I want to talk to your husband is—"

She had already gone into the bedroom on the other side of the wall. Its door had a hasp and a staple on the outside, which made it look more like the door to a storage room than a bedroom. She came back tuning a radio set.

"Music," she said, but left the dial on an English program on the mating habits of the African elephant.

Souza had to raise his voice over it. "I want to talk to your husband about my brother-in-law. Maybe he knows something about him." He showed her a photograph of Martin. "Have you seen him around here?"

She seemed confused. "He comes eat, too?" She hardly knew any English. "The children come very soon," she said, and left him to eat alone.

The stench from the plate forced him to put the food aside. He drank one of the sodas while the radio program's moderator explained: *The African elephant has large internal testicles. They can weigh up to five kilograms each.* A radio program aimed at tourists on safari, no doubt.

Souza worried about the possibility that not even the Sub-Chief had heard of Martin. He would have to go back to Mudoga then, to get the exact location and name of the village. It would really complicate things if Mudoga was as angry and important as he had claimed.

African elephants sometimes discharge sperm while not mating. It's believed to be a sign of stress.

Two young children filed into the room with a thermos and a cup. They took short, cautious steps toward the stranger until their mother appeared behind them. The safety of her presence changed them into inquisitive creatures who soon marveled at the hair on Souza's legs. They lifted the legs of his pants to examine him and laugh.

The woman served hot tea from the thermos while her children ran their hands over his arms, giggling at the sensation the curly down gave them. They had never seen body hair, she tried to explain.

The youngest one played with Souza's hands and fingers. He weighed them, caressed the knuckles, then turned them upside down with a jerk. The red cushions rising up from the fingertips astonished him. He said something to his older brother and they laughed together. Their mother joined them with a frivolous roar. Souza didn't see the humor in it.

"Like a cat," the older boy said. "You are a cat-man."

Souza tightened his fists with regret. It did not amuse him at all. They had already assigned him a descriptive label. Others would soon hear about the cat-man, maybe even Martin. Not a good thing. Martin could easily deduce who a foreigner with paws might be, and flee again.

"Cat-man, cat-man, cat-man," the children yelled in unison. Souza made them hush. He knew that one couldn't ask children to keep a secret, but did so anyway. "Don't tell a soul the cat's not away. I want that mouse to play till I surprise him."

The boys did not seem to understand.

2

Martin heard Soi's whistling and thought of how little he had seen of the school's watchman in the last few weeks.

Soi spent his days in a beer stupor, forever shirking his duties.

Dawn was still about two hours away. Martin noticed how the cool morning temperature had completely fogged the window panes. So much condensation never took place when he slept alone in the room.

He rubbed his eyes and yawned at length before turning to Rebecca. He could barely see her, but his lips knew instinctively where hers were and he kissed her. She complained in her sleep with a moan, a sound that made him think of that first night with her weeks ago:

Father Reeves stood there with the jar of honey in the paper sack. Behind him, Rebecca disappeared with Benjamin, and Martin looked on, desperate, unable to do a thing about the loss.

An act of pleasure was about to take place here, Father. Please leave! Martin wanted to yell at the priest. But did nothing, and wasted the rest of the afternoon brooding the missed opportunity, angry at himself for allowing a boy and a priest to ruin his bliss.

In the evening he went to bed with the hopeless feeling that a long night lay ahead of him. The fantasy he had rehearsed a number of times in his mind was just not going to take place. Not that night, anyway. Instead, he only had a pillow to embrace as he waited for sleep to free him from his disappointment.

The anger he felt, though, was a powerful tool against slumber. In his rage, which came to him in cycles, he could only see the lost chance of fondling the girl, of prying her thighs open with his hips, of filling his needs. Cravings of that nature became a painful burden when they went on un-satisfied.

He tossed in bed for what seemed to him hours, until desire and imagination drove him to pretend with the pillowcase. The same white fabric had covered her legs. He felt a fool for undressing a pillow, for thinking it a girl. But no one would see him. No one would tell.

Only the insistent taps on the window brought him back from the depths of his fantasy. When he looked outside, he found Rebecca.

Martin had not seen her face again. Her nightly taps on the window soon became nightly knocks on the door, and they came only after he turned out the lights.

They rarely spoke more than a few words to each other, observing the same routine every night: she arrived, undressed, and submitted passively under his weight. Then she left before dawn. Intercourse became an unconscious activity, like shaving or taking a breath. He hardly recalled any of it in the morning. Only the idea of pleasure lingered, like her scent did in the bed. He needed nothing else. With this type of stimulation, he knew he could last in Africa long enough to be completely and forever forgotten in America.

Chapter V

1

"You have no right to endanger other people's hard work," Megan said with a touch of anger.

Martin rubbed his forehead and listened quietly. She had come to see him on her own, but it seemed obvious that Sam had sent her.

Word of Martin's intrusive behavior, she said, had already spread beyond Keptembei. Even some residents in the distant provincial capital had heard his name already.

"In the few months you've lived here," she said, "you have managed to create resentment so deep that it rivals that felt in colonial times. Foreign interference is strongly resented in this country."

"So it is. But I resent them, too." Martin stood next to the stove to pour sugar into a boiling mixture of milk and tea. "I resent them for using me as a trophy in their school. Teachers go about saying, 'We have a white man in our school, we have a little monkey. Come see him perform tricks.' And then an endless parade of obscure government officials and teachers from other schools come requesting a tour of the school—as if this were some exemplary institution—demanding that I conduct the tour. I resent their using me for this purpose. So if they dislike my actions—then we're even."

He blew the flame out and removed the pot from the stove. "Do you care for some tea?" He spoke with the tone lovers use when they are not talking to each other but must, for some reason, communicate.

"Is it sufficiently boiled? I'm terrified of brucellosis."

Megan looked pale. Her hair did not have the same luster as when he had first met her. She seemed abandoned, a neglected wife, overly distracted. Martin imagined Sam spending all hours of the day in that study, leaving her to boredom and monotonous inoculation rounds.

"It would be acceptable," she said as she took the tea, "if only one of your actions had caused resentment. But you're trying to change too many things too soon."

"My promoting respect toward women? You of all people should agree with that, you so-called humanist, as you define yourself."

"Telling them to refuse sex to their husbands and to force the men to wear condoms is not the proper way to gain respect here. You must stop confusing them. These are simple people."

Martin gritted his teeth audibly. Why, when he was enjoying his role of reformer, should moralists come to ruin his act? "There's no such thing as simple people, Megan. Even the most seemingly stupid fool in this world has a complicated mind. And even if they were simple, it's time they complicated themselves some. Isn't that what *you* are here for? You seem to be too much into accepting things as they are. I thought missionaries were all about change, about conversions."

"Changes must come piecemeal."

"That's nonsense. If reforms are to stick at all, you have to act swiftly. You have to hack away at their taboos, knock down their obsolete beliefs. That's what *I'm* doing—confronting their views, letting them know that their ideas are more than eighty years behind in a world where women have already become presidents and astronauts."

Megan took a piece of paper from her breast pocket and unfolded it.

"I'll give you an example," Martin said. "I went to the Ministry of Social Services and came away with a large case of condoms from their Family Planning Office, an office that has been functioning for twenty-five years without visible results. Villagers are having as many children today as they ever did. What's needed is an aggressive campaign to promote the idea of birth control." Martin spoke enthusiastically, as though he had finally found his vocation.

"What are you going to do with those condoms?" Megan said with a sign of alarm. "May I ask?"

Martin almost smiled. "A demonstration of their use at the village market on Wednesdays, when everyone is there. I'll tell women about their rights."

"You can't—"

"I won't expose anyone. Volunteers from the audience, women, will fit them on a banana. That's all. They'll laugh as they learn, by far the most effective educational approach. Then I'll distribute them."

"You can't do that. You're a guest here, a foreigner. It's against—"

"You're absolutely right. And only a foreigner could get away with it. And I will. It's my contribution to this community. What have *you* done to free the local women from the treatment you so hate to see imposed on them?"

Megan played with the sheet in her hand and almost dropped it. She seemed about to say a lot but was brief: "I pray for them." Her eyes were moist.

"I don't think you do. What you do is beg for them, passively requesting that they be saved while you stand around, doing nothing. *That* is begging. Or maybe praying and begging are the same thing?"

Dusk had darkened the room quickly. Martin wished Megan would leave now. He knew Rebecca would arrive soon and be forced to wait outside.

He had not seen the girl in three days. For some reason, she had changed her hours and now came to see him earlier in the evening. She had also begun to skip the same three days of every week from her regular visits. When he asked her why, she refused to explain.

Their relationship ran like a schedule—sex four days a week, no visits on the remaining three. And the three days without her only made him long for her more.

Perhaps she was out there now, waiting. Megan was in the way.

He set a pressure lamp on the table and filled it with kerosene from a Coca-Cola bottle. He pumped it quickly and put a match to the mantle. In seconds the room turned bright with light and he could see that Megan's eyes were no longer moist. She seemed to have gained determination. Her back was erect and her legs crossed in a way more feminine than Martin had ever noticed in her. Her voice, clear and loud, spoke over the noisy breathing of the lamp.

"The point of my visit," she said, "is to tell you that your actions are endangering our work. There are far more people than you think who resent your doings. And because Sam and I are white, as you are, they've begun to resent us as well, by association. People whom we've known for some time have come to us with complaints, thinking that maybe we can do something about you. I wrote those complaints down because they're too many and my memory isn't very good."

She paused to read from the sheet. "Some of these things are unbelievable. To think that an educated, mature individual like you would come up with these harmful lies. For example, we heard you told people that policewomen in America go about killing babies."

Martin chuckled. "It was just a fable about how taxes affect the birth rate. They didn't get it."

"You've taught children to yell back at their teachers. You told people to demand political changes from the government. Don't you know that such behavior is considered subversive here and is absolutely forbidden?"

"I—"

"You put a lock to the only water tank in the village, a tank that everyone used before your arrival. What good does that do? There's so much water in there, you'll never need it nor use it all yourself."

"The Chief told me to lock it. I was tired of children coming around with empty pails, knocking on my door."

"Now it's the mothers who have to go to the creek for water and walk two or three miles bent over under the load. What does that do to your trying to help the women?"

"Things will fall into place."

"And the Chief," she said, "is only backing you because you've promised him funds for that hospital, which he claims he'll build for the community. You are very naive if you believe this. He's a corrupt man, and will just pocket the money."

Please leave, he thought.

It had turned completely dark outside. Martin needed the girl. He said, "Why have *you* been told all these things? No one has come to me to complain."

"They're shy. They don't want to offend you. You're a white man." She turned her eyes to the list again with a nervous twitch on her forehead. She might even be sick, Martin thought. Some tropical diseases grew on you with the casual speed of a snail. It could take years before the mind began to deteriorate. And these small signs—the raised eyebrow, the unsteady fingers, and the almost hysterical rate of her breath—could easily be considered the first symptoms.

He tapped his fingers on the table. Moths were circling around the lamp with persistence. They needed the light like he needed the girl. The windows were all shut, but the insects had managed to come in somehow. If only he could be as successful as they were in satisfying immediate needs.

Megan said, "You told them we have flying cows in America."

Martin laughed. He couldn't help himself. They had believed everything. "I simply told them they had wings."

"Why? What's the purpose in lying like that?"

"I was trying to explain low-fat milk."

"With lies? What *is* the purpose?"

Suddenly he had had enough. He needed the Bakers as friends, but friends were useful only if they were good company. Better to have an army of enemies before a handful of nagging, moralistic friends. Time to be rude, he thought. She had crossed the line.

"The purpose," he said, "is that I'm sick of being asked the same stupid questions, by the same people, over and over again. Questions such as 'Are there cows in America? Are there trees? Are there chickens? Are there bees?' I try to at least entertain myself by coloring my answers with some fiction, if only to save my sanity." He stood as if to indicate that it was time for her to leave.

Megan did not move.

"This isn't the greatest place to live in," he said. "You know that. I can tell how you suffer here, with your allergies and disease phobias. You only stay for your husband's sake, because *he* wants to be here. This place is hell."

She stood and replaced the piece of paper in her pocket. "Then why on earth did you come here? Why don't you leave?"

"For the same reasons you don't. I can't. You have Sam. I have my reasons."

They faced each other for a few seconds, studying their intentions the way wrestlers do before engaging their arms. Megan averted her eyes first and said, "But your worst sin, and why I finally decided to come see you, was your telling them that Americans had developed an eternal-life vaccine. Don't you know the struggles I've had trying to convince these people that immunizations are good for them? Now that you have told them shots will make them live forever, they mob my house with requests. Hundreds who don't need shots now demand them. I can't cope."

"You always complained about how they didn't trust shots. I just wanted to help you solve that problem."

"But what about the mother who comes back later with her dead child, blaming me because *my* eternal-life shot failed?" Her voice resounded through the room over the hissing of the lamp. The louder she talked, the more Martin lowered his voice. He felt an urge to keep a balance.

"I don't see why," he said almost whispering, "you and Sam are so sensitive to my activities. Father Reeves doesn't seem to mind."

"Leave that honey priest out of this. He's senile, a man who loves bees more than human beings. You're endangering our work and the work of all other non-Africans in the area with your behavior. You—"

A succession of blows came from outside the door. An almost unintelligible voice accompanied it, saying, "My wife, my wife!"

Megan rolled her eyes as though she had suddenly understood something that had been clear all along. She said, "So that's why you've been acting like this, putting down my words with terse remarks, tapping your fingers on the table—so obviously eager to see me leave. You have a woman in your bedroom, somebody's wife!"

"Nonsense. It's only that drunk, my neighbor."

"I don't believe you!" She ran to his bedroom. "Who is she?"

"Nobody. Don't go in there!" But she had already entered the room. "Just come to see this," he said, and opened the front door. The pathetic, drunk figure of Mutai stood there in the red sweater. He babbled as he held his crotch.

Megan came back from the bedroom as hurriedly as she had gone into it. "I apologize," she said. "I had no right to—" The sight of Mutai made her lips turn rigid with repugnance.

Mutai entered the building and advanced toward Megan, pointing an accusing finger at her. He yelled at Martin, "You in bed with my wife. You in bed with my wife," but kept on pointing at Megan as though she were the woman he referred to in his tirade.

The sight of the drunk had an emetic effect on her. She gasped for air in her nausea until Martin felt pity for her. She had come here to intimidate him, he thought, to accuse and scold. Perhaps she had even believed that she could easily force him out of the village and the country, back to the U.S. But how could she in good conscience tell him to go away? Martin had as much a right to tamper with local mores as any missionary. After all, weren't they all here to push their own goals?

"My wife is a bad one," Mutai said. "She is not a good wife. A whore, she is. A whore!"

Martin twisted Mutai's arm brusquely. "That's enough," he said. "Nobody invited you in."

He led the drunk out of the house, gave him a swift kick in the buttocks, and shoved him until he was on the other side of the fence.

In the darkness Martin whispered Rebecca's name in the hope that he could ask her to wait. No reply came.

Back inside, he turned the lamp off before walking Megan out of the house. She was shaken. "I feel faint," she said. "That man—he was so repulsive. I could smell him—the alcohol, and the smoke, like kipper."

"Be quiet and take deep breaths."

They were below the starlit arc of the night. Martin looked up at the scintillating stars. He had never seen so many of them in one place. "Are you well enough to drive?" he said.

"Yes. I think it's just another mild attack of ague. It comes and goes."

He watched the beam of light from the car's headlights grow dimmer and disappear in the distance. When he turned toward the house, the warm body of a woman blocked his way. He immediately recognized the scent.

As usual, he took her hands and led her into the bedroom. But this time he noticed a mild resistance in her. He might be a rapist, he thought, pulling a reluctant partner to bed.

"What's wrong?"

"That woman. You were with her."

"Don't be jealous. She's from the church. You know church people. They never do bad things."

He helped her undress with anxious tugs at her clothes. For the moment, pleasure was all that mattered. The Bakers and their piety didn't concern him. He had come to Africa to save only himself.

2

Martin woke with the smell. He tried to turn over but the girl's back blocked the way. His first thought was of how little pleasure she had given him last night, lying beneath him, still and clammy with sweat—wholly unsatisfying. Now Rebecca sat at the edge of the mattress with her head buried between her knees. She had just vomited on the cement floor. The smell grew more acrid as he regained consciousness.

"What's wrong?" he said.

"Pain."

"Where?"

"Here—and here." She was pointing somewhere but he couldn't see. He switched on a flashlight. The bulb burned with a weak charge from batteries he had never replaced. He examined her eyes and placed his palm on her forehead. Nothing wrong with her, he thought, until he noticed her belly. It had expanded, though the growth was almost imperceptible. He could not be sure himself.

"Is there someone in here?" he said, touching her abdomen.

She did not understand. Her face twisted with the signs of nausea. Martin took a pencil from the desk and drew a stick figure on the cover of a book. He added breasts and lines flowing down from between the legs, then showed it to her. "Has this happened to you lately? Any blood? Your period?"

Her eyes fixed on the stick figure—a blank stare that meant nothing. She had no clue. Martin added a large belly to the sticks. "A baby?" he said. "Pregnant?"

Rebecca leaned forward and sobbed indistinctly. He couldn't tell whether she was laughing or crying.

"Be quiet," he said, and took her outside.

The sky was still dark but the stars not as visible as earlier in the night.

"Go home now," he said, hoping that she never came back.

The unbearable smell of vomit drove him to carry the mattress out of the bedroom and set it next to the kitchen table. He tried to go back to sleep without success. He could only think of the belly. If a child was on the way, it would only complicate things. How ironic. In a few days he would be giving a public demonstration of condoms as a means to control unwanted pregnancies. There was that large case of them in the bedroom, and *he* had not bothered to use them.

He had almost fallen asleep when the screams brought him back. They came from nearby—a series of horrifying wails, as if someone were being flayed alive. For a few minutes, they drowned every other sound around him. Then they died off and the usual concert of crickets and bats resumed its permanent play.

Martin imagined he had dreamt it all until the frantic barks of dogs started. He felt like a blind man. Sounds came and went at different volumes and intervals, and he could only imagine what lurked outside. The dogs yapped louder, relentlessly, as if announcing the coming of an earthquake or natural disaster only they knew about. Then came the loud knocking on his door.

Rebecca was near a state of shock. He made her sit on the mattress and rocked her back and forth in an effort to comfort her. But her crying soon put his nerves on edge. He groped for the first-aid kit and the phenobarbital—both gifts from Megan; she had insisted he be prepared for anything. Martin made the girl take some and had a dose himself.

Rebecca calmed down gradually. A long time elapsed before she said, "He killed her."

The victim was Mrs. Mutai, the hapless wife, the mother of four children, expecting a fifth. Rebecca knew nothing else. She became gloomy and quiet.

Martin tried to make her lie down but she refused. She said she wanted to leave.

"You can stay here as long as you want," he said, and felt stupid for making such a meaningless offer. He knew nothing about her aside from her name and the possibility that she might be pregnant with his child. He had no knowledge of her dreams or desires. Nor did he know how much of a nuisance she might become living with him, if she accepted the offer.

"No," she said. "I go back now, before the light comes and my family finds me outside."

Foolish girl, he thought when she had gone. If you're pregnant, they'll know anyway.

The last, terrifying cries from Mrs. Mutai had upset the balance. He sensed things were no longer right. Perhaps there was a god somewhere playing with the weights—with the burdens of life—shifting them onto Martin's pan. His side tended to become heavier when he least needed the weight.

He shut his eyes without realizing that dawn had almost arrived. He would have to teach a class soon. But exhaustion, like selfishness, released one from all responsibility. He could claim sickness and take a rest.

3

A week later, Martin kept on having the same nightmare. His several wives wanted him killed by his two hundred children. The women commanded, and the children obeyed with zealous determination, all dressed in fraying red uniforms. Like lemmings, they surrounded him while his wives gave the orders: "Castrate! Castrate!"

He got out of bed thinking of Mrs. Mutai. The gossip had already spread in the village, reaching even him. Mr. Mutai, the drunkard, had kicked his wife to death, in the abdomen, where their fifth child awaited birth. The police did not consider it a crime to kill an unfaithful wife in this manner. Mutai was already back in the village a free man, after only two days in police custody. He had been fully exonerated, and was already looking for a new bride. Most villagers agreed. His wife had deserved to die for making a cuckold out of him. *That* was a crime.

Mrs. Mutai's presumed lover was Martin. The fetus the drunk had so furiously aimed at was believed by all to have been the result of Martin's love affair with her. For that, she had deserved death. But no one had raised a hand against Martin. He was a man, a white man. His only punishment came in the form of reproaching looks, which followed him everywhere he went.

The school had closed for the last six days. The village stayed in mourning. Aside from Mrs. Mutai and her unborn child, several others died in that week, most of them eternal drunks whose livers finally succumbed to cirrhosis. At least one drunkard passed away daily, and the village shuffled from one funeral to the next. Three infants who died of diarrhea were also buried quickly. The death rate had tripled, as though nature had decided to clean up a filthy place. *It's the work of God*, Soi told Martin one morning. All the sudden deaths were the work of God, including Mrs. Mutai's. No one was to blame.

Martin felt guilty about her death all the same. It had been the shadow of Rebecca entering his house every night that the drunk Mutai had taken for an unfaithful wife.

He returned to bed. Rebecca slept peacefully—her breath loud and rhythmic. She was pregnant. He had no doubt. But at least she would not be another hapless Mrs. Mutai. He would do his best to protect her.

In her innocence there seemed to be no remorse. She might even be proud to be expecting his child. He worried about her spreading the news too readily, or boasting about her status of concubine to a white man. He had enough problems dealing with the ghost of Mrs. Mutai to take on another burden.

Up in the corner where the two walls met with the ceiling, a firefly sent signals of distress. The insect struggled in the snarly hold of a cobweb.

That's me there, Martin thought. The only difference is that I'm spinning my own.

He struck a match and studied the girl's face. Her skin glistened with perspiration. He touched the greasy moisture on her forehead. Was it really hers? He never knew where that constant luster came from—Vaseline or sweat. At any rate, he no longer saw Rebecca as an object of physical pleasure. And that distressed him. There wasn't much more he could do with the girl.

The sudden shattering of a window made him get up.

"People are honest in America," a voice yelled outside. "No one tell a lie in America!"

Martin recognized the words as ones he had once spoken himself. Benjamin's voice repeated them now. Another window shattered, one out in the kitchen. Glass spread over the concrete floor like a sprinkling of hail.

"Benjamin!" Martin called out as he pulled a machete from under the mattress. He had to stop the boy, he thought, before the rest of the village came. "Benjamin!"

The answer came in the form of a rock hurled onto the iron-sheet roof. It rolled down the slant with a thunderous rumble. Martin approached one of the broken windows prudently and aimed the weak beam of his flashlight outside. He saw Benjamin's teeth first. The boy might have been a feral beast foaming with rage. He had no shirt on. And a sheath of sweat, like the one on Rebecca's forehead, made his chest glisten.

"Have you gone mad?" Martin said calmly, directing the light at the boy's eyes.

"You don't tell a lie in America."

"That's right. We don't."

"But in Africa, you lie!"

"What you heard isn't true. Mutai killed his wife because he wanted to get a new one. I never slept with his wife. He's a murderous drunk."

Benjamin picked up another rock.

"Put that down, Benjamin."

"In Africa, you lie!" The boy approached as if to fling the stone through the broken window. Martin cringed and the beam of light fell to the floor with a fleeting dance on the walls.

"You were only going to *cook* with her." Benjamin yelled and pointed at a terrified Rebecca. She had stumbled out of the bedroom with a pillow in her arms.

The balance, Martin thought, is tipping at this very moment. His side sank precipitously. The weight of his actions had finally taken effect. It annoyed him that the girl did not cooperate. "What are you doing here?" he said to her. "Go back to bed."

Benjamin's words were louder. "Whore!" he yelled as he cast the stone at her. Rebecca stopped it with the pillow before it fell on her foot, making her scream with pain.

"Whore! Whore!"

"Leave her alone!" Martin rushed to help her. But in her distress, she ran outside into the darkness and he dared not follow her.

"Whore!" Benjamin shouted relentlessly.

It occurred to Martin that the words could be heard all over the village. Soon an audience would come to watch.

The rumbling of rocks on the roof replaced the loud accusations. Another window shattered before Benjamin's voice reached in again. "Liar!" And the boy cast another stone.

Missionaries had failed dismally in their work, Martin thought. Didn't the Bible say not to cast the first stone? Not to make accusations?

Another blow resounded from the iron sheets above. Martin recovered the flashlight and used the pillow as a shield. For a moment, he believed the attack to be a village effort to scare him away. But when he listened more closely, he realized it was only the rumbling of the roof that made it seem like a barrage from several people. Benjamin was alone.

"Stop this at once, Benjamin!" Martin aimed the light outside hoping to see the boy.

"Liar."

The last rock had rolled off the roof and the house became quiet again. Martin took advantage of the lull to charge out in search of Benjamin. He was determined to give him a beating, no matter what the consequences.

The batteries were running low. He waved the weak beam about like a searchlight atop a prison's turret.

"Benjamin," he called out. "You're not a good Christian, casting the first stone. Look what you've done to my windows." He turned the light to the flower beds. Someone had trampled the seedlings and smashed the trellis.

"Look at this," Martin yelled as he walked around the house. "You have destroyed the Kingdom of God!"

To speak like this was a way to make light of the situation, to amuse himself. Christspeak, he thought. The mantra of the missionaries. It had become more the local language than any other the villagers knew. With a Bible and a pulpit, the young were being taught to judge without shame.

"Benjamin! Look what you've done. God's going to be upset with you."

No one was there to listen. The impudent boy had left, probably terrified of what a white man's wrath might do to him. He had surely heard from the village's elders about the vile punishment white colonists had once dispensed.

Martin lowered his voice gradually and said at last, "You stained the name of the Lord."

A voice said, "And what have *you* stained, Mr. Bloom?"

Francis appeared. He spoke with a tone of conceited self-righteousness, holding Rebecca in his arms like a helpless creature whom he had to protect from evil.

"My house has been attacked. That boy broke my windows."

"Do you know this young woman, Mr. Bloom?" Francis spoke with dignified self-control. He seemed a different man from the Francis Martin knew. "*Do* you know her?"

"She's visited a few times. We cooked together."

"She is my daughter, and she is fifteen years old."

Martin grimaced at the number involuntarily. It had never occurred to him to find out her age. She seemed mature enough. "She never told me you were her father. I thought the Chief had sent her."

"The girl has been defiled by you." Francis spoke slowly and clearly. Martin could tell he had carefully prepared this speech for several days, if not weeks. Diction seemed more important to Francis than emotions, as though he believed that speaking well alone might make him superior to those he tagged with blame.

Francis said, "She now belongs to you. You must pay me the bride price, which is twenty heads of cattle and a vehicle."

Martin laughed. "I don't have that kind of money."

"Then you must ask someone in America to send it to you. Americans always have money. This bride price is not very much to you. You must pay." Francis pushed the girl toward Martin. "Take her."

"I can't take her. I'm already married. In America, you can't have more than one wife. It's against the law. Take her back with you. I won't touch her again, I promise."

"One cannot return used goods, Mr. Bloom. She belongs to you." Francis turned quickly away and was already out of sight when he yelled, "You must pay the bride price soon."

Martin aimed the flashlight at Rebecca and kept it on her until the batteries, at the end of their charge, became so weak that only a flicker emerged.

"You didn't tell me you were so young, or that your father was—" He pressed the feeble light against her eyes. Interrogators did that to elicit a response or extract information, but Rebecca retained her usual unemotional presence.

Martin knew she was waiting for a command, for an order from her new husband. If he told her to cook now, she would cook. If told to clean, she would clean. She had become his maid, but he would not stand for it. If the village wanted to force the girl on him, he would show them what he could do with her. If they had never seen a woman in tight shorts before, they would soon. He would send her out to market in them. If no woman was allowed to smoke, he would light her cigarettes in public. If they disapproved of long hair on a woman's head, he would groom Rebecca's in long braids. If they wanted scandal, they would get it through her. He was going to show them what development really meant—what the Bakers, the priests, and all the other foreigners in this country had come to spread.

When the flashlight finally died, he pressed it into her hand and said, "Do whatever you want with yourself." He went back to bed and locked her out of the bedroom.

Before he fell asleep, he heard the breathing of the pressure lamp and the faint scratching of broken glass on the cement floor. Out in the kitchen Rebecca was sweeping what remained of the windows.

Her housekeeping has already begun, he thought.

It might be impossible to get her to parade in shorts after all. As young as she was, the cultural conditioning had already set. Without a word of complaint, she would serve her husband to the end of her days.

4

The cow had lain dead on the other side of the fence for over two days. Martin watched the four men dig a large grave as though he were watching television. His only activity, now that the doors of the school were closed to him. Francis had told him to stay away from the innocent.

The Chief still came to see him daily about the funds for the local hospital. Martin reassured him the grant was on the way. Money was the only leverage he had. With the promise of it, he could stay in the house and in Keptembei for a while. No one ever contravened the Chief's wishes.

Francis came with equal frequency to demand his bride price, getting the same response from Martin. Like the Kingdom of God that missionaries had promised them, the money was always on the way.

The diggers stopped their work to take a rest. The mound of soil opposite the cow had grown to a height almost twice that of the animal. The hole was deep enough for burial.

Martin waited with anticipation and wondered how they would move the heavy mass to the edge of the hole. He turned back to see if Rebecca was watching and found her stooping over the flower bed, repairing what Benjamin had destroyed. She seemed to have no interest in burials. Village children witnessed frequent deaths. Funerals were nothing new to them.

He studied her legs with interest. His pants did not fit her well. But they were a first step toward making her free. No woman in the village was allowed to wear pants. He had sent her to market in them. And through Soi, the school's watchman, the village's gossip had already reached him. Martin reveled in it. It gave him a feeling of triumph, and some mindless form of entertainment.

The plastic sheets over the windows fluttered noisily with the occasional gust of wind. The sound reminded Martin of a flag. He had flown one at half-staff at his parents' home, the day after their funeral.

He turned back to the cow. Three of the men were still resting. The fourth had begun to tie a rope around the hooves of the animal.

"It's their own way of rustling cattle," Father Reeves said. He had arrived quietly and placed his freckled hands on the fence. "Thieves don't actually steal the animal from you. They kill it with poison instead. That way no one finds out who committed the crime. It's a lot more difficult to hide a cow than to murder it."

"Why would they do that? What use is a dead cow to a thief?"

"The point of it, obviously, is not to rustle the animal—but to hurt its owner. Whoever wishes you ill comes during the night, and poisons your cattle while you sleep."

Martin could see a jar of honey under the priest's arm—another gift, no doubt. Rebecca had already finished the first jar. She would appreciate this one, he thought. She liked sweets more than he did. "Why don't they cut it up and sell the meat, Father?"

"It's too late for that. Besides, these men didn't kill it. God did. You can eat what you slaughter, but not what God kills."

"You just said someone poisoned it. Surely not God?"

"No matter. They still think God took its life."

The four men pulled at the rope with no visible result.

"It would be easier," the priest said, "if they used three ropes—one around the hind legs, one around the fore, and one around the neck. It would triple the pulling force, like the Holy Trinity. Three-in-one makes strength."

Father Reeves hardly seemed to notice his own religious analogies. They emerged automatically and without thought, like advertising slogans a salesman parroted by rote.

The four men exerted one last time and the bloated mass of flesh tumbled into the hole with a thud. They cut the rope free and began to shovel soil back into the opening.

Martin said, "When I die, I would like to have a funeral as simple as that." He looked back at the fluttering sheets of plastic over the broken windows. "Most funerals are a lie, Father. Your people have turned dying into a religious rite, when it's no more than the disposal of rotting flesh and bones. When I die, just give me a simple cremation. No pomposity, no morbidity, no tears, no pain—and no one dressed in black."

Father Reeves nodded as though concentrated on the last wishes of a dying man, of someone to whom he was about to give the deathbed's anointment. He said, "Before you die, however, won't you marry the girl?"

Martin did not answer. He was trying to imagine being in the cow's place. Four men above him, swinging their arms in rhythm as they gradually extinguished the light from the sky. Life had reached its end.

Father Reeves seemed pleased. "Should I take your silence as a sign that you will?" he said. "Should I post the banns?"

"Mind your own business, Father."

"In your country, you would be in jail for having done what you did to her."

"I'm not in my country."

"Then why so much spite? What have these people done to you?"

"They've made me feel vulnerable—exposed. I came here to be left alone."

"Only God knows what type of atrocity you committed back home. Few crimes give a man the incentive to hide for long in a place he hates."

"I committed no crime."

"But you have! A moral crime. Marry the girl. For you maybe it means nothing. But for her—it's a dream for a local girl to marry a white man and be taken away from here." He pulled the jar of honey from under his arm and fit it tightly between two lengths of barbed wire. "I know you won't last much more in this place. These people despise you. You will leave soon. So make up your mind to take her with you. Don't leave her here to rot in her shame."

"What difference does it make? I could take her or leave her whether I'm married to her or not. Since when has marriage been so essential to life? *You* chose not to wed, didn't you? What makes you so special?"

"My marriage is to the Church, something altogether different."

Two of the grave diggers were now stamping on the mound of soil that rose from the covered hole. The others collected the shovels and rope and walked away.

Father Reeves said, "What about the bride price, then? If you don't adhere to the Church, at least do so to their secular traditions, out of respect."

"Her father wants too much. I can't afford her."

"You're a foreigner. As a white man, you're expected to afford more. Be a decent man. Have you no relatives from whom to borrow some money? Make an effort to afford her. Everyone knows she's expecting your child." The priest's tone grew more emotional, as though he were talking about his own daughter. "Marry the girl."

"I don't love her, Father."

"It's not a matter of love but morals. She's with child."

"I'm willing to help her abort it."

"Blasphemy!" Father Reeves bowed his head and closed his eyes. It occurred to Martin that he was saying a prayer. That was what they all did in the face of frustration. When they failed to convert, they prayed.

Martin took the jar of honey and opened it. Light from the sun went through the liquid with a golden glow. He could not resist dipping his finger in it. But the taste disappointed him. Honey was always too sweet. "Haven't you ever lied, Father? We can tell people it was a miscarriage. This place is teeming with children. There are so many of them that their parents have begun to treat them like animals. The last thing this village needs is another child—bastard or not."

Father Reeves' lips moved slightly. He was praying after all. He raised his freckled hand up to his eyes as if to help the eyelids open from a heavy sleep. His pale blue eyes turned to Martin with a deepness of thought that gave them a sanctified look. "You're a selfish man," he said. "You must have suffered much in life. Only a man who lives in great pain could be as selfish as this."

"It doesn't take much suffering, Father. A little is enough to make you start thinking of only yourself."

The priest walked away without a word. He stopped next to the flower bed and asked Rebecca to stand.

Martin watched with curiosity. He felt a sudden fear that the priest might take her away. Perhaps his words had been too harsh. He really needed the girl. Without Rebecca there would be no challenge for him, no mores to change, no distraction.

Father Reeves took her hand and led her to Martin. Rebecca kept her head down. Martin had not yet been able to get her to look up all the time, to stare at others as an equal, with self-respect.

The priest said, "Won't you at least—" He waved at her clothing. "No one can stand seeing her walking in and out of your house like this. And the cigarettes—it's just not done."

"You've been here too long, Father. Speak your mind like priests do in the rest of the world. Don't involve others in your judgments. Just say that it's *you* who can't stand seeing her like this."

"It's not done. They may harm her—to retaliate against you. She's vulnerable looking like this. Concubines get little respect in this country. Remember Mutai—what happened to his wife."

Martin imagined an angry mob entering the house. They could easily do to Rebecca what the drunk had done to his wife. And they would also be justified.

A sudden feeling of parental pride went through him: she was carrying his child. What tricks the mind played. He could want the child aborted one minute, and care about it the next. The thought of Mrs. Mutai and the dead fetus disturbed him. He said, "Don't worry, Father. I will take her away for a few days until things calm down here."

The priest took the honey from Martin. "Don't think I harbor any hard feelings for you," he said. "You can come to me any time you wish." He pressed down the lower line of barbed wire to cross through the fence. On the other side, he approached the fresh grave and contemplated it as if the animal had been part of his life.

Martin recalled the cultural ban on public display of affection and hugged Rebecca with exaggerated passion. He kissed her on the lips and said, "Pack your things. You're going to be living in a hotel room for a few days."

Chapter VI

1

Martin returned to Keptembei late at night, exhausted from the long journey. He felt irrelevant in the darkness and solitude of the dirt road, in the boring emptiness of rural life. He already missed Rebecca and regretted having left her behind, unnecessarily, and without a plan in mind. He would have to go back for her in a day or two anyway. His funds had nearly run out.

He felt responsible for the girl against his will. Guilt was a powerful enemy and an invincible warrior. Martin knew that it would eventually corner him, force him to negotiate a bride price with Francis. Perhaps the village would allow him to pay installments on the girl. He hoped so. He needed the support of the local people.

Keptembei was really a good place in which to hide. He had used a faulty strategy in stirring up so much animosity. His approach had backfired. Lies in a small community could only go so far. The local butcher knew who ate the meat he carved. The storekeeper remembered how long ago you had bought your last bar of soap. Even children could tell who drank too much—and the righteous and pious pointed out the sinners on sight. It had served no purpose to alienate himself from people, to be the object of nasty comments every time he went outside.

He walked past Mutai's shack. It seemed ghostly and desolate. The drunk and his new bride were surely in bed right now. Newlyweds rarely stayed up late, lest life cheat them of the business at hand. Martin heard no sign of Mutai's dog, either. Perhaps the animal had belonged to Mrs. Mutai, and the drunk had kicked it to death, too—a last hateful act against his unfortunate ex-wife.

The lack of light from cooking fires seemed unusual. He saw no flickering flames behind the thicket or beyond the fence to his right. He sniffed the air. It smelled fresh. No trace of smoke lay over it. Where was everyone? He could understand if Mutai were in bed, involved in privacy, but the rest of the villagers were ignoring their routine. If they were mourning somebody, he didn't hear the usual drumming and wailing, the native dirges that commonly went on all night. Only the crickets gave signs of life.

Perhaps the village was celebrating with a silent prayer, giving thanks for the white man's recent departure with the pregnant girl, requesting that he never come back. But how wrong they were, he thought. I *am* back—here to stay.

He had a difficult time with the key. Opening the door required all his concentration. He never heard the quick succession of cracks behind him, the rushing sound of shoes treading over dry twigs.

He felt the first blow in the stomach. His knees jabbed the cold concrete below him, then someone dragged him backwards onto a patch of grass.

The blows seemed to last forever—angry kicks from many feet that skillfully reached the most sensitive and painful part of his body. He was unable to see his attackers, but he knew who they were. He could smell their hate. There was the acrid stench of the red sweater, of home-brewed millet beer and dirt. He recognized the smell of sweat and smoke from the women's parched legs. These were the villagers who despised him. They had come to seek revenge.

He drew his arms up to protect his head and waited, patiently, like a sheep forced into a shearing shed. Only his fleece did not fall like a sheep's. It merely bled.

2

"You will forgive me for telling you this," Megan said, "but this is much more pleasant than the monotony of giving shots." She was dressing Martin's wounds with the tenderness of a loving young mother toward her only child. Most of the bruises were on his back and thighs and she covered them with arnica. Martin offered her a wan smile and a whimper whenever she pressed the tender spots too hard. She swabbed around a large laceration on the elbow with a lump of cotton dipped in water and soap. "This is the only bleeding cut you have."

"They were only trying to scare me, not kill me. I guess they want me to leave."

"Then you should heed their warning," Sam said as he came out from the study. He wore a bathrobe and his face was pale and haggard, as if he had been in bed for weeks without food or a bath. "And the sooner you leave the better," he said. "Although I must confess I'd be very interested in seeing what these people do to you if you stay." He placed two glasses on the table and poured large portions of brandy.

"Don't scare him," Megan said. "It's a peaceful community. They won't do anything."

They sat in the living room and Martin drank his brandy quickly, hoping that it would act as a painkiller. He tried to prop himself carefully on the sofa to avoid the discomfort that came with contact. And while he partly succeeded, the effort made for a comic spectacle at which only he laughed.

The couple watched him grimace in silence, with a quietness that distressed him. It extended far beyond a normal pause in conversation. They really had nothing to say to each other. Martin knew he and the missionaries were separated by a wide stretch of lies—all of them his. He had endangered their work and yet they had still helped him in this moment of need.

"So will you *leave*?" Sam adorned his boyish face with a curious glance.

"To go where?"

"Home. Where in the States did you say you came from?"

"I can't go home."

"You don't have to worry about that. If it's a question of money, we can help—"

"I *can't* go home." Martin took the brandy bottle and filled his glass. Why not tell them? he thought. They might feel pity and help him if they learned the truth. He needed their help with Rebecca. The girl needed a place to stay—far from Keptembei, but close enough that he could at least show some responsibility for her. He had to tell them something, if only a half-truth.

Sam said matter-of-factly, "Legal problems?"

"You could say so. I owe more than money to loan sharks. Home wasn't big enough to hide from them. The country itself was too small. I had to come here."

"How much do you owe them?" Megan asked as though she were ready to write a check for the amount and end the matter there.

"Too much. Some debts are not meant to be paid off with money. I can't go back." He grimaced and let out a painful moan as he shifted his body to one side.

"You're hurting," she said.

"No. I exaggerate. It's only the idea of pain that hurts. It will go away soon." *Soon*—the word had lost its meaning in Africa. Every aspect of life in this continent seemed to take place behind schedule. Even death procrastinated here.

"Things could be worse," Sam said. His arms rested in his lap like heavy logs. He spoke with the aloofness of an analyst who knows a subject beyond facts. "Back home you'd be in jail for the rape of a minor. Here, all you owe is a negotiable bride price. Once you pay it, you're off the hook."

"How do you know about the girl?"

Sam laughed uncontrollably, almost mockingly. "Come on. Everyone knows about the girl. Even her father probably knew all along. You just fell in a trap. Foreigners are a good catch."

"But they're Christians. Her father seems genuinely pious."

"So he is. Piety never stopped anyone from pursuing a more comfortable life."

How ironic, Martin thought. Elizabeth had accused him of rape when he had not even touched her. Rebecca was younger, pregnant with his child, and all her father cared about was economic reparation. Buying respect always seemed easier than earning it, even here. He wondered how the indigent paid for their brides.

Megan said, "What are you going to do?"

"I don't know. Make peace with the village somehow. I don't want to have to leave anytime soon. I'll do whatever they want, even marry her. I'll talk to Mudoga, the man who got me here. He's the girl's uncle, an important politician in the capital. He'll talk to them, make them give me the job at the school back, maybe even help me pay the bride price."

"Don't grow so desperate, my man." Sam sat back with an air of professional pride. "There's no need to do all that. Remember you're a white man and, as such, you're entitled to certain freedoms here, especially at the village level. If you don't want the girl, just give her back to her family. Locals do it. Why can't you?"

"I already tried that. Her father said something about used goods—"

"That just shows he's determined to get money out of you. Return the girl to him. He'll have no choice but to take her back."

Martin turned to Megan searchingly. "Do you agree?"

"Reluctantly. I would never encourage irresponsible behavior like that."

"Then?"

"In this case—" She looked for words. "You'd probably not last married anyway. Think of how little the two of you have in common. Children gain nothing from parents who stay together solely for their sake. I've seen it. When a husband and wife don't care for each other, their children can tell. Is that what you want for your child?"

"We've seen too many mixed marriages collapse," Sam said. "You have the white, educated foreigner enthralled by the sensuality of black loins, and he tries to build a marriage on that—taking the local girl back home with him, full of pride, disregarding the fact that she's no more than an ignorant farm girl who will never be accepted by anyone in his family or group of friends. It's disastrous. You'd do better to send the girl some money from time to time after you leave her."

"But in the meantime I can't leave. What do I do for company without her?"

"Meet other whites, or urban blacks. Go to the capital on weekends. Fulfill yourself with prostitutes, whatever. Just don't get involved with locals beyond a friendly chat." Sam had grown warm and amiable. He seemed to enjoy giving advice.

"Where is she now?" Megan said.

"I left her in a hotel in Maobei. The room's paid for until tomorrow. Won't you go get her for me? Perhaps you could intercede with her father, or keep her living here with you until I work things out."

Sam's friendly manner vanished with a rush of formality. He stood and moved to the window. "We can't help you in that way. I just said that it doesn't pay to be more than a casual friend to locals. We can loan you money if you like, but we can't afford to endanger our work here by getting involved in your mess."

Martin knew he had made them feel shame. Compromising situations were not a strong point with missionaries. They seemed to have little experience with blunt requests. Their awkward responses and facial expressions were no match for a good lie.

He said, "I thought helping others in distress was what your work was all about. I guess I was wrong."

They stood quietly. Megan's mouth gaped with indecision. Sam took quick steps into his study and brought back a small and faded cardboard box with him. A string held it together like a package that would otherwise soon collapse. He gave it to Megan.

"What are you doing?" she said.

"He needs to protect himself. Hold it for a moment."

Martin observed them with curiosity—two adults in the role of children. One moment they were giving him advice, the next they were pacing nervously around the room, unable to explain themselves.

"We're not really missionaries," Sam said. "We would help you if we were but—all we can do is let you borrow this." He took the box from his wife's hands and placed it in Martin's lap. Martin pulled the string off and opened it. A small revolver lay inside.

Sam said, "In case you're in trouble, you don't even have to show it to them. Locals fear guns like they do the wrath of God. Just tell them you have one and shoot at the ceiling inside your house. If they are outside—trying to break in—and if they hear the shots go off, rest assured they will flee."

"Missionaries?" Martin said with a tone that wavered between derision and disappointment. "Don't you know firearms are strictly forbidden in this country?"

"We do. But we didn't want to take any chances. You shouldn't, either. Mob justice doesn't give you a chance to explain. This will. Take it."

"No. I'm not a violent man." A memory flashed through his mind. He was in the bathroom with Alfie, letting him bleed to death through the gash he had cut. Yet he wasn't violent. A handgun had a more definite air of lethality to it. He couldn't take it. "If not missionaries, what are you then?"

Sam returned the box to his wife. Megan tied the string around it and took it back to the study with extreme care, as though the gun were part of the family heirloom, a piece from an invaluable collection they kept somewhere out of sight.

When she returned she said, "I *am* a nurse. Don't think I was giving immunizations without adequate preparation."

Martin glanced at Sam, who had a blank stare fixed in his youthful eyes.

"My work here," Sam said, "is research for a book dealing with what I call reverse ekistics. Instead of basing urban development on social and economic factors, I aim to predict human reactions to sudden development. Say that these scattered villages switched almost overnight into a set of sprawling urban and suburban neighborhoods. What would happen to this community if we were to transform its surroundings into a New York in a two-year span? What would such a sudden shift do to these people's psyches, to their social and cultural values, to their birth rates, death rates, and to many others aspects of their lives? These questions are the ones my work will try to answer. Part of the task involves the development of a computer program that will project the effects of these changes, to let us peek into a fictional future, as it were. The charts..."

Sam continued the explanation in a monotonous, humming tone.

Martin lost interest and turned his thoughts to the ingenious act of his hosts. Why had he not thought of it himself? As a missionary, he could have wielded much more power over the community. Members of the Church were allowed certain freedoms. Rebecca might have been less of a problem had he been a lonesome man of God.

The world was fraught with people like him—liars misrepresenting their identities with nothing but self-interest in mind. The Bakers had gone even farther. They were using God as their shield, charity and benevolence as their mask. They had found something new. It had never occurred to Martin that one should have to lie for the sake of writing a book, for an irrelevant, scholarly treatise based purely on speculation.

Megan said, "They would give us biased responses if they knew the real reason we came here. As a missionary, I have complete freedom to talk to women while I immunize their children. Believe me, sometimes I've felt ready to act against the injustices done to them. But we can't risk our research when we have only a few more months to go. And one can't do much to change things here anyway, can one? We've seen where it got *you*."

"I suggest you go get the girl," Sam said, "and take her to Father Reeves. He should be able to do something about her."

Martin spoke without thinking. "Yes. Perhaps that would be best."

"Sorry we can't help you. I hope you understand."

3

The people of Keptembei had something wrong with them, Souza thought. Their initial friendliness disappeared the moment he mentioned Martin. They took a surly look at him, as if to remember his face, and walked away. Was Martin in the village or not? No one would say.

He walked along the dirt road past a number of shacks—bars, two-table restaurants, stores and a carpenter's shop. Then the village came to an end.

He turned around and paced like a soldier on guard duty. Villagers studied him with what seemed utter distrust. The children stared at his hands. They had heard already: the cat-man had come.

He approached a group of girls—young students in bright blue uniforms and bare feet. They giggled in the comfort of each other's company, apparently not afraid of him. Souza held Martin's photograph in one hand and a stack of fresh bills in the other. "Have you seen this man? If you tell me where he lives, I'll give you all this money."

The girls laughed and exchanged elaborate comments in their own language, all of which Souza missed.

"Money," he said. "It's all you people want, isn't it? Where's the white man? Tell me."

"Leave them alone," a drunken voice said. The stooping frame of a man followed it, tottering into place between Souza and the girls.

Souza could smell the acrid stench of home-brewed alcohol on the man's breath. He studied the old red sweater. It looked stiff with grime—a crust that had long ago taken the shape of the body it dressed.

The drunk stared at the bills as he scratched his groin. "We don't need another white man here. You only bring death."

"Move out of the way. I'm talking to these girls."

"Our girls are not whores for the white man. They don't sell their bodies to you." Mutai ordered the girls to disperse with a grunt and a jerk of his arm. Then he coughed up a gob of phlegm and spat it on Souza's left shoe. "This is what we think of you."

Souza watched the drunk stumble away. Better not react to the insults of these people, he thought. I need them to help me find Martin. That's why I'm here. Martin, nothing else.

He replaced the bills in his pocket and entered the nearest restaurant. Someone had hand-painted the words *Graceland Hotel* on the corrugated iron wall. Two communal picnic tables filled the space inside. A pair of young men ate hungrily at one of them. A man in an old suit and hat sat alone at the other. Souza waved the flies off a spot and sat next to the youths. He ordered a deep-fried dough ball and a glass of water.

The two young men seemed to be making their meal a speed contest. They forced large amounts of food into their mouths and swallowed without chewing. Souza compared them to the man in the suit and hat. A visible contrast.

The generation gap held true across all races and cultures, even among siblings distanced by only a few years. The younger ones were always more impudent and reckless. They never listened to those with more experience in life. Alfie had died for that very reason.

Stupid jerk, Souza thought. I gave him step-by-step instructions, exactly what to do to kill Pete and Martin. He couldn't have botched the job had he followed my advice.

The waiter brought him two dough balls on a plastic plate. The smell of the stale shortening in which they had been fried arrived with them.

"I ordered one," Souza said.

"You leave what you don't want." The waiter poured water into a glass from a soiled plastic container that had once held motor oil. The logo of the petroleum company was still visible on it.

"Where does that water come from?"

"The river."

Souza had seen the river. People and cows bathed in it. Women did the family laundry.

"We boil," the waiter said.

"Bring me a soda."

The waiter moved quickly and pried the cap off an orange soda bottle with the few teeth he had left.

Souza ate slowly. He would sit here all day if necessary. At some point, the restaurant would have to fill with customers. Then it might be easier to talk to these villagers. Unlike animals, people were often friendlier while they ate.

The youths next to him stood abruptly and left, like firemen summoned to duty by an unheard bell. He reached for their salt shaker—a soda bottle refilled with salt and sealed by a punctured cap. All around he had seen the ingenious recycling of garbage. It showed how practical rural dwellers were. He did not believe they wouldn't take money in exchange for Martin, wherever Martin were.

Souza had just bitten into the second dough ball when Mutai stumbled in. One can only expect trouble from a drunk, and Souza was ready for it.

Mutai stood between the two picnic tables as if at a pulpit, ready to preach. His body swayed unsteadily in its inebriated state. He hacked some phlegm up but swallowed it quickly upon noticing the waiter's disapproving stare. "The white man has come to steal our women," he said, "to fornicate with our wives." His arms went up as he spoke. He was reaching for something. "Before, we were his slaves. Now we are free. But the white man still wants the black people of all Africa to suffer. *He* came to Africa with the AIDS disease, to spread it amongst our peoples." Mutai pointed at Souza. "From America he comes loaded with disease. From America, where all their perverted acts bring on the wrath of God, where all the men are homosexual, now he brings himself here to destroy Africa!"

Souza turned to the waiter and said calmly, "Get this drunk out of here or I'll smash his head." He placed a bill under the soda bottle and walked toward the back door. "I'll come back for the change."

In the back he looked for the outhouse. He often got an urge to relieve himself near a moment of violence. It calmed his nerves. This time it would also give him a minute to decide whether smashing the drunk's head against the counter was worth the trouble.

He stepped in holding his breath. The iron-sheet walls around the pit were smeared with excrement.

Only drunks could be so unconscious as to wipe themselves with the walls, he thought. What filth this is.

Flies buzzed happily about him. He exhaled every drop of air from his lungs to delay inhaling.

When he went back in the restaurant, the waiter apologized for Mutai, who was no longer around, and returned his money. The meal was on the house.

"You have to forgive some of our people," the man in the suit and hat said. He looked out of place sitting at the blue picnic table, among the swarm of flies. "Sometimes, they can be ignorant and fall into the claws of alcohol." He stood with an effort and walked outside with Souza. "I of course am different," he said. "I have *been* in America, in your country. A very wonderful place, it is. I was there in 1965. My name is Joshua Mungo." He took his hat off and tried to reshape it in vain. He gave the impression of someone who had once been important, someone who yearned for the past.

Souza listened while he stared at the other side of the road, at the hovels behind the row of stores. The red sweater played there, moving incessantly from left to right and back, like a target at a fair's shooting gallery. It made Souza want to aim and fire.

"I was in Chicago, Detroit, New York—" the man in the suit said. "Part of a delegation from my country—very important, you know? For development. Of course, your country has boomed since then. Here—nothing changes."

He had a consumptive figure—a man bitter with a life that had gone wrong.

Souza nodded at the man's comments and took a step away from him with every nod, eager to leave.

The man said, "Are you a friend of that white man you've been asking for?"

"A relative. He's in trouble. I need to find him soon."

"Well, you are right. He is in much trouble. He defiled the young daughter of a respectful, religious man in our community—made her pregnant—and has delayed paying the bride price. Blames his bank in America for not sending his money quickly. But I know he's lying. I've been in America and know your banks are efficient organizations that give you your money when you ask for it, just like that. Who knows what he's up to? Maybe he doesn't have any money."

Souza could hardly control the urge to smile. Martin lived here. Revenge was only a matter of days now, maybe hours. "Where is he?"

"The rumor is that he got into a fight with some of our people. Now he comes and goes. I think he took the girl away to some hotel for a few days, to try to appease us. But it won't be long before he comes back. If it's true he has no money, he won't be able to pay any hotel."

"And—" Souza was ecstatic. Things could not have worked out any better. If Martin was really away, he could wait for him inside his very house and kill him the moment he returned—just as Alfie should have done at the beach cabin. "And where does he live when he *is* here?"

The man pointed at a group of cinder-block buildings on the slope behind the village. "The one to the right, with the blue door."

Souza planned the execution as he walked from Keptembei to the village where he was staying. He had doubts about which method to use. The most painful methods, the ones that made the victim beg for death, were the most time-consuming. It would be cumbersome to keep Martin suffering for too long, especially if a pregnant girl were present. A quick job would have to do then. And why not? After all, that was why he had bothered to smuggle the throwaway. A single shot through the head made more sense.

When Souza entered his rented room the throwaway was gone. Someone had taken everything from the room except the furniture. He kicked the door and rushed outside in search of his landlady.

Why didn't I take it with me? he thought. Why?

He knew it would do no good to complain to the landlady. She had probably arranged the burglary herself. Her grown children had come to him daily to borrow the small radio set he had brought from America. *Share your radio with us Africans, white man*, they had said. Souza had refused, and now the radio set and his clothes and the gun were probably in their possession.

Damn the gun, he thought. If it's gone then I'm meant to make that bastard suffer. And to hell with his girl. If she is present while I take care of him, then she'll learn something. Maybe even his bastard child will be observing from the womb. When he grows up, he'll know better than to cheat and lie like his old man.

More than pain, Souza wanted to see panic in Martin's eyes. A branding iron would work, but he dismissed it as too complicated. Burns didn't kill unless they covered most of the victim's body. There might not be enough time to do that. He thought instead of the shotgun going off accidentally, of Alfie's left leg disappearing with the blast, of the blood and the panic. Maybe he could use a machete to sever one of Martin's limbs, then let him bleed to death the way Alfie had.

Whatever he did, he had to act soon. He would never forgive himself if Martin managed to escape this time.

4

Martin didn't know what he would say to Father Reeves. He felt no need to prepare a speech for the priest. A confession, a conversation, a plea for help—it made no difference. Unlike the Bakers, the priest could not refuse him help. A real clergyman had to forgive everyone everything, to give a hand even to Satan if there were signs of regret.

He stopped to look back. Rebecca lagged behind at the last bend, over the stone bridge and the abandoned flour mill. He knew she was doing it on purpose. She seemed to know why they were going to the mission. Martin felt sorry for her—a girl so young and already pregnant. But he recalled the Bakers' words and used them under his breath: "Sorry I can't help you. I hope you understand."

The words absolved him. He felt free. Some situations in life were just too much for weak, inept mortals to handle. Better to entrust them to higher powers—to religion and the Church—and let the clergy solve the mysteries of sin, regret and shame.

"Hurry up," he called out to her. "I want to get there before dusk."

He waited and took her hand. People might object to it as a public display of affection, but he could think of nothing else to keep her walking at his same pace. Besides, if teenage males were allowed to hold hands in public, why not he with Rebecca? He had done enough already to please the priest. Rebecca was modestly dressed in white muslin. Martin had even asked her to cover her head. Nothing distinguished her from the other women now. He felt he had lost her. Keptembei had prevailed.

They climbed the steep road together. With the lack of rain, the soil had crumbled into rocky islands in an ocean of crevices. The drought had even begun to affect the plantations. The tea shrubs in the distance gave off a yellow hue.

Village elders gathered daily to vote on what to do about the dry spell. They believed it was all up to them now. When Christianity failed them, they set it temporarily aside to invoke their own ancestral beliefs. Hope for them came from many sources. When one source was exhausted, they went on to the next.

Yesterday, the drought had been blamed on some evil cow that had suddenly died. Today, they might blame Martin, and not even the Chief nor money would be powerful enough to allow him to stay in Keptembei. If the gods did not answer the prayers and invocations with copious showers soon, the choice seemed clear—the white man or rain. And if getting rid of Martin did not work for the elders, tomorrow would be time to blame something else. The process was a long one, a series of steps. Blame this, get rid of it. Blame that, get rid of it. Eventually, meteorological conditions would bring on a cloudburst that the elders would credit to the steps. All the sacrifices made along the way would have been worth it then.

Martin looked up at the clear skies. It seemed a waste of time to try to win the elders' approval at this point. If the drought continued and they blamed him, he would have to leave even if a saint.

The large white cross atop the campanile was Father Reeves' only religious billboard, the beacon that drew all the catechumens of the surrounding villages to pray. The lime-washed walls soaked up the waning rays of the sun.

Martin and Rebecca crossed the field. A group of youngsters played soccer on it with a ball fashioned out of rags. Some of the boys belied their malnourished frames with the exulting way in which they played, constantly running from one end of the field to the other. Their game ceased only when they stopped to listen to the faint droning of an airplane, a sound they had perhaps heard only a few times in their lives.

Martin stopped, too, and looked up. The sky was a clear pale blue that had nothing to offer, not even freedom. The sound of the airplane made him long for a trip, for flying high above the village and the problems it held for him.

Father Reeves had turned the mission into an apiary. Part of the land behind the white building was overgrown with weeds. The rest grew a thin layer of green that gave the impression of moss. Rows of hives ran across it. Despite the symmetry of the rows, an air of absolute disorder lay on the place. Martin got the feeling no one was in charge. The priest, he had heard, devoted most of his time to keeping bees. His work in Africa was based on obscure chantries. No one knew where the funds came from, and Father Reeves did not seem to use them for the intended purpose anyway. His passion was bees. Sermons and homilies were incidental.

Martin released the girl's hand and continued alone toward the colorful rows of wooden hives. The priest's gangly figure hid behind the white fabric of overalls, gloves and a hat. The net that came down from the rim of the hat wrapped around his bony shoulders to protect his face and neck from the insects. All that protection gave the idea of a dangerous job. Keeping bees was how the priest added adventure and risk to the slow pace of rural life.

"Don't come any closer," Father Reeves called out. He was busy blowing smoke into a hive. "They're particularly violent today—quite unpredictable." He uttered the warning with a tone of childish excitement. He appeared to be in a good mood. His hands danced around the bees with graceful movements, as if directing the insects in an orchestra. The smoke was his baton.

The sight made Martin wonder what the priest fed on. Gloom never seemed to sting him.

"I need to talk to you, Father." Martin pointed at Rebecca, who had just arrived at his side.

Between puffs from the smoker, the priest looked up and noticed the white muslin and the feminine headdress. "I see you've decided to marry the queen."

"I'm afraid not, Father."

Father Reeves set the smoker aside. The bees appeared to have calmed down. "Then the dissolute drone has come to shirk his Christian duties?"

"I've come for your help."

"An absolution, perhaps? It's easy to be foolhardy, isn't it, when you have the Church behind you to exonerate."

"None of that. I want you to take her back to her father. *He's* a Christian. Maybe you can convince him to learn to forgive."

The priest placed a new wax frame in the slot where one heavy with honey had sat. He was absorbed in his task and spoke casually as he covered the honeycomb with a cloud of smoke. "It's true that drones don't have much use for the queen after fertilization. You know why that is?"

"No."

"Because they die right after mating. The queen tears off their sexual organs and most of their bellies once she's done with them. Sometimes one wishes sexual intercourse in humans worked the same way."

"I didn't come for a sermon, Father."

"But don't worry. The drones are never missed by anyone. They don't even contribute to the household with the production of sweets. The queen raises the brood on her own. The girl will survive, too." Father Reeves paused to replace the roof on the hive. He drove the remaining bees away from the thick honey frame before placing it in a bag. "Don't you envy her simple form of happiness?" he said. "The girl's, I mean."

"Don't start, please."

"She would be more than overjoyed if you made her your wife."

"Tell her father that I will contribute with what I can now. I will go see the girl's uncle in the capital and borrow as much as possible from him to pay a reasonable bride price. Then, eventually, when I go home, I will support her from there until the child becomes an adult. Tell him all that, and to learn to forgive, and to make peace. I want to teach at the school again."

"That is too long a wish list, Mr. Bloom. You should be more realistic."

A series of whistle blows and drumbeats started in the distance. The priest took off the hat and net and cocked his head to listen. "That's the preparations for the circumcisions. A lot of boys will be cut soon, and possibly many girls, too. You'd never think that cutting girls is illegal,

when so many of them get cut every season. And a dangerous practice it is. Last year one bled to death from the
incisions." He seemed fascinated and lost in the sounds.

Martin observed the priest and wondered how anyone
could still marvel at every detail of a culture after so many
years of being buried in it. He held Rebecca by the waist
and moved her in front of him. "Let's talk about her,
Father. Please."

Father Reeves took a deep breath. "I'll visit her father.
But at this point, I don't know if it will do any good.
There's a council of elders who likes to decide on these
delicate matters. I'm afraid neither the Church nor her uncle
in the capital have much influence over them. You know
how stubborn a clique of old men can be."

Dusk moved over them. The drums and the whistles grew
louder with every beat. Martin waited for another word
from the priest. The next step would be the departure, the
return to the village leaving the girl behind. He wondered
what the Church would do with her if Francis refused to
take her back. He said tentatively, "I will leave her with you
then, Father, if you don't mind."

"If you must. I think we can accommodate her with the
mission's cook. She's a good woman and will take care of
her. For one, this girl needs to eat more. You have to be fat
to marry in this land. A thin girl like this one lacks the
strength to work her husband's farm." The priest spoke
with youthful detachment, the way a brain surgeon might
casually describe a surgical procedure over lunch. "It may
not be too difficult to find a man interested in her after all.
The child of a white man in the house *and* the prospect of
alimony payments from America may make her much more
attractive than you think."

A cool breeze arrived with the dark before they could say goodbye. Martin had seen the last of Rebecca. Like Elizabeth, she now belonged to the past.

On his way home, the shrill calls of fruit bats accompanied him in the near darkness. The animals emerged nightly from under the roofs of the shacks.

The tom-toms and whistles reached him with more clarity as he neared Keptembei. The voices sounded like an army of children being brainwashed, drilled in preparation for an onslaught. All part of their circumcision ceremony.

He wondered what he should do next. The obvious was to go see Mudoga—a humiliating necessity. Martin blamed him for all the troubles he had encountered in Keptembei. Mudoga had sent him here, had encouraged him to fill his solitude with the sexual company of a village girl.

Mutai's house was again dark and desolate. It gave Martin a bad feeling. A rustle of corn husks came from the field behind. It could be cattle or locust feeding on the dying crop. Or it could be villagers, lurking.

As he neared the front door of his own house, the sound was replaced by that of pouring water. It irked him that they might have broken the spout of the water tank to circumvent the lock.

But the padlock was in place, as he had left it. He looked up to find a young boy standing on top of the tank, urinating into the water intake. Martin gripped his ankle and brought him down with one violent pull.

They're trying to contaminate my water, he thought. Bastards!

He felt no mercy for the boy, whose thigh and back scraped the coarse surface as he fell.

The boy got up immediately and limped away without a sound. Children never cried in Keptembei. They put burning coals on their arms at an early age to silence themselves for life.

"Where is the money, white man?" The Chief called out from the other side of the fence. He sat on his motorcycle and switched the headlight on to blind Martin. A few shadows in tribal dress stood around the Chief. Martin was relieved to hear words and not blows. He had time.

The Chief still seemed to believe that a grant was on the way—funds that only Martin could withdraw and transfer to the Chief's account. As long as greed was a factor, things would be fine. It rested on his ability to lie well to keep the Chief's greed alive. He said without faltering, "That grant I told you about has been canceled because a new one was approved—twice the money. I was able to convince them you needed a larger building and requested this new grant. It will be wired to me within a month."

The Chief did not seem impressed. He started the motorcycle and gunned the engine. "You have one more week to get that money. Otherwise, my people will be free to deliver justice. Forgiveness comes only with atonement through good deeds. Do something good for our village and you will be forgiven. You know what I mean."

He turned slowly before speeding away in a cloud of dust. The silhouettes of the other men superimposed the dimming beam of light as they followed the motorcycle on foot.

Martin listened to the ominous silence. The circumcision carols had stopped. The dogs were quiet. Insects seemed to no longer exist. He got the idea the world was holding its breath to see him take the next step. A surprise party. He would enter the house and the lights would go on instantly.

The merriment and the noise would follow. Guests would crowd the living room and embrace him warmly. Pete and his parents would be there. He imagined the past.

The moment he shut the door a blow struck him between the shoulder blades. How stupid, he thought, to be surprised at all. How much more obvious could it be? The Chief had planned it this way.

He felt the blows strike him in the same bruised spots that had resulted from the previous attack. But now only a few large fists hit him, not the cowardly feet of a mob.

Pain was not what made him cry. The few tears that flowed from him were merely a sign of desperation. He could only see and hear the image of Christ. *We won't leave you alone. We won't leave you alone.* The hoodlums abandoned the woman they had been trying to rape only to lunge at him like wild animals in search of a blood feast. Christ and the two old women with bullet holes in their heads pounded him with clubs. They wanted him dead.

He felt large knuckles strike against his chest—and the sharp pain caused by a bulging piece of metal, a bulky ring on a large, perfumed hand. Martin knew the smell. These were not villagers. They smelled of aftershave, of American hyper-hygiene.

He made an effort to scream when he heard a voice say, "Okay. Slash and burn."

Two shadows dragged him by the feet into the bedroom and onto his bed. His arms fell over the side of the mattress and he gripped the handle of the machete that lay beneath. The idea was to swing it at his enemies, but he lacked the strength.

The two shadows went about their plan with confidence. Their voices grew more familiar to Martin as they spoke.

One said, "Let's move the mattress to the center of the room."

Martin dragged the machete as they moved him. He had difficulty trying to lift it, but found the incentive to do so when he heard the snap of a switchblade.

He hacked at the shadows like a cane cutter rushing to finish a tedious job. No one yelled. He only knew he was hitting his target from the shocks he felt in his arm with every new strike he gave.

It hardly mattered when the machete fell to the floor with a loud clang. He had been cutting the air for some time. The shadows had fled and he could relax, if relaxation was at all possible for an injured man.

He felt as though slowly waking from a nightmare. But his crying and tears were real. The sobs of a man who could find no relief.

What good does it do to flee if one is always found out? he thought.

Life was a losing game. He had played it long enough to realize that it was not the Souzas who were successful at locating his hideouts. It was God. And God was on *their* side.

He struck a match to get a quick view of the room. A few drops of blood stained the cement floor, but none of them appeared to be his. He found only one cut, on his hand, and a trickle of blood from one side of his lips. He was probably in better condition than his attackers.

The match went out the moment he saw what looked like a large rat gnawing at the bedroom door. He struck another and observed. The animal stood still. It might be dead. He kicked it to discover that it was only a black baseball cap. It filled him with sudden confusion. He recalled the bulky ring, the aftershave, the black canvas cap. They belonged to the retired football players, the men in sunglasses, the FBI agents who had arrested him for Elizabeth's alleged rape.

Chapter VII

1

"It's a real shame," Father Reeves said when he returned to the apiary and saw Rebecca waiting for him. His meeting with her father had proved fruitless. Francis had his mind set on a substantial bride price. Greed sometimes overtook even the most devoted Christians.

He rushed inside the building to avoid the girl and to change into the bee-keeping uniform. He wore the white overalls and the netted hat more than he did his religious habit. The demands and responsibilities of the parish exhausted him. The bees were his only relief. He could talk to and advise the girl or any other faithful, without strain, only as long as he worked with the insects at the same time. He had often thought of hearing confessions out in the middle of the apiary. If only the idea were not so radical.

He asked Rebecca to follow him to the hives and to stand at a safe distance while he harvested the honey. The whiffs of smoke calmed him as it did the bees. He spoke with a soothing tone. "You will have to go back to the white man. Your father wants you to be his wife."

She understood and made a move to start the long walk home, back to Martin.

"Wait," the priest said. "If he doesn't want you, come back here. You can live and work with us. Take a jar of honey with you. Tell him it's a gift from those who care."

2

Souza stood quickly when he heard someone enter the house through the window. The plastic coverings had already torn under the intense heat of the sun and the force of the wind. No barriers were left to stop burglars from coming in.

Rebecca climbed down slowly into the living room on her bare feet. Souza made sure she saw his pocket knife open and ready. "Who are you?" he said.

She seemed afraid. The jar of honey in her hands almost fell. "This is my house—with my husband."

"The white man?"

"Yes."

"Why didn't you use the door?" Souza had used the window, too. A large padlock secured the door in addition to the regular lock. It seemed incongruous, he thought, when so many of the windows were broken or missing.

"No key," she said. She looked around as if to study what was missing.

"Where is he?" Souza said.

"I don't know. He come soon." She stepped away from him, visibly shaken.

Souza followed her into the bedroom. He had been in it already. The bed sat in the center, next to the dry drops of blood. The bloodstained machete lay on the mattress. Souza didn't know what to make of it but hoped that Martin would be back soon. He was tired of waiting.

He observed the girl as she tidied up the room. "What's with the blood?" he said.

"I don't know blood." She seemed unconcerned, going about the house with the same contemptuous detachment of a maid who knows her job well—to dust and scrub and not to meddle in the affairs of her employer.

She isn't worth killing, Souza thought. Even as Martin's wife, she probably knows less about him than I do.

"I'm an old friend of your husband's." He put away the pocket knife. "We go back a long way, to childhood. Used to play monopoly together. He always lost. Owed me a great deal of money afterward."

The girl swept the room and threw the dust and the baseball cap outside. She placed the stained sheets in a basin to let them soak.

"Has he ever told you about me or why he left his country?"

She shook her head and lit the kerosene stove. The flame flared up high for a moment. She was not yet familiar with the technology. In a pan, she poured corn kernels, red beans, some salt and water.

"That looks very good," Souza said. "Maybe I should stay for dinner."

He sat to watch her deep-dark arms and legs move about the house. They were busy with the same chores he had seen his mother perform all his life. But his mother was a Portuguese woman, a human being who showed dignity in the household work she did for her family. There was something repulsive to him about this girl. She seemed to strut from room to room, parting her bony thighs like a mare's hind legs, inviting a breach.

To Souza, the idea of copulating with the girl almost equaled the abomination of bestiality. It made him despise Martin all the more to know that he had made this girl pregnant, that he slept with her. The thought made him spit with contempt on the concrete floor.

Quietly, Rebecca came to wash off the spittle.

"That's a good girl," he said. "Make the house gorgeous for the stud who mounts and rides you. Turn this into his kingdom, that he may soon lie dead in it and make it also his tomb." Violent words relaxed him like a warm glass of milk before bedtime.

He was able to ignore her and concentrate on his work, the butcher job he planned to perform on Martin with the pocket knife. He had discarded the idea of the machete. A small blade would inflict more pain.

It's my duty to make him suffer, he thought. A man has to deliver justice the way God intends it. That's what the Bible says. I shall not show pity—*Eye for eye, tooth for tooth, hand for hand, foot for foot.*

He was justified in cutting off a living man's limb. It qualified as sadism only when one did it for sport. This was justice.

3

Martin stepped difficultly over the fallow cracks of the road. He could see very little, and the matches he struck from time to time didn't help at all.

"The bold lie that I told..." he said, and repeated the verse several times, unable to remember the ones that followed. He was exhausted, tired of coming and going to and from Keptembei, tired of walking back to the village again and again this late at night.

A round-trip journey to the capital often took a whole day, sometimes even more. He had spent much of this one crammed inside public transportation vans, enduring the countless stops they had made along the way—all for nothing. As a mission for funds and moral support, the trip had been an absolute failure. Mudoga had refused to talk to him. The only message conveyed by his secretary had been an offer to pay for Martin's immediate departure from the country.

Martin had rejected it categorically, but felt foolish now for having done so. Why let pride control everything? There was no longer a reason to stay here, especially now that he knew the truth about the phony FBI men, the football players Elizabeth's father had sent.

On his way home through Maobei he had picked up Elizabeth's letter. It explained it all in a poem. *The lie...* He had forgotten even the first verse now. He struck a fresh match to try to read the words again.

If I had only received this earlier, he thought.

The postmark was almost as old as the one on the only letter he had mailed to her months ago. She had answered it right away. But sometimes even letters addressed to provincial capitals took long. Not much he could do about it now. He read.

The bold lie that I told
Far away from here did take you.
I regret the harm that's done
By the thugs my dad has sent you.

It was too late when Rufus told him
For when dad learned of my lie
The thugs were paid and gone
On your trail to make you die.
Sorry.

The anger he had felt upon reading it the first time was no longer with him. The poem, as badly composed as it was, seemed to him a statement of freedom. His freedom. He

                    A.R. Eguiguren

had fled America for fear of encountering a pawn of the Souzas' in jail. If Elizabeth had admitted her lie, he should no longer fear imprisonment from a charge of rape. He was a free man, free to return to his country.

The thought of leaving Keptembei gave him an immense sense of pleasure. No more would he have to tolerate the rural grudges, the sight of the murderous drunk, or that twisted form of Christianity they practiced here. Back in America, he would become an anonymous man again, a human being at whom children would not laugh.

I'll leave first thing tomorrow morning, he thought. There's little sense in staying here even one more day.

Rebecca would be out of his hands by now. The Church had probably taken care of her. He had no responsibilities, no debts—and Mudoga's offer struck him as more than sensible. He felt a strong urge to return to the capital right now, to eat his pride and accept the offer at once.

A tall figure came running behind him with desperate steps. "Wait a minute," Father Reeves' voice said. The priest's profile came to an abrupt stop next to his. "I think you should know before you reach home." He was panting, his lungs whizzing a tune. "You will find the girl waiting for you. I tried to talk some sense into her father but failed. He's a proud man. I suspect it is riches. A fat bride price. That's what he wants."

Martin felt disappointed. The Church had failed him and he would now have to deal with the problem himself. In truth, he was afraid of confronting Rebecca, even of walking away from her. Her protruding belly would surely be pointing at him as he left, making a life-long claim for support and paternal guidance.

"Can't you keep her for a few days, Father? It would be easier for me not to see her."

"You're leaving us, aren't you?"

Martin nodded, though he wasn't sure the priest could see his head in the dark. The last match had gone out.

They said nothing for some time. Gusts of wind had begun to blow. Clouds were finally coming in.

"Well," Father Reeves said, "if you abandon her, I cannot in good conscience offer you a hand. The least I can do for her is to make it harder for you. Who knows? Maybe she'll follow you as you leave, with her arms tight around your waist, crying desperately. You'll have to drag her with you until she drops from humiliation, or until *you* do. The whole village will be watching, and you'll never forget it."

"I will send some money to her, whenever possible. You'll take care of it, Father, won't you?"

The priest did not answer. Martin heard the whizzing of the lungs and the steps grow fainter in the distance. Then, among the sounds of wind-battered leaves, the priest's voice finally yelled from afar, "Oh, a man came looking for you this afternoon. Said you were his brother-in-law. I didn't ask, but God bless her soul and protect her—his poor sister, your wife. God knows in what conditions you left *her* behind. You're an evil man, Mr. Bloom. Your brother-in-law said so himself. I saw what you did to his hands. Only the Devil himself would try to dip a relative's fingers in acid like that. The sooner you leave here the better."

The voice died out gradually, the way the steps had.

"It's all lies!" Martin yelled. "Who was he, Father? Who?"

No need to ask. Martin knew who it was.

The time had come once more. It almost seemed a relief to him. If Souza was really here, he could no longer afford to worry about the girl. He was excused.

He began the journey back to the capital with a sense of purpose, hoping that Mudoga would receive him. The Souzas would lose a few days waiting for him in Keptembei before they realized he was not coming back. He had time.

As the wind grew louder, he recalled the plastic sheets flapping on the windows of the house. Rebecca had helped him put them up. She had swept away the broken glass. She had restored the garden, cooked for him, cleaned the house.

I wonder what she's doing right now, he thought. Waiting for me with a hot meal on the table? She better not have gone home. If Father Reeves sent her there, he probably directed Souza to the house, too. She could be in danger.

Martin turned back toward Keptembei without thinking. How absurd to let guilt make him risk his life. He had never let emotions intervene like this before. The girl had nothing to do with him. She was not his wife, nor his child. He had even imagined, many times, that her pregnancy was the result of her sleeping with some other man.

Martin knew he did not love Rebecca. Then why go back? Why *run* back?

As he ran, panic pounded in his chest. His legs weakened, and gusts of wind almost felled him whenever he made a turn on the path. Why was it that he feared the Souzas so much? The football players had shown the same murderous intentions toward him, yet he had managed to scare them away by fighting back. They meant nothing to him. Elizabeth had said so herself. They were mere thugs, hired hands who didn't have it in them to fulfill their end of a contract. They failed once and gave up.

The Souzas were different, a family that fed on revenge. And Martin would have to confront them. If he didn't try to save the girl, no lie in the world would ever clear his conscience of her death. And if *he* died in the process, that would be that. Human beings were doomed to lose the war against death anyway. His parents had lost it, and so had Pete and Mrs. Mutai.

To die for the girl might even redeem him. He envisioned a hostage exchange—the girl for the village's bane. No villager would interfere with Souza if it came to that. They would be happy to see anyone take Martin away.

He ran toward Keptembei without as much as a simple plan of action. Perhaps, he thought, death meant nothing once accepted—and accepting it did not mean he had to die. His killer might act ineptly, like Alfie had. Martin could save Rebecca and still have a chance to flee.

4

Souza placed a cigarette between his lips. Night had fallen and Rebecca had fled the house quietly.

Instead of daydreaming, he thought, I should have killed her. She may warn Martin of my surprise.

He caressed the cigarette with his damaged fingertips. "This one's yours, Alf, remember? Haven't smoked it yet, as I promised. I'll light it as soon as that bastard's blood starts flowing."

It had been a long wait since that day at the beach, when he had found the cabin's door locked.

Souza stood the moment he heard the sound from outside. The time had come. He tightened his grip on the pocket knife and held a lump of rags ready to use as a gag. He would have preferred to enjoy Martin's screams of pain, but it was wiser to muffle them, lest the noise draw attention from the village and force him to hasten the murder. Without the girl as a witness, he could now extend the operation for as long as he wished, cutting slowly into the flesh, allowing the pain to go on for eternity.

The remains of the plastic on the windows began to flap noisily with a sudden gush of wind. Souza had a difficult time hearing the hands that fumbled with the padlock outside.

The door opened quickly, violently, as though a bull had pushed against it with a choleric thrust. Souza had hoped to enjoy the moment, to hear Martin enter the house in a sort of slow motion, so that he could trip him and kick him before using the knife. But the suddenness of the entry forced him to lunge at his target instead. He had to act fast. If he felt a need later to extend the torturing, to slow down Martin's bleeding for the pleasure of it, he would do so by using a tourniquet. Like a spigot on a wine barrel, a tourniquet would give him complete control.

The important thing now was to inflict the wound, to tap the barrel and let the cheap wine flow. With a firm grip, he sunk the blade twice in his enemy's arm. He could see little in the darkness, but realized almost with glee that he could smell the blood. What he saw was the bathtub, the white porcelain smeared with Alfie's blood, the gash on his brother's arm—a festering wound that he now tried to imitate with the aid of the pocket knife.

Every stab Souza gave had a purpose. One thrust for Alfie, one thrust for his father, and one more for all the suffering his mother had had to endure. He thanked God for the opportunity to avenge those whom he loved so much. The journey was over. He finally had Martin's life in his hands—and absolutely no mercy to spare him. *I shall not show pity*, he thought. *Eye for eye, tooth for tooth, hand for hand, foot for foot.*

But the wounded man refused to fall. Souza lost confidence. His legs grew limp and he tripped as easily as he had done on that hunting day in the country. His eight-year-old brother walked ahead of him, in front of the shotgun. "Alfie!" he yelled. But Alfie's leg had already been replaced by a shower of blood and the frightening prospect of a long, guilt-ridden life. Souza panicked with the thought. A mistake, only a mistake. Life was based on mistakes. He had forgotten to unload the shotgun. He had sent a diffident Alfie to eliminate Martin and Pete. It had all been wrong. And now *this* was a mistake.

He stabbed at the moving mass with unchecked fury, but impatience made him miss repeatedly. One should not try to kill a man in a hurry.

The strong smell of aftershave overpowered his thoughts. The blow on the back of his head came unexpectedly, only a moment after he realized that the large moving mass under him was not Martin.

5

The football players struck with calculated blows. They had no intentions of failing a second time. They kicked Souza to the ground with the intense, sadistic joy of drilling soldiers beating on a punching bag. This had turned out to be a difficult contract for them, but they were proud of their work. As professionals, they never took the money and ran. A matter of sheer vocational pride with them: complete every job no matter what. And though usually they did not allow personal emotions to mix with work, kicking this victim made their task a pleasure. The bastard had had the gall to fight back.

"Slash," one of them said.

They dragged the body onto the mattress in the bedroom and made deep cuts on the neck, wrists and calves.

"Burn."

Still in the dark, one of the men rushed outside for a heavy container filled with kerosene.

They splashed the fuel on Souza and the bed first. Then, as volatile fumes filled the air, they poured the rest of it on every piece of furniture in the house. Flames engulfed the mattress almost the moment they put a match to it. Alfie's cigarette rolled on the concrete floor and caught fire right away.

6

Martin watched the roaring fire from a safe distance, far behind the fence and concealed among the wilted leaves and stems of the corn field. Little of the house he had once shared with Rebecca remained. The flames rose high above the structure, fed by all the useless things he had accumulated.

Most of Keptembei had gathered around the fire—hungry spectators who had not seen anything exciting in a long time. Martin knew that many more would arrive soon, from surrounding villages, from Father Reeves' mission, perhaps even from as far as Maobei. Martin Lane, known to them as Pete Bloom, the evil white man, had come to Africa to entertain them. He had soiled their dignity, impregnated one of their girls, derided them, and laughed at their faith. For that reason they gathered now—to speculate on what new evil the white man was up to, what sin of his had caused his house to burn.

Martin felt the heat on his face even from the distance at which he stood. Fire was a merciless judge. It burned what it fed on indiscriminately. In purgatory, it might purify the sinner. But on earth, it punished him with the eternal pain of a burn.

He feared for Rebecca. If he had only arrived earlier he might know for certain that she was alive. He tried to distinguish the faces in the crowd hoping to see hers among the cheering smiles. But the light flickered constantly on them. More than ever, it seemed to him that the villagers were hiding in those same, indistinct noses and eyes.

Behind the flames he saw the open front door, the one he had locked with the extra padlock. If Souza had burst it open, Rebecca had surely walked into a trap.

Martin lost hope. Where was she? What could he do to find her? Souza had probably killed her and set her and the house on fire. A grisly death. A warning to Martin so that he knew in advance what was in store for him.

Mutai's red sweater stood out from the crowd, more from its constant movement than from its color. The drunk walked dangerously close to the fire, circling the burning house several times as he preached a sermon of doom. Only the words *white man* and *evil* reached Martin. The rest were lost in a mixture of human growls and the roaring breath of the fire.

Mutai swaggered among the villagers with arms pointed at the sky. Very few paid attention to him. The flames that began to emerge from the bedroom windows offered something much more interesting. Whenever a new piece of the ceiling crumbled to the ground, the crowd clamored a note, almost as if they were about to start a religious song or a melodious prayer.

Someone had brought a sledgehammer and a few men took turns to strike at the bedroom wall. The audience waited with visible anticipation. Aside from their glee,

Martin could not say what other emotions stirred in them. He had never learned to read their passions, their feelings, or their fears.

Mutai, seemingly eager to see what lay inside, took the sledgehammer and rammed the wall. When he managed a hole large enough, everyone took a step closer to get a better look.

"A body!" a voice yelled, and the crowd leaned forward to confirm the report.

Martin swallowed the saliva he had consciously secreted to keep his mouth moist. The fire *had* killed her then.

He thought he heard the sound of a knell. Rebecca lay in her pyre, free from scorn. The simplest of funerals—death, cremation, and a quasi-religious ceremony at the same time. She had died *his* death.

He lamented the loss as though the girl had been his wife, a lifelong companion who had shared with him numerous children and countless good times.

He even said a silent prayer for Rebecca, and it surprised him how readily religion engulfed him. It mattered little how deeply God was buried in one. Faith always lived there, ready to emerge upon request.

The villagers formed a ring around the burning house. They held hands and went on in what seemed a circular procession of joy. Their song had a melody. Even a tone of gratitude filled their voices as they trampled on the flower beds. They were celebrating his death, not mourning Rebecca's. They didn't know any better.

Poor fools, Martin thought. They will regret this premature celebration later, when they find out the truth.

The wind picked up strength for a moment. It swayed the dead corn around him with a sonorous rustle. It fanned the flames, turning them inward. The house began to glow like a hearth.

He felt the first drops of rain and then a storm broke out. The dry spell had come to an end. The village was saved.

Chapter VIII

The cathedral's garden lay almost bare under the light of the late-fall sun. Martin sat on the edge of a stone bench and shivered. He wore a thick wool sweater. The months spent in Africa had ruined his taste for cold days.

Down by the hedge a quiet gardener knelt and planted tulip bulbs. A priest in habit stood next to him giving directions. He wanted only red tulips on this side, he said, and yellow ones across the pathway. His stern eyes hid behind thick glasses, magnified by an overtly self-righteous attitude. Everything about this priest seemed immaculate, a man not at all like Father Reeves. This was a city clergyman in a developed country, a pious man far removed from the madness of a village mission. He crossed through the flower beds onto the path and past Martin. "Beautiful day, isn't it?" A porcine smile rippled the flesh on his face. The Church fed the brothers well.

"More than beautiful," Martin mocked him. "Makes one feel like being born again."

The priest did not reply. Apparently, the greeting had only been a formality. He was out of sight with a few more steps.

Martin sat still. He had nothing to do but wait for his future. And to a man in permanent hiding, the future came stuffed in an envelope, delivered by a suspicious-looking man. He looked around for such a man, but he had not come yet.

Martin liked the idea of being told where to go, what to do, and for how long. Independence and individualism counted for nothing. With them came full responsibility for one's deeds. There lay the true appeal of belonging to a church or living under the protective wing of the government. No one was ever responsible for anything in those organizations.

Tito's heavy frame appeared suddenly from behind the hedge. He approached Martin as fast as his weight allowed it, and betrayed an air of urgency in his gait. He said, "No need to get up. We can talk here," and sat slowly on the bench with a noisy pant. "I've got your documents. Do you want to talk first or do you want to listen?"

Martin wanted neither. He said with effort, "I'll listen."

"I gave you my word you'd have a choice." Tito took out a set of papers from his breast pocket. "You can sign these and legally terminate our relationship right now."

Martin took the papers and studied the first page. Nothing made sense to him.

"Or—you can take on this new identity we've worked out for you." Tito handed him a sealed envelope. "It's up to you. And remember, you'll be safe, under full protection, if you accept it."

Martin opened the envelope and read its contents—a number of forms neatly typed. His picture and a new name were on top. The rest described his new life, one better suited for him than anything he had been offered in the past. Its background and experience had to do with books.

Tito said, "If you want it, we have already made an appointment for a job interview at a small bookstore. They need someone like you. A quiet job—considerably safe. I'm sure you'll get it."

Martin stared at the photograph. An old one. He looked much younger in it, a different man. The face belonged to the inexperienced hustler who, along with his gambling parents, had turned to games of chance to escape the boring realities of life.

"The old man Souza died in jail, you know?" Tito made it clear which choice he wanted Martin to take. "You'll be safe with us. Their family structure is crumbling. The elder son, we heard, has been missing for weeks. We think maybe he was bumped by a warring family."

"Then what do you need *me* for?"

"We still have convictions to hand down. You know that. And you owe us."

Martin read. His doubts emerged successively, like bubbles of freed air from a diver's purge valve. Tito was wrong, he thought. Souza was still alive. No warring family had killed him. He had been in Africa and would soon be back.

Martin held the two separate sets of documents in each hand. He had grown to distrust decisions. Every single one he had made so far seemed to have turned him toward disaster. All the lies he had told had given him no benefit. Nothing had changed. And again he faced the same options he had always had.

"What should I do?" he said.

"If I were you, I'd take the new identity. You'll be safe."

"You said that long ago."

"We had a leak. The man was found out and convicted. We've gone over this."

"I just want to make sure. How about Pete's death? And the two old women's?"

"You're clean."

"I don't know, Tito. How clean? I have a feeling you'd tell me anything to make me commit to this, to participate in your filthy mess of legal trials and convictions." Martin folded the new identity documents, stuffed them in the envelope, then in his pocket.

Tito took and crumpled the other choice. "You don't seem excited to be back with us."

"Would you be if after much effort to make things different you found that very little has changed in your life?"

"Don't fret, Martin. At least you're alive."

They left the garden. Martin followed the burly image down the flagstone steps and out to the street. *If you love your life a little...* He tried to remember the poem Elizabeth had once written for him.

Tito opened the sedan's door courteously and they got in. A wave of warm air blew inside. The driver had kept the car running and the heat on.

Martin took off his thick sweater, feeling as though he were back in Africa. A comfortable sensation. Suddenly, the verses flowed back from memory as if part of an unforgettable nursery rhyme: *If you love your life a little, God will stay with you today.* He thought, I *am* alive, and wished he could say the same for the others—Rebecca, Pete, even Alfie. And his parents, of course—those two incurable gamblers who had foolishly brought him to life.